MW01174676

MAKING MARRIAGE MEANINGFUL

MAKING MARRIAGE MEANINGFUL

Insights and Secrets from a Forty-Year Marriage

Robert O.A. Samms, Ph.D.

iUniverse, Inc.
New York Lincoln Shanghai

MAKING MARRIAGE MEANINGFUL
Insights and Secrets from a Forty-Year Marriage

Copyright © 2005 by Robert Oswald Anthony Samms

All rights reserved. No part of this book may be used or reproduced by any means, graphic, electronic, or mechanical, including photocopying, recording, taping or by any information storage retrieval system without the written permission of the publisher except in the case of brief quotations embodied in critical articles and reviews.

iUniverse books may be ordered through booksellers or by contacting:

iUniverse
2021 Pine Lake Road, Suite 100
Lincoln, NE 68512
www.iuniverse.com
1-800-Authors (1-800-288-4677)

ISBN-13: 978-0-595-34289-1 (pbk)
ISBN-13: 978-0-595-79192-7 (cloth)
ISBN-13: 978-0-595-79059-3 (ebk)
ISBN-10: 0-595-34289-2 (pbk)
ISBN-10: 0-595-79192-1 (cloth)
ISBN-10: 0-595-79059-3 (ebk)

Printed in the United States of America

Permission for copyright uses was granted from the following authors and/or
publishers

Dr. William Betcher and Robie Macauley. *The Seven Basic quarrels of Marriage*. New
York: Villard Books, a division of Random House, Inc.

Dr. Barbara DeAngelis. *What Women Want Men to Know*. New York: Hyperion Press.

Linda Dillow and Lorraine Pintus. *Intimate Issues*. Colorado Springs: Waterbrook
Press.

Dr. James Dobson. *Marriage and Family*. Carol Stream, IL: Tyndale House Publishers.

Laura Doyle. *The Surrendered Wife*. New York: Simon & Schuster.

Dr. John Gottman. *Why Marriages Succeed or Fail?* New York: Simon & Schuster.

Dr. David Schnarch. *Passionate Marriage*. New York: W. W. Norton & Co.

Nancy Van Pelt. *To Have and To Hold*. Hagerstown, MD: Review and Herald
Publishing.

Dr. Judith S. Wallerstein and Sandra Blakeslee. *The Good Marriage*. New York:
Houghton Mifflin Co.

This book is dedicated to the numerous marriages, like ours, that have endured decades of difficult marital relationships successfully and have proved that love, loyalty, and commitment to spouse and children pave the path to lasting pleasures, enduring relationships, and marital success. We trust that those seeking success in their marriage will benefit from the experiences related in this book as well as the strategies advanced by marriage professionals for dealing with marital challenges and promoting successful relationships.

Contents

Acknowledgment

The author is indebted to numerous persons and sources for the contents of this book. In expressing my thanks, I will not attempt to be exhaustive.

Of great significance is the fact that our allegiance to God greatly enhanced our survival and success as a family. Without that spiritual undergirding, we would have been devastated by the ever-increasing moral decadence and negative forces aimed at destroying families in our communities and the nations around the world.

This book would not be possible without Pamela, my wife of four decades, who should be credited with much of my personal and professional success. She has been a rich resource and has given spontaneous support for the contents of this book and the project itself.

My children have not only been supportive but they have sacrificed time from their own pressing schedules to add written opinions to enrich this work. Their contributions are completely their own. I am grateful to all eight of them for holding tenaciously to such high moral and religious principles in their own lives and for passing them on to their children and others. Whenever they encounter setbacks, they seem to rely strongly on those principles for renewal and advancement.

I am indebted to several of my relatives and my parents for the invaluable lessons I have gleaned from their experiences and counsels, especially lessons relating to family relationships. Elsada, our mother (my wife's mother), is steadfast in her religious devotion and has a positive influence on our family. Keith, Violet, and Gloria, my older siblings, as well as my deceased father, influenced my life significantly. Keith, who has endured seven decades as a bachelor, taught me much over the years. Violet gave me the love and care of a mother (I lost my mother when I was four). Sergena Obas, my former secretary, who is a certified Family Life presenter, and Dr. Don Drennon-Gala, a writer and educator, have assisted with preliminary editing. Stephen Bosch, my son-in-law, has aided me in the technical use of the computer and has helped with the cover design. Sherine Samms-Bosch and my wife, Pamela, did some of the planning and organizing. My parishioners have broadened my concept and exposure to the real needs of families and have been a main source of my emerging strategies to cope with marriage and family counseling. My appreciation goes to the numerous marriage and family professionals from whom I have learnt much during my years of research.

To those mentioned here and the countless others I have omitted for lack of space, who have helped me in sundry ways, let me render my heartfelt thanks. Finally, I must mention Ross Clark, a coworker, who is responsible for introducing to me the idea of reaching couples through motivational speaking. Finally, I am doing so.

Introduction

"What is love?" I asked my wife, Pamela, as we sat close to each other on our thirty-eighth wedding anniversary. Without replying, Pam leaned over lovingly and gave me a warm lingering kiss. "What is love?" Pam asked in her soft melodious voice. This time I leaned forward and pressed my lips against hers in a long loving embrace and replied, "Whatever it is, I love it."

That was Saturday evening, February 2, 2002. We separated briefly to prepare for the evening's celebrated event—dinner theater on the Gaylord Entertainment's famous boat, the *General Jackson*. Yes, indeed, today is our anniversary. For my New Year's resolution, I had pledged to begin writing this book on our anniversary. I did. This delightful day provided the necessary motivation.

Purpose and Format

The main purpose of this book is to view the dynamic inner workings of a modern family—our own. In so doing, I have extracted fourteen salient facets that best describe the functioning of our forty-year marriage. These fourteen issues depict vividly and comprehensively the strengths and weaknesses, as well as successes and failures, of our marriage for the purpose of enriching the marriage of successful couples or to serve as a sounding board for those who may need help with their faltering family. This may also serve to give those contemplating marriage a few sound principles to ponder.

The format is the same for each chapter, except the conclusion. The chapters begin with the author's personal experience, followed by researched information on the topic for that chapter. Each chapter will end with family members' response to at least one practical question based on the issues in that chapter. All family members will participate. The purpose of including the researched information is twofold: To accentuate the positive aspects of our interactions and to show how other marriage professionals' strategies would improve our poor or problematic interactions. The contrasting or collaborating dynamic should serve to stimulate and inform our readers. As the conclusion will point out, our marriage benefited immensely from the writing of this book, and I trust that all those who read it will enrich their lives and their marriages.

This book focuses on the period of our marriage considered as the summer of marriage. This period is the time between our wedding and the departure of our last child from home. That is between February 2, 1964, and January 1, 1999. I met Pam for the first time when I was eighteen years old. I had just graduated from high school and decided not to consider serious friendship until I graduated from college. That idea was short-lived. When I saw Pam for the first time, she was so graceful, modest, and charming that I told my friend Vincent that I must try to meet her again. I did. Our friendship lasted for five years before we were married. Our four children have developed noble characters and are all contributing to society and raising their families. (More is said about them at the end of their first contribution. Their comments appear at the end of each chapter.)

Let's explore together those exciting events related from our marriage. Before we do so, however, let me indulge myself with my musings on love. I penned these few lines to my wife on April 19, 1985. While browsing through my files recently, I saw a handwritten copy of the following note with the observation scribbled at the bottom: "Given with a weekend gift after a little misunderstanding in the morning." The note reads as follows:

To my wife, Pamie,

Due to human limitations and mundane vicissitudes, the expression of love may be variable as the wind: true love is as constant as the rising and setting of the sun. It can neither be overpowered nor superseded. True love is as pure as a lily, sincere as a saint, faithful as a martyr. Having found it, cherish it and secure it within the secret chambers of your heart—forever.

Robert loves you.

This was written after twenty-one years of marriage. It must have worked because we are still in love with each other in our fortieth year of marriage and the forty-fifth year since we began our friendship. Let's take a look at the concept of love, from various sources.

1

What Is Love?

What Is Love, Really?

True love often appears to be complex and, at times, contradictory. As we set out to explore its true meaning, consider these poetic lines:

> I do not wish you joy without a sorrow,
> Nor endless day without the healing dark,
> Nor brilliant sun without the restful shadow,
> Nor tides that never turn against your bark.
> I wish you love, and strength, and wisdom,
> And gold enough to help some needy one,
> I wish you songs, but also blessed silence,
> And God's sweet peace when every day is done.[1]
> Author Unknown.

After reviewing much of the voluminous writings on love and marriage, I was somewhat disappointed that no clear definition of love had emerged. Although some of the authors attempted to explain it, most of them wrote on the subject without even attempting a definition. Since I had struggled with understanding what love really is or how to determine with some degree of certainty when two people are truly in love, I hoped that some of the writers had arrived at a more thorough understanding of this mysterious experience. Perhaps, throughout history no other human experience has absorbed more intense interest or created a more curious quest. The elusive charm of love has escaped the desire of the wealthy, befuddled the most brilliant scholars, resisted the most persistent suitors, shipwrecked the lives of countless individuals, and rendered helpless many mighty conquerors. Yet this mysterious passion for love has pacified political disputes, lifted the human spirit, led to the surrender of the hardened human heart and even influenced the course of history. The power of love is available to the humblest peasant and the wealthiest prince or princess. True love cannot be bought or sold. Still, we cannot fully comprehend it. In this section, we will focus on a few writers' views in an attempt to gain a better understanding of the experience.

I once read the story of a hardened criminal who came in contact with a mother and her three-year-old daughter. The man had an unattractive physical appearance. His beard was unkempt and his clothes were shabby. His unwelcome presence startled the woman. But the little girl suddenly broke from the grasp of her mother's arm and ran up to the man with outstretched hands, exclaiming gleefully: "Take me up, man! Take me up!" He reached down and picked her up in his strong arms. She stroked his beard, threw her arms around his neck, and kissed him on his cheek. Then she whispered in his ear: "I love you, man. I love you." Tears started trickling down his cheeks. The little girl's innocent expression of love had melted the heart of a hardened criminal.

I once read how Norman Vincent Peale illustrated the true power of love. He related a personal experience, which took place at the beginning of his career as a clergyman. During a job placement interview, his bishop told him that he had two churches available. One was a lovely congregation located in a beautiful New England town. "I'll take it," Peale exclaimed. "Hold on," said the bishop. "Let me tell you about the other one." He explained that it was located in the mill district of Rhode Island where a strike had been going on for more than a year. The church had financial difficulty and there was dissension among the members. In fact, he explained, the church was divided down the middle, and a minister was badly needed to unite them. You guessed it! Peale accepted the challenge.

Peale reported that "sometimes it seemed the people all just sat there on Sunday mornings on opposite sides of the main aisle making faces at each other. The hate that filled that place was pretty awful. So I bombarded them with love. I preached one sermon after another on love." He concluded that "love conquers all."

Very few people would remain unmoved when experiencing or even viewing the powerful passion of true love. Which of us would not be moved after viewing the passionate display of love by the characters in *Gone with the Wind, Titanic,* or *Romeo and Juliet*? After reading the story of Ruth and Naomi in the Old Testament, or after listening to the account of Edward, duke of Windsor, who chose to surrender the throne of England rather than abandon his lover, who would remain unmoved by their passionate appeal?

What is love? The definition may be elusive, but in some strange way, most of us have a self-authenticated understanding of love. Of course, different people experience love in different ways and with different types of relationships. The word *love* is used in such a variety of ways, from a child's love for his pet to one's love for God. Therefore, we should delineate our area of interest in this book. Our main purpose is to deal with the marriage experience of a man and a woman. We will also include, to a lesser extent, other relationships within the family.

Toward a Definition of Love

Theodor Bovet, a Swiss physician and marriage counselor, explained that:

> When we speak of love, we must distinguish between three different aspects of it. Unfortunately, these are often confused with or opposed to each other. Just as every human personality has a physical, a psychological and a spiritual aspect (or dimension), so within the organism or union of two persons in marriage there are three aspects—sex, *eros*, and *agape*.[2]

The words *eros* and *agape* are adapted from the Greek language. The Greek language is much more accurate in its use of words than the English language. Since a significant number of English words are derived from Greek, it is frequently enlightening to look more closely at the origin of some of these words. By using the word *love*, in English, we may mean to refer to sexual attraction, physical admiration, friendship, deep regard for others, or devotion to God. Biblical Greek (known as Koine Greek) employed different words to specify the intended meaning or more precise meaning of a broader concept. *Philos*, from which the English word *philanthropy* is derived, refers to brotherly love. *Eros* refers to the love shared between spouses. *Agape* is considered to be divine love. *Agape* is directed toward its object with no expectation of something in return. *Agape* is truly unselfish love. In the English language, we use the word *love* to describe all three of these aspects of our relationships.

Dr. Bovet has certainly pointed us in the right direction in our attempt to understand this elusive experience we term love. Although in modern society, we tend to merge various passionate and even friendly relationships under the banner of love, we could benefit from even a cursory view of what our relationships mean. It is precisely at this stage—differentiation of our feelings for another person—that many youth and even adults falter and fail. For instance, strong sexual attraction is often confused with love.

Sex is the physical aspect of the relationship. Sex is generally self-centered. The aim of sex is, to some extent, the satisfaction of lust and sensual desire. Dr. Bovet informs us that sexual expression transcends individuality mainly in so far as it attempts to please the partner or aims at procreation. In contrast, *eros* is concerned with the other person.[3] *Eros* focuses on the whole person, including his/her attributes. It is erotic to focus on grace, kindness, and charm in a woman and chivalry, courage, gentleness, and attentiveness in a man. Whereas the aim of sex is self-satisfaction, the objective of *eros* is relationship. "*Eros* finds its fulfillment in the relationship of love. It gives pleasure to both partners at the same time, enables them to give themselves to each other, stilling their own egos for the sake of each other."[4]

The art of love will require a balance between sex and *eros*. Whereas sex is egocentric and *eros* is partner oriented, *agape* provides the bond of loyalty that operates beyond sex and *eros*. It is a spiritual bond that rises beyond itself.

One of the problems of our modern culture is that it teaches youth to confuse love with sexual impulse. *Sensuous* should not be confused with *sexual* and *sensual*. Many spouses miss this distinction and pay dearly in their relationships. Men and youth tend to focus more on the body of a woman than on the person—body, mind, and spirit. Women more naturally focus on the *eros*, the sensuous aspect of relationship with the person they love. The challenge of men and youth is to progress beyond sex to *eros*, sensual to sensuous.

Many marriages have failed due to the lack of understanding of *eros*. In marriage relationships, "most husbands are prodigies in sex but almost complete morons so far as *eros* is concerned. And so their wives, who live more by *eros* than by sex, become psychologically disillusioned and, therefore, physically repelled by their husbands."[5] What is considered frigidity in some wives may well be due to their husbands' emphasis on sex rather than on *eros*. The art of love requires a balance between sex and *eros*. Whereas sex is egocentric and *eros* is partner oriented, *agape* provides the bond of loyalty that operates beyond sex and *eros*. It is a spiritual bond, a bond that rises beyond itself. "It maintains loyalty between couples even when one party no longer desires to be loyal."[6] Carl J. Jung concurred with Bovet concerning the difference between sexuality and *eros*. Jung stated:

> Most men are erotically blind in that they commit the unpardonable error of confusing *eros* with sexuality. A man thinks that he possesses a woman when he is possessing her sexually. But never is he possessing her less, because for the woman only the erotic relationship is truly significant. For her, marriage is a relationship, and sexuality an addendum.[7]

In her attempt to define the experience of love, author Nancy Van Pelt dissected it. From the outset, she posited the view that love cannot occur at first sight. While this may be true in most cases, I believe love can occur at first sight. That happened to me. Even in such cases, the couples experience only the first stage of love. But they possess the qualities for building a lasting relationship.

Many marriages have failed due to the lack of understanding of *eros*, the relationship aspect of love.

The popular term is "falling in love." Van Pelt expressed that "when we use this term, we usually mean that they have fallen in love only with their 'hearts.' But falling in love with the heart is only a portion of the love process. When you fall in love, you must fall in love with your heart and your head."[8] Van Pelt admitted that "it is difficult, however, to state with any degree of accuracy precisely what love is." Echoing George Bernard Shaw, she pointed out "that love was the most misused and misunderstood word in our vocabulary."[9] The authors of *Family Matters—A Guide to Family Life* stated: "Defining love in rational terms is about as difficult and elusive as catching a rainbow. No wonder so many books have been written, songs composed, and films made, all attempting to describe the many facets of the experience of love."[10]

According to Nancy Van Pelt, love is experienced through a process of five stages.[11] First is the infantile stage. This period occurs when the person is pre-occupied with filling his/her own needs. Second is the parent-love stage. The person expects the parent or spouse to make him/her the center of attention. Third is the buddy-love stage. This emerges as the person begins to explore the experience of sharing the interest of other friends. The home, parents, or spouse lose their center of interest, and the person may spend several nights of the week with friends, club, church, or work. The fourth, the adolescent stage, occurs when a person develops greater interest in the opposite sex. When a spouse remains at this stage, that spouse may react negatively to his/her partner because of his/her insecurity. He may begin to criticize his wife for not dressing like other women or he may gaze for longer periods at other women. She may begin to compare her husband to other men. Finally, in the fifth stage, the mature-love stage, the emphasis on physical attraction is superseded by emphasis on emotional and psychological factors. The spouses shift their focus from what they can get from the relationship to what they can give to it. Your partner's interest takes precedence over your own. You act with your partner's best interest at heart.

Developing through these five stages of love takes time. Some people get married before they grow into mature love. Some couples marry while one or both are still in the infantile stage of love. Some people progress through these stages more rapidly than others. However, assessing where you are on the ladder to mature love may help improve your relationship. For marriage to succeed, the couple needs to develop beyond sex and *eros* to *agape*. Miroslav Volf said it this way: "Marital love is more than *eros*. It has to do with how you treat each other when dishes need to be washed or garbage taken out, when misunderstandings arise and when one has transgressed against the other. Love is not the desire to be united with the other, but action on behalf of the other, and constancy in the pursuit of his or her well-being."[12]

However, assessing where you are on the ladder to mature love may help improve your relationship. For marriage to succeed, the couple needs to develop beyond sex and *eros* to *agape*.

Love or Infatuation

Webster's Dictionary defines love as "an intense affectionate concern for another person." Infatuation is defined as "short-lived powerful but foolish and unreasoning passion or attraction." By these definitions one may deduce that love and infatuation are very similar at the time of their origin. There is intense or powerful attraction for the object of the would-be lover. Hence, at that point it is very difficult for individuals to discern whether their experience is truly "love." According to Van Pelt, sufficient time is needed in order for the relationship to reveal its true quality. She observed:

> Love and infatuation share three similar symptoms: passion, nearness, and strange emotions. Passion may be present without genuine love. It is entirely possible to feel passionate or to have strong sexual feelings for a person you have not even met. Necking and petting increase the urgency of erotic feelings until sex may become a prominent part of your association together. But these feelings do not necessarily indicate genuine love. Sexual attraction can be as urgent in infatuation as it is in genuine love.[13]

Apart from the biblical principle that maintains that sex should be reserved for the sanctity of marriage, the fact that a premature sexual relationship could overshadow and distort the development of a true love relationship is likely the strongest argument for abstinence. Sex preceding marriage only complicates the normal process of discovering whether the couple is genuinely suited for each other.

Sex preceding marriage only complicates the normal process of discovering whether the couple is genuinely suited for each other.

Infatuation frequently ends when the couple is faced with reality. But sexual involvement confuses that process and may influence the couple to remain together, especially if pregnancy occurs. Many people make the serious life-changing decision of marriage based on emotion born out of infatuation.

In a study about marriage failures, 48 percent of the wives felt their marriage would succeed and 70 percent of husbands felt that their marriage would succeed. Although men fared much better than women, the numbers that cherished high expectations for their future together reveal that something is lacking in the premarital phase of a large number of relationships.[14]

In one of Ann Landers's popular newspaper columns, a sixteen-year-old requested that Ann republish her views on love or infatuation.[15] Subsequently, the youth expressed regret that she had not seen it two years before. In the article, Ann Landers pointed out that infatuation is instant desire. "It's one set of glands calling out to another. Love is friendship that has caught fire. It takes root and grows—one day at a time."[16] Whereas infatuation is accompanied by a lingering feeling of insecurity, doubt, and unanswered questions that are left unexplored for fear of spoiling the dream, love is the quiet understanding and mature acceptance of imperfection. Because love is real, it grows and becomes stronger, even when the two persons are separated by distance. Infatuation begins with a hasty sexual passion mixed with the fear of losing the relationship. Love patiently builds a lasting mature friendship based on trust, confidence, and patience.

> Infatuation begins with a hasty sexual passion mixed with the fear of losing the relationship. Love patiently builds a lasting mature friendship based on trust, confidence, and patience.

The book, *The New Couple*, by Maurice Taylor and Seana McGee, is based on the idea that ten laws of love are vital to the success of a marriage. They are chemistry, priority, emotional integrity, deep listening, equality, peacemaking, self-love, mission in life, walking, and transformational education. Although these guidelines are difficult to achieve, we should consider them the ideal to strive toward. In so doing, we improve our relationship as we move toward marital success.

The Paradox of Love

Even in our present hedonistic and amoral society, there is a deep-seated quest for true love. As Tom Eisenman put it: "The paradox in the sexual revolution is that what is really wanted and needed and sought after by men and women cannot be achieved in the experience of free sex. True intimacy and irresponsible sex are a contradiction."[17]

The elusive reality is that the lasting pleasure and passion people want can be found in the enduring love that people really need. But they lose what they need in their unbridled pursuit of what they think they want in order to satisfy their insatiable pleasure-seeking urges. In effect, if they should pursue and capture what they really need, most likely, they will simultaneously obtain what they want.

Even to the casual observer, it should be obvious that traditional marriage is increasingly under attack by various factions and forces in our society. A special issue of *Newsweek* magazine at the end of the 1980s all but declared the death of the traditional family. It left the reader with the impression that the new forms of family such as a single-parent family and same-sex couple were leading to the abolition of the traditional form of marriage and family. William J. Bennett, in his book, *The Broken Hearth*, posited as his core argument that the nuclear family, defined as a monogamous married couple with children, is vital to civilization's success. Bennett pointed out that "like the breakdown of the family itself, this cultural destruction of family life and its purposes has no historical precedent. It has left us open to doubts about some of our most basic understandings: about the parent-child bond, about marital permanence, about the link between marriage, sex, and procreation."[18] While these attacks on the family are continuing unabated, the desire to fall in love, get married, and establish a family remains entrenched in North American society.

Tommy Franks, who led the American forces in a spectacular victory in Operation Iraqi Freedom, retired after serving thirty-six years in the armed forces. In his retirement speech on July 7, 2003, which was broadcast to the world, he said: "A man has no greater treasure than his family." In many studies in which Americans are asked what they value the most in assessing the quality of their lives, they place marriage first. Marriage is named ahead of money, jobs, and friends.

Yet in the book, *You Owe Me*, the authors compared correctly the dissolution of marriage unfavorably with the wear of Michelin tires. "The average steel-belted radial tire lasts approximately 45,000 miles, or 3.5 years of normal highway use. The duration of the average American marriage is but 2.3 years—which translates into around 30,000 miles of friction and wear. Either way you look at it, we apparently have a more enduring, and often more endearing, relationship with our Michelins and Pirellis than we do with our chosen life partner."[19]

A Roman Catholic bishop was assisting a priest in administering confirmation to a group of young people. He asked a nervous child, "How does the Catechism define matrimony?" "It is a state of terrible torment, which those who are compelled undergo for a time to fit them for the better world," she replied. "No, no," said the parish priest. "You are mixed up with the definition of purgatory!" "Let it be," smiled the bishop. "How do two priests like you and me know that the child is not right?"

On the contrary, love can bring the enduring bond of friendship and fidelity to a marriage relationship, if the two parties are passionately committed. An aspiring poetess approached an editor in an attempt to get her poems accepted for publication. "What is love?" asked the editor. She readily responded: "Love is gazing on the lily pond, with lilies of purest white and delicate shades in full bloom, with the moonlight streaming down and…" "Enough," said the editor. "Love is getting out of bed at two-thirty on a cold, frosty morning to fill a hot water bottle for a sick, restless child who has awakened the whole house, so that the mother can get some sleep. That's what real love is. I don't think I can use your poems!"

One committed lover has said: "I bind myself to thee for life. Having chosen as I pleased, I will now spend the rest of my life endeavoring to please whom I have chosen."

We may not be able to define love precisely, but we can catch a glimpse of its essence in the unsurpassed lines of Solomon:

> Set me a seal upon your heart, as a seal upon your arm;
> For love is strong as death, jealousy is cruel as the grave.
> Its flashes are flashes of fire, a most vehement flame.
> Many waters cannot quench love, neither can floods drown it.
> If a man offered for love all the wealth of his house, it would be
> utterly scorned.[20]

Family Interview

How would you express what love means to you?

We struggled to define love because we concluded that love is dynamic and multifaceted. We also agreed that romantic love (*eros*) is a combination of attraction (physical, personality, etc.) and friendship. As the love relationship matures, it becomes less dependent on attraction and more on friendship. We notice in our relationship that our love is increasingly enhanced by our commonalties, shared experiences, and good "chemistry."

Contributed by Richard and Alicia

Although Richard is our first child, he was the last to be married. He married Alicia. Richard insisted he was waiting to find true love. And he really did. Alicia is in many ways the perfect choice. Born in Trinidad, she migrated with family members and relatives to the United States. They met in Atlanta and immediately began to form a lifelong bond. They were married within a year and have an adorable daughter. Richard is an attorney, specializing in discrimination law and Alicia is a paralegal. They operate a private legal practice in the greater Atlanta region.

Over the years the girls were attracted to him and he enjoyed their association, but he never made the final commitment at the altar. We discussed the matter until he was annoyed with me. My contention was simple. With over three billion women in the world, it should not be difficult to choose a partner. He disagreed. Either way, "all is well that ends well."

2

Commitment

The view that marriage is potentially the most difficult ongoing human experience could generate heated debates. Viewed at a glance, some could consider this statement absurd, given society's romantic concept of the marriage experience.

Within the matrix of most cultures, people are bred to believe that marriage is by far the most delightful of human experiences. And so it should be. Nevertheless, recent marriage statistics indicate that about 50 percent of first marriages and over 60 percent of second marriages fail. (See Statistical Abstract of the United States, U.S. Census Bureau, 2004–2005). Why? Since marriage is such a romantic and exciting experience, why is it not equally enduring?

The reality is that despite our confirmed experience and observation, we do not come to grips with the inexorable elements built into most relationships. Stated laconically, marriage is one of the most difficult and challenging ongoing human experiences.

Just consider for a moment some of the elements involved when two people get married. When they exchange vows at the altar or before a marriage officer, the setting is saturated with smiles and satisfaction, smothered with ecstasy. At least, that's how we expect it to be. Remember the global euphoria accompanying Prince Charles and Princess Diana's wedding? Isn't the desire to mirror their experience even in a minuscule fashion shared by the humblest bride and groom? Yet in the heart of the eternally joyful expectation lurks the potential for inimical forces to invade and destroy the marriage. Since these negative forces are likely dormant and imperceptible, the couple may be oblivious to them. The bride and groom may feel completely secure in each other's love as they swear before God or a judge that their marriage will endure the onslaught of anything human, inhuman, or even superhuman. Based upon their belief system, many newlyweds feel that even death will not end their commitment to each other.

Despite this seemingly irrevocable covenant contained in the wedding vows, frequently, the couple does not have a complete knowledge of his/her marriage partner. This is not due to a lack of preparation or even to any failure on the part of the bride or groom, even if they have lived together for a time. Reality is that we are not like a vessel already shaped by the potter, rather we are like the clay in the hand of the potter, ready to be shaped in any of a thousand ways as we face life's unpredictable forces. Therefore, as good and valuable as marriage counseling may be, there remain the silent secrets of the inner self, often unrevealed to even the most trusting lovers. Although well intentioned, a marriage faces enormous odds against achieving the expected eternally enduring happy and successful relationship.

The fact that both bride and groom were born and bred in completely different circumstances and environments is rarely taken seriously or even considered. Their parents likely shared different values and subjected them to different training and discipline. During their years of schooling, they likely had different friends, thereby being exposed to different influences. In some cases, they were affiliated with different religions and accepted or rejected different doctrines. The profound impact of culture, race, politics, and language on an individual should be taken into account. These factors, along with moral training or the lack thereof, could lead to different dormant, deep-seated personality traits. We could even add the potentially devastating effects of hereditary or predisposed illnesses—psychological, physical, or emotional—to which many people are subjected. Then there are suppressed childhood traumas and various phobias. What of strong likes, dislikes, desires, prejudices, and ambitions or lack of ambitions! What if any of these influences, or a combination of any number of them, surfaces early or late in the marriage, especially at an unwelcome, critical, or embarrassing moment?

This is only a peek into the prism through which I view the vast complexity of marriage. What is fascinating and even enigmatic is that although these factors that may influence the marriage relationship are self-evident, we usually ignore them and proceed with our relationships somewhat oblivious to their incalculable impact. The result is frequently a futile fight for survival.

I have come to view commitment as the key principle in the endurance of a marriage relationship. That's what kept Pam and me together during the dark, difficult days. We had burnt our bridges behind us and provided no escape route. When we got married, there was no serious discussion of where we would live, the number of children we would have, the amount of money we needed, or who owned any item in our possession. To us, getting married meant a permanent lifetime bond.

> When we got married, there was no serious discussion of where we would live, the number of children we would have, the amount of money we needed, or who owned any item in our possession. To us, getting married meant a permanent lifetime bond.

There was no discussion that led to that conclusion. We simply shared that principle of total commitment, regardless of the outcome. Obviously, as the reader will observe, after our wedding, this principle would inevitably be discussed and debated, tested and tried, stretched and strengthened.

Our commitment was tested on the first night of our honeymoon. As the excitement of the wedding slowly subsided, Pam and I knew it was time to leave on our long-looked-for honeymoon. We hugged all the guests (about fifty), kissed the only two relatives attending (Pam's mother, Elsada, and sister, Melissa) and took our leave. Sitting comfortably in the rear seat of Professor Walter Comm's large American-made car (I think it was a Ford), we felt engulfed by the darkness. Professor Walter Comm and his wife, Dorothy, hosted our wedding reception in their home, located on the Andrews University campus in Berrien Springs, Michigan. Since both were our college professors, we felt comfortable with them. Knowing that the tension and excitement of the day were over, I began to unwind slowly. Suddenly sobs penetrated the silence. How could that be? Only moments before, we sat silently enjoying each other's presence and the delightful reality that we were married at last. I reached over with a loving embrace and tried to discover the reason. My first reaction was that Pam felt insecure now that she would be alone with me. Speaking softly between sobs, Pam assured me that she felt her mother didn't look her usual self. She wondered how life was really going for her in the "Big Apple" (New York). Perhaps, Pam was crying because she was overwhelmed by the pressures of the occasion. Since I was in college in Canada until the week of the wedding, she did all the planning while taking a full college course load. Fortunately, she soon overcame her sadness.

We arrived at the Four Flags Hotel in Niles, Michigan. A soothing sensation saturated my mind and body as I realized the most precious days of my life had truly arrived. Since we had waited until after our wedding to experience sex together, this moment was memorable. I still remember that Pam did not feel comfortable undressing in front of me. Of course, I was impatient, anxious, and curious, although I couldn't reveal my true feelings lest I made matters worse. Having waited for five years for our first sexual encounter, surely I could wait a few minutes. Happily, our experience at Four Flags Hotel was exceedingly exciting and set the trend for a lifelong experience together. We cannot soon forget the setting. The room was peaceful and pleasant. Rapturous instrumental music enveloped the room in an unbroken flow of mystical melody. We didn't leave the hotel for the four-day stay, except to buy food, which I bought and brought back.

Awakening that first morning, we realized that we had only a few dollars (I think about twenty dollars) and that neither family members nor wedding guests had given us money, even though we were both college students. We received many gifts but no cash. Having spent all we had for the wedding, our limited finances were exhausted. Now it was my responsibility to provide the needed funds to get our lives together started. We spent the few dollars sparingly for our meals, which consisted of sandwiches and juices. We were so completely comfortable with being together that we were never concerned about the money we needed to travel to Edmonton, Canada, until a day before our departure. Placing a call to Hubert, a friend attending Canadian Union College in Lacombe, Alberta, I explained that I needed a short-term loan. He immediately sent me one hundred dollars by Western Union. This was sufficient to pay Greyhound bus fares for both of us with enough left to pay for our meals. At least, that's what we thought.

Our first surprise struck near the end of a four-hour wait in Chicago at about five o'clock in the morning. We had fallen asleep with our suitcases and boxes containing our gifts at our feet. Checking the items, we realized that one box was missing. Regrettably, among other things, it contained the bridal bouquet. We couldn't even speculate how or when it disappeared. To our amazement, about one week later, the bouquet arrived in the mail without the other items. Whoever snatched our package had a heart and took the trouble to mail the bouquet to us. Perhaps, our address was on the tag attached to the package.

The next surprise came the following night as we continued our two-day journey to Edmonton, where the Alberta Conference of Seventh-day Adventists promised me a job as a colporteur. This required selling religious, health, and children's educational books from door to door. We arrived at a small country town in North Dakota about two o'clock in the morning where we had to change buses some four hours later. Despite our plea to remain in the station until the next scheduled bus, we were told that the bus station was closed to passengers until 6:00 A.M. After a desperate search to save ourselves from the uncompromising cold in midwinter, we found a nearby hotel. Since we had to sacrifice to pay for this unexpected service, we had to settle for a room that was questionable in terms of safety and cleanliness. Exhausted from the tedious travel, we fell asleep readily.

The third surprise came when we arrived at the immigration office in Emerson, Manitoba. Although I had a letter of employment, which met the approval of the immigration in Edmonton, we were subjected to about two hours of questioning before receiving clearance. This experience was exhausting and frustrating but exhilarating once we realized we had crossed the border into Canada.

Throughout these difficult circumstances, neither Pam nor I shared any feeling of regret regarding our decision to marry at that time. As I recall, Pam's mother, Elsada, affectionately called Aunt Sada, requested that we postpone the wedding until she had enough funds to help with the expenses. Our view then and now is to limit the influence of money on important decisions in our lives. Our view regarding decision making was to look at all the relevant factors that affected the proposed plan of action. After determining our best option, we then considered the feasibility of financing. We found that should we elevate finance to priority status, our creative concepts would be curtailed, especially since funds were frequently limited. Pam and I felt we were ready to be married. We did so, despite our financial constraints. We were completely committed to each other's happiness and we intended to use our limited funds to support our goal.

Burning Our Bridges

For us, marriage meant burning all bridges behind us. Although the future was uncertain, we understood marriage to be a lifelong experience. Therefore, we were fully focused on the future with no thought of life separate from each other. Needless to say, during our marriage, several situations arose to cause us serious reflection with reference to the permanence of our relationship. Let's explore some examples.

Early in our friendship, I discovered that Pam did not want to marry a minister. I made it clear to her from the outset that I would become a pastor. On the other hand, Pam chose to study elementary education and I preferred to see her study secondary education. She changed to a secondary education major in college and eventually completed her degree in that field. She even taught English and literature at Harrison Memorial High School for several years. Nevertheless, nine years after our marriage, she obtained diplomas in elementary education and special education from McGill University. Later, she obtained a master's degree in special education from the University of Alberta and taught elementary school for most of her teaching career. My education blended theology and business administration. During my career, I worked in both fields with equal dedication. We learned to accept each other's profession, and we gave full, unconditional support to each other. In fact, I would attribute much of my success in ministry to my wife, who very graciously won the hearts of my parishioners and gave public as well as private support. Our career choices confirmed our commitment to a significant extent. If our commitment were shifting rather than stable, superficial rather than certain, or limited rather than enduring, the vicissitudes that awaited us would have destroyed our marriage in the cruel crucible of conflict and change that characterized my ministry. The same could be said for the endless energy Pam's decades of dedicated teaching demanded.

> However, the more the challenges intensified, the closer we were drawn together. This does not mean there were no moments of crisis. There were many, but our marriage emerged intact.

However, the more the challenges intensified, the closer we were drawn together. This does not mean there were no moments of crisis. There were many, but our marriage emerged intact. Later, we will explore some of the factors that aided in our success and some of the problems that threatened to separate us.

A very important factor affecting our family was the constant relocating due to job transfers. This is a common practice for some evangelical church organizations. They require that the clergy be reassigned to different congregations in order to avoid complacency, undue attachment to the man rather than to the movement and the message. Frequent reassignments of pastors provide exposure to a broad-based experience and a more even distribution of the ministers' strengths and weaknesses. The ministers also get the opportunity to develop professionally, thereby receiving invitations to serve in more responsible positions. The weakness of one may be the strength of another, hence as ministers rotate, each congregation is exposed to similar pastoral leadership, and the ministers are able to move, often to greener pastures.

What may prove good for the church and pastor may pose a serious challenge to the minister's family. Fortunately for me Pam was extraordinarily accommodating. She'd never murmured nor complained. I consider this one of my greatest blessings in our marriage. What is even more remarkable was her willingness to leave her teaching job and move to a completely different region (we lived and worked in four countries, as well as in several locations within those countries).

Commitment to our marriage resulted in creating a cementing bond without consciously planning to do so. Let's bear in mind that most people who go to the altar to take a vow to live together—"until death do us part"—are sincere. There is no justifiable reason to believe otherwise. When scores of couples approached me over the years with their request for marriage, they appeared to have a sincere passion and deep yearning for lasting happiness. Rarely did they display any tentativeness. If I detected even a slight uncertainty on the part of the couple, I used the marriage assessment evaluation test to determine the area of weakness in their relationship and counseled them in dealing with the issues involved. In some cases the couples delayed the wedding. After counseling one couple in 1984, they decided to delay their wedding for six months. To my knowledge, that couple is still together today. The point here is that couples tend to overlook flaws in each other before marriage but pay the bitter price of dealing with these irritants during marriage.

> Unless the differences are completely irreconcilable, with enduring commitment to each other, the marriage could and should survive.

That is precisely the reason a deep sincere commitment to the marriage relationship is invaluable. Unless the differences are completely irreconcilable, the marriage could and should survive with enduring commitment to each other. Unfortunately, many couples are sincere about their relationship and expect a lasting marriage at the time of their wedding, but they have neither contemplated nor determined their level of commitment. When a soldier enters into battle, he/she should expect to destroy the enemy. However, that soldier should come to terms with the possibility of being pinned down in a no-possibility-of-retreat situation. There is also the possibility of being captured and tortured by the enemy. Otherwise, he/she could be caught unprepared should he/she be forced to face those crises. During my military training many decades ago, I was taught a strict rule concerning my response to a command given by a superior officer. You obey promptly without any provision for protest. Protest is considered only after the command has been executed. That would be a problem, of course, if obeying the command led to your death. However, soldiers are trained to face any eventuality in the execution of their duty. What if marriages had a similar level of commitment? What, then, would be the divorce rate in the United States, for example?

While attending a boys' boarding school during my teen years, I heard much discussion about boy-girl relationships. One troubling topic of discussion that seemed to contradict the glowing quest for love and marriage was the prospect of long-term marriage. The dialogues returned occasionally to the idea of living with one person for a long time. As boys, we felt that we would lose interest in the same wife after a few years. After being married for forty years, I have the opportunity of reviewing my boyhood concern. It has now occurred to me that our view of love was limited to the birth of love. As teenagers, our concept of love and marriage was fixated on ecstasy and passion to the complete exclusion of growth and maturity within the bond of marriage.

Four centuries ago, William Shakespeare, often considered the greatest writer in English literature, gave his assessment of the birth of love. His comments appear to be remarkably contemporary. In *A Midsummernight's Dream*, the poet penned the words:

Thing base and vile, holding no quality,
Love can transpose to form and dignity.
Love looks not with the eyes, but with the mind;
And therefore is wing'd cupid painted blind.
Nor hath love's mind of any judgment to taste;
Wings, and no eyes, figure unheedy haste:
And therefore is love said to be a child,
Because in choice he is so oft beguil'd.

Just ask two young lovers how they know they are in love. Invariably, they will give an answer similar to the seventeen-year-old girl whose reply was: "I know the boy I'm going out with is the right one for me because whenever I meet him, I tremble all over like jelly!" During three decades as a marriage officer, I have conducted scores of weddings. In every case the couple appeared optimistic about their future together. Possibly, those with doubts ignore them in favor of their more exciting present experience. While serving in my first parish, I was initiated in my marriage counseling experience with a couple, who appeared to be godly, moral, and sober but gave up on their marriage. As I attempted to get the husband to remember the early days of their marriage, which were full of hope and excitement, he remarked coldly: "I know that God did not sanction our marriage." Soon afterward his wife passed away. Possibly, his uncaring attitude aided her demise. I can imagine the excitement they shared on their wedding day. How tragic was the loss of such youthful optimism!

Several writers on the subject of marriage have reminded us of the inevitable changes that occur in the experience of married couples. One writer suggested that marriages develop through three phases. I agree. Let me attempt to describe them.

Mutual Enjoyment

The first phase is mutual enjoyment. This is the period when love is blind. During this honeymoon period, everything is bright and jolly. The flowers are blooming, the birds are singing, the trees are swaying in the balmy breeze, church bells are chiming, and the problems of life seem to vanish into thin air. The lovers are lost in a frenzy of ecstasy and a world of fantasy. The love partner appears to be the most beautiful, most sublime, and most glorious in the world. Reality is denied.

Mutual Adjustment

The second phase is mutual adjustment. In common parlance, the honeymoon is over. Marriage now takes on a clashing and joining phase. This is manifested in disagreements and conflicts or merely in the discovery of each other's differences, likes and dislikes, failures and faults. This period, known as "the cooling off of love," fosters disillusionment. It is a time of disappointing discovery. At this time the lethal question imperceptibly creeps into the mind:

"Did I marry the right person?" Many rush to the divorce court before waiting long enough for an answer. According to Nancy Van Pelt, "Most couples find that within a few days after the honeymoon, the return to reality hits swift and deep. Yes, they feel elated over the excitement of settling into their first home, but they must also be prepared for the disillusionment that will surely follow—a letdown from the cloud nine of bliss, glamour, and all-absorbing interest they have had in each other."[1] She claimed that men suffer more severe symptoms of disillusionment than women. They are concerned with loss of freedom, the task of household obligations, and the burden of financial worries. Brides begin to feel that their husbands take them for granted. "The masks that each may have worn prior to marriage soon drop away. The put-ons gradually disappear, and the real self of moods and temper appear."[2] The first year may well decide the success or failure of the marriage since it is usually the most challenging and the couple has the least experience.

I remember counseling couples on the verge of separation because their petty attitudes had accumulated. During my sessions with them, they related many unfortunate incidents. One couple related that upon returning from their honeymoon, they entered their new home. The groom, pausing beside a closet near the entrance, claimed it as his. The new bride felt she needed to assert her claim to it as well. Another couple told of the conflict between them at bedtime. One wanted the light on, and the other wanted it off. Consequently, the couples found it difficult to live together because of their failure to resolve normal disagreements. Another couple's difficulty was that the wife preferred to be awakened in the morning by loud music from the clock radio and the husband detested it. One study revealed that 26.5 percent of all divorces in the United States were granted to couples married two years or fewer and 51.3 percent of divorces were granted to couples who had no more than five years of marriage. These statistics support the view that "disillusionment sets in early, hard and fast."[3]

> How can a couple pass successfully through these three phases of marriage to become and remain happy, well-adjusted husband and wife? The main thrust of *Making Marriage Meaningful* is to search for and present viable answers to that very question.

Mutual Fulfillment

The third phase of marriage is mutual fulfillment. This is actually the grown-up phase of marriage. The couple learns to accept each other, communicate, and develop strategies to resolve disagreements. They have become friends and have developed trust in each other.

How can a couple pass successfully through these three phases of marriage to become and remain happy, well-adjusted husband and wife? The main thrust of this book is to search for and present viable answers to that very question. In this and the following chapters, we will tackle issues that are vital to the success of married couples and, to some extent, the success of families.

Apart from love, the most important ingredient for the success of any marriage is *commitment*. Of course, the order of importance of each element of a marriage relationship may vary in the view of professionals who study the marriage process. Based on my experience, I have concluded that, apart from love, commitment is preeminent. The escalating failure rate of marriages in recent decades has led to a plethora of theories regarding the reasons for the modern or even post-modern marriage predicament. It is not surprising that marriage professionals may place more emphasis on different aspects of such a complex problem.

Nancy Van Pelt considers preparation of primary importance. "Why do marriages fail? There are many reasons, but the main reason is a lack of preparation."[4] She explained that couples need to see successful marriage as a difficult task to attain, but not unattainable. Too much ignorance exists regarding the complexity of marriage. Many people believe that marriage is a lifelong quest for lasting bliss. They think love alone will take them through. Often their hopes are dashed. "Marriage is demanding. It calls for knowledge, combined with effort and maturity and patience, in order to achieve the reward it offers. It also requires outside guidance and support."[5]

Eric J. Cohen and Gregory Sterling supported this view, the primacy of preparation. They compared the emotional debt in a marriage relationship to financial debt. "In the same way that we take on financial debts without weighing their real burden, we are also predisposed to falling into emotional debts without any awareness of doing so."[6] They explained that in a business transaction the terms of the agreement are clearly stated, including the penalty for failing to abide by the terms of the contract and what is expected from each party named in the contract. Yet in this most difficult of all human relationships, frequently very little study is given to the requirements of the marriage relationship. "It is amazing how much spontaneous intuition and magic people expect in their human relationships."[7]

In most cases, because no clarification of the terms of the marriage takes place, expectations are assumed. When marriage partners fail to fulfill each other's expectations, conflict begins. Cohen and Sterling mentioned that when these perceived promises are broken, they may lead to broken hearts, which in turn lead to shattered relationships.

In most cases, because no clarification of terms of the marriage takes place, expectations are assumed. When the marriage partners fail to fulfill each other's expectations, conflict begins.

When considering the input needed for marriage renewal, Jim Conway placed time at the head of the list. Not far behind, in second position, was commitment. Conway claimed that time is vital for the couple to work on challenging issues. Lack of time is often used as an excuse to avoid the hard work necessary to rekindle the dying marital fire.[8] Renewal of a couple's relationship demands that time be preeminent since the early passion for each other has subsided and the couple is preoccupied with work, finances, children, and other distractions. However, in the early stages of a couple's relationship, much time is spent enjoying each other's company.

The main purpose for spending time together during courtship should not be merely to look into each other's eyes, to whisper sweet nothings in each other's ears, or to engage in petting and sexual relations. Rather, the time should be spent discovering who the other person really is and whether this person is really suited to be his or her life's partner. This is the time of discovery to determine whether they should proceed into the commitment phase of their relationship.

The main purpose for spending time together during courtship should not be merely to look into each other's eyes, to whisper sweet nothings in each other's ears, or to engage in petting and sexual relations. Rather, the time should be spent discovering who the other person really is and whether this person is really suited to be his or her life's partner. This is the time of discovery to determine whether they should proceed into the commitment phase of their relationship.

Whether commitment or recommitment, the sorting out of issues must precede the decision to proceed together. Most authorities in the marriage field recommend the assistance of a marriage counselor or marriage therapist depending on the circumstances. But the crucial commitment comes from the partners themselves. Without commitment, the marriage has no solid foundation. It is like the proverbial house built on the sand without adequate foundation. Like this building, marriage will be unable to withstand the ravages of nature that, most surely, will arrive. Conway pointed out that "some people, unfortunately, try to make their mate into the ideal person...All of these attempts are unrealistic and guaranteed to fail. Commitment means a willingness to understand the other person's unique personality, a desire to see the spouse's needs and understand what will help the spouse enjoy life more completely. The commitment must be to work with this particular person, at this age in life, in the society in which we live."[9]

Romantic Marriage

In a review of the evolution of marriage, John Townsend pointed out that "in all societies throughout history the fundamental basis of marriage has been a contract between two family lines that has assigned rights and duties concerning property and children."[10] With the help of Ralph Linton, Townsend noted that the concept of romantic love did not appear in Europe until the thirteenth century, and until the eighteenth century, marriage on the basis of romantic love played a minor role in European marriages.

Townsend believed that with the exception of a few earlier cultures, which included an intense emotional bond as a part of the marriage concept, American society is alone in using romantic love as a sole basis for marriage. In other words, marriage in most societies was an economic affair. "The primary purpose of the traditional family was to produce the next generation and transmit to it property, position, and knowledge."[11] With those marriages, the family lineage is important; the individual's feeling is not. Men and women performed different functions. Hence, both husband and wife were interdependent in order for the home to function properly. Of course, the Industrial Revolution and recent technological advancements have aided in bringing about the sexual revolution.

Since most North Americans have considered their culture and countries superior to most other nations of the world, excepting a few Western European allies, little effort has been expended to explore the fundamental elements in the functioning of other cultures and countries. Undoubtedly, North America's economic power and technological advancements have created societies unmatched by any other country in any other era of history. However, if it is true that this continent has formed, fashioned, and fostered the system of marriages based solely on romantic love as several researchers have claimed, we should be prepared to evaluate the outcome of this experiment as it passes through various stages in its metamorphosis. As our system of marriage progresses, is it enriching and supporting our advancing culture or does it contribute negatively to the deterioration of the moral, spiritual, and social underpinnings of the American society? Furthermore, should the American marriage find itself floundering in the dawn of the twenty-first century, how does a married couple find their way to a fulfilling experience, despite the escalating number of marital failures (about 50 percent of first marriages and 60 percent of second marriages)? Or, do we just surrender to the inevitability of our marriage adding to the failure rate?

Judith Wallerstein, in her book, *The Good Marriage: How and Why Love Lasts,* coauthored with Sandra Blakeslee, revealed an experience that took place at the genesis of the book project. She had the notion of writing a book about successful marriages. Entering a room with a hundred or so of her professional colleagues and friends, she announced her project idea and requested that some of them volunteer as subjects for the study. The room exploded with laughter and undertones of cynicism, nervousness, and disbelief. They were quite likely wondering if anyone thought there were still good marriages in society today. However, Wallerstein became perplexed when she saw that "when their sons and daughters decided to marry, these same women announced the marriages with great pride and accepted heartfelt rounds of congratulations from the others in the group. No one acknowledged the apparent contradictions involved."[12] Most of us learn to live with the duality of hope and despair for the future of marriage. Yet we see only optimism for the future of our children as they grow up and marry. They have yet to face the reality of marriage. Those who have married children soon witness their children's struggles and are reminded of their own marital challenges. Contrast our system of marriage with cultures in which parents choose a mate for their children. Do the brides and grooms in such cultures with a low divorce rate consider their system superior to ours? Or, do we feel that our system, despite a 50 to 60 percent failure rate, is superior to theirs? It is said that Americans fall in love before they marry, and in other cultures, they marry and then fall in love. Either way, love and commitment are needed in a successful marriage.

The Vow

How can we better ensure a long-lasting romantic marriage? Or, how can we recapture romance and foster security in our marriage? *Commitment!* When we consider that more than 50 percent of marriages fail and an additional number stay in an unhappy relationship for various reasons, such as children or fear of being alone, something significant is being overlooked. Most of those seeking divorce would likely confess that they were optimistic about the future of their marriage on the day of their wedding. Most likely, they were committed to marry their partner at that time. However, was that commitment thoroughly informed and completely analyzed? How much thought was given to the true reality of life together after the wedding?

Usually before marrying a couple, I would ask them to take a marriage pre-diction assessment, followed by counseling based on their responses. On one occasion, however, I agreed to perform a wedding for a young man and a young woman who were referred to me by a family I knew very well. Because they lived several hundred miles away, formal counseling was impractical. I believe we had only a few brief meetings. After checking for any legal impedi-ments, I agreed to perform the wedding. When I arrived at the church, the groom was present and the guests were beginning to arrive.

To my surprise, a young woman approached me to inform me that she was there to stop the wedding. She claimed that the groom had three children with her and was living with her up to the week prior to the wedding. He assured her that he would marry her soon. From her point of view, she should be the bride and she would find some means to stop the wedding. Although I was sympathetic with her situation, I had to explain that since they had duly obtained a marriage license, I would need the groom's consent to delay or postpone the wedding, unless she had legal grounds to prevent the groom from contracting a legal marriage. In addition, at that late stage, I had no way of verifying her claim unless she provided adequate proof with a legal basis. Having children with her and reneging on his promise to marry her appeared insensitive, immoral, and even cruel, but it did not provide legal grounds for halting the wedding. With earlier notification, I would have withdrawn my services until the matter was resolved and adequate counseling could take place. At this point, I did not deem it wise to do so.

I encouraged the groom to resolve the matter with her, but all attempts failed. We became concerned when she threatened to use unconventional means to stop the wedding. The groom called the police. I proceeded with the wedding with two police officers flanking the bride and groom. After that incident, I was very cautious about the backgrounds of those who requested my services to marry them. This couple is an example of the low level of awareness people can bring to the marriage process. How much do couples know about each other before committing to marry? If a lack of knowledge surrounds the parties, is their marriage destined to fail when their true characters are revealed?

> In the case of marriage, a long-term pleasant experience requires flexibility, adaptation, forgiveness, growth, and a willingness to endure various vicissitudes. With the exception of extreme circumstances, such as violence, abandonment or adultery, the marriage commitment should be for keeps.

By using the term *commitment*, I mean, "the state of being bound emotionally and intellectually to a way of thinking or course of action." In the case of marriage, a long-term pleasant experience requires flexibility, adaptation, forgiveness, growth, and a willingness to endure various vicissitudes. With the exception of extreme circumstances, such as violence and abandonment, the marriage commitment should be for keeps.

That is the reason for a vow and a binding legal contract at the beginning of the marriage journey. If either party is insincere or superficial, the marriage is doomed from its inception. Alstair Begg pointed out that it is necessary for couples contemplating marriage, as well as those in troubled marriages, to recognize that American marriages based on emotional surges and physical attraction are open to the possibility of disintegration when warm feelings evaporate and bodies succumb to the ravaging effects of nature.[13] "On the other hand, the likelihood of survival is markedly improved when marriages are grounded in friendship, companionship, and the awareness of an unending covenant, no matter what."[14]

Alistair Begg further indicated that when the Bible speaks of love within marriage, it refers to the will rather than the emotion. The biblical model is closer to the arranged marriage in which the families participate in the choice of the mate. "In stark contrast is our Western arrangement where newly engaged individuals stun their friends and family by announcing the name of a person with whom they are planning on spending the rest of their lives!"[15] Begg added that "the vows become very important. They provide walls of protection when threatening emotional winds and waves begin to beat upon the relationship. The traditional vows have stood the test of time because they aptly summarize the commitment that is involved."[16] Husbands and wives can increase their chances of enjoying a lasting marriage if they choose to abide by their marriage vows.

Dr. Fred Lowery concurred fully with my conclusions, which I stated earlier concerning the difficulty of the marriage experience. He stated, "I want to be gut-level honest with you: Maintaining a loving, intimate relationship between two selfish and imperfect human beings is the most difficult, most complex, and most time-consuming challenge any of us will face in this lifetime."[17] The authors of *A Lasting Promise* support my other contention that most married couples understand that commitment is the glue that keeps them together.[18]

Dedication Not Constraint

In the book, *A Lasting Promise*, the authors specified the type of commitment needed. There are two types: *dedication* and *constraint*. Commitment characterized by dedication should provide the basis for the marriage relationship. The partners are imbued with an intrinsic desire "not only to continue the relationship but also to improve it, to sacrifice for it, to invest in it, to link personal goals to it, and to seek the partner's welfare, not simply one's own."[19] Commitment by constraint refers to forces that obligate the persons to remain in the relationship whether or not they are dedicated. Constraint commitment fosters negative forces, which in turn lead to unhappiness, dissatisfaction, and lack of freedom.

Covenant or Contract

Fred Lowery took a different approach in order to reach a similar conclusion. His approach is based on the covenant as presented in the Bible. It is no secret that the North American principles and procedures regarding marriage were rooted in biblical concepts. It is the Genesis account that sheds light on the creation of a man and a woman as the first married couple. God performed the first wedding, and in blessing the first couple, he said: "Be fruitful and multiply, and fill the earth and subdue it...."[20] The biblical record also states: "Therefore a man leaves his father and his mother and cleaves to his wife, and they become one flesh."[21] This sets into motion a pattern for subsequent marriages. Lowery made the point that the term *covenant*, though mentioned more than three hundred times in the Old Testament, has an extra-biblical origin. "For thousands of years, the practice of making and keeping covenants has been used by civilized societies to promote understanding, resolve conflicts, and provide parameters for relationships."[22] However, the Bible relied heavily on the use of the term covenant. As an example, Jesus made a covenant with those who accept his promises and his sacrifice for their sins. He covenants: "I will never fail you nor forsake you." [23]

A covenant is different from a contract. Both are usually involved in a wedding. In the Christian wedding, a covenant and a contract are separated by the law of the state, which requires a contract, and the church, which performs the wedding vows based on a covenant made between the two parties. A contract is an agreement based on lack of trust. The parties set limits on their responsibilities, their rights, benefits, duration, liability, and even their escape clause. A covenant is based on trust, love, and loyalty and sets no limit to their own responsibility. A covenant marriage "is unconditional, unlimited, and unending. A covenant marriage is more about trust than terms, more about character than convenience, more about giving than receiving."[24] To be successful, a marriage may begin with a contract but must be sustained by a covenant.

In the prologue to their book, *Good Marriages Don't Just Happen*, the authors told their story. Pointing out that marriage is currently approached as a business venture, they proceeded to show how their experience was different. The popular approach in our society is to have a contract duly signed before witnesses with stipulations made and expectations defined in case one party fails to live up to his/her part of the agreement. Rather than considering marriage a contract, they claimed they approached marriage as a covenant made with each other as a permanent unconditional commitment.

> We chose to be with each other in a never-ending relationship. We chose to love the other in a relationship that would strive to make each of us better individuals. We also chose to integrate God into all aspects of our lives, not understanding at the time of our wedding how integral God's love and spirit would be in the growth of our relationship. We've experienced the richer and the poorer, the good times and the bad, health and illness, sadness and joy, fulfillment and disappointments. The commitment we both made to our relationship enabled us to weather the hard times and grow stronger in our love. Building a loving, lasting, joy-filled relationship entails effort and a constant commitment by both spouses. Good marriages don't just happen.[25]

After coming to terms with her own marital challenges, Iris Krasnow wrote *Surrendering to Marriage*. In her book, she wrote: "Yet, my fantasy of marriage as a wellspring of contentment has completely disappeared, and so should yours. Thinking you get happiness ever after is a ticket to divorce."[26] From her transforming relationship, she learned four things:

1. *Marriage can be hell;*

2. *The grass is not greener on the other side;*

3. *Savor the highs, because one thing you can count on—the dips are just around the corner;*

4. *Nobody is perfect, so you may as well love the one you're with.*[27]

Krasnow developed these principles after a lot of work and tears. She confessed: "I surrender to this imperfect marriage, because I love it more than I hate it and I am committed to this man with a promise that I need to, we all need to, do our best to fulfill."[28] If marriages were approached with this kind of commitment, would our escalating divorce statistics occur?

Commitment Phobia

When considering commitment in a relationship, it would be instructive to take into account that some people are unable or unwilling to commit completely to a life partner. Researchers have documented this issue adequately. The well-known *Shere Hite Report on the Family*, published in 1994, for instance, supports the theory that boys experience a separation trauma when at an early age they have to break the bond with their mother. "Leaving the mother causes a paralysis in boys, a trauma of guilt, which can make it hard for them to love and accept love later, and creates conflict in almost all relationships with women (including those at work), because it brings up feelings of guilt and fear of 'entrapment' in the women's world."[29] The report claimed that since mothers had to kill physical intimacy with their son as society demands, some boys develop the feeling instinctively that love must have an ending. Hence during friendship or marriage, they may abruptly sever the love connection with their mate. "Many women report a pattern in men which they find extraordinarily confusing and irrational. The man behaves with undeniably real and intense passion toward them (not only sexually, but also emotionally), only to turn around and close down his feelings almost in the middle of love...."[30]

In a *New York Times* bestseller, *Men Who Can't Love*, Stephen Carter and Julia Sokol portrayed this lack of commitment by some men as *commitment phobia*. When dealing with this type of man, some women believe that this lack of sustained commitment happened only to them. But they are wrong. These men do that to every woman with whom they develop a relationship. Carter and Sokol believed this behavior to be so common that most women have encountered at least one such man during their dating or marriage. They seek to expose this problem so that women could recognize it and avoid serious relationships with these men.

The relationship may seem quite normal at first. She may see in him a man who seems to need and want love. He may even appear vulnerable so that she is convinced that it is safe to respond. But "if his fear is strong enough, this man will ultimately sabotage, destroy, or run away from any solid, good relationship. He wants love but he is terrified—genuinely phobic—about commitment and will run away from any woman who represents 'happy ever after.'"[31] Some women will try to be their therapists but often to no avail. These men may need professional help. The woman who surrenders to such a man may be one step away from serious heartbreak, depending, of course, on how much emotional and economic investment is made before his true character is unveiled. This is another reason that couples should take the time and effort to discover the true character of the other individual before committing to a serious relationship. You need to be certain that both of you are equally committed to make the relationship succeed.

> You need to be certain that both of you are equally committed to make the relationship succeed.

I believed for many years that no one runs away from love. Research results have caused me to modify my views. Individuals who want to enjoy lifelong happiness in a marriage relationship should reflect carefully on their intended partner's capacity for a long-term commitment. "Building a marriage is much like building a house, and the plans you follow are shaped by the vision you have in mind. The vision you construct for your marriage will shape the life you have in it."[32]

Family Interview

Of what importance is commitment to your relationship?

Based on our personal experiences and observations, we believe that commitment is the most important factor in the success of any relationship.

As a newly married couple, we feel very committed to each other and to making our marriage succeed. Given our religious beliefs, we both also strongly believe that marriage is forever. Before making our ultimate commitment at the marriage altar, we occasionally entertained insecurities and questions that caused us to evaluate the viability of our relationship. That's probably healthy in the premarital phase of our relationship. But that changed on our wedding day.

Because of our irreversible commitment to our marriage, events and questions that previously threatened the permanency of our relationship are now merely minor challenges to overcome together. Rather than second-guessing our marriage decision, we talk candidly and constructively and put the issues to rest before bedtime.

We observe that many unmarried couples and some married couples lack that commitment and, consequently, their relationships are damaged or ruined by even the smallest challenges. But it is because of its power to overcome such challenges, that we feel commitment is the most important aspect of our relationship.

Contributed by Richard and Alicia

3

Conflict

Much of our forty years of marriage contained serious conflicts—emotional wars—but we never seriously contemplated retreat. To be sure, at times the possibility of separating perched perilously at a tantalizing proximity prodding either one of us to pick that perilous path. Needless to say, it never became an option. Like soldiers on a clearly defined mission, we didn't only endure the battle, we reveled in the victory. There is something to be said for the victorious human spirit. It is revealed frequently in several aspects of life—business, politics, religion, adventures, and numerous other ways—frequently resulting in admirable outcomes. Just think that some persons would endure bitter criticisms, sleepless nights, and constant bombardment by ever-escalating and unrelenting problems in a political position without quitting. Similarly, other persons would choose to endure incredible pain, panic, and problems in climbing the daunting Mount Everest or in reaching the freezing North Pole but would not tolerate the inevitable problems that marriage presents. Since emotion is the universal language of humans, there should be a logical expectation that in a close relationship, conflict is at least likely, if not inevitable. What experience has taught me, however, is that when conflict develops in a marriage, frequently each spouse seeks to claim the high ground of innocence—it's not my fault syndrome. Even if it's clear who is at fault, the guilty spouse will tend to avoid the consequences, which is the humble role of being sincerely sorrowful and following through with a genuine apology. In fact, one of the most difficult experiences for me even now is accepting the wrong, especially if I think the guilty party may be my spouse. The high ground should be to develop an attitude of seeing myself as a peacemaker. Consequently, when a problem develops, my reaction should be to deal with my attitude to resolving it rather than seeking to blame my spouse. In the end it doesn't matter who is wrong, the moment a misunderstanding occurs, the path of wisdom would be to seek an early resolution. This would save us both from the stressful saga such sensitivities bring. There usually emerges the problematic process of hurting, blaming, withdrawal, avoidance, reticence, tit-for-tat, unpleasantness, cooling off, warming up, unspoken forgiveness, bonding, and, finally, back to loving.

> What experience has taught me, however, is that when conflict develops in a marriage, frequently each spouse seeks to claim the high ground of innocence—it's not my fault syndrome.

This process may be limited to two or more aspects or it may be full-blown, lasting from a few minutes to several days. After one special incident, the hurt to recovery process lasted about six months. It is truly amazing to me to discover that someone so near and dear to me, in an instant, appeared to me cold and distant. I lay much of the blame on my shoulders since I know my own feelings and, to me, this path is mainly selfish and unproductive. Even though theoretically, I know how to handle conflict, especially since during decades of counseling other families I have seen several positive outcomes, there was still that lingering lack of personal victory. That is not to say I had not obtained numerous victories over my feelings. The issue remains that there are still times of abject failure. Fortunately, they have now become fewer and much milder. Experience certainly teaches wisdom. Of course, we must search incessantly for the lessons that experience always brings and seek to find ways to apply them to our lives.

Hurt Feelings

Let's explore hurt feelings within our spousal relationship. In our case, this issue has dominated the cause and duration of conflict. Regardless of the cause of any particular incident, soon the matter is forgotten unless one of us feels hurt. Often the hurt grows either gradually or suddenly by succeeding words or actions or even a glance or silence. Anything intentional or incidental may trigger an escalation of the perceived perpetrated wrong.

We had just arrived in Edmonton, Alberta, Canada, after our wedding. We rented an apartment from a lady who was an art teacher at the University of Alberta. Since we were alone on the lower floor of a single family home in a middle class neighborhood, we felt quite secure and comfortable. I soon realized that spending time together with a wife in the same living space was significantly different from meeting Pam for an evening date. There were several areas of adjustment needed. In retrospect, it appeared that we needed to begin a whole new experience. Our periods of friendship and courtship served only as preparation. Now the real process of pulverizing, sowing, mulching, pruning, waiting, and harvesting all lay ahead.

Soon after we settled in, Pam started to recount the situations that arose between us in college that made her uncomfortable. (We were classmates in high school and the first two years of college.) The discussion became intense when she insisted that I ignored her for two girls in whom I had showed much interest. I'll admit that my philosophy of dating was difficult for Pam. I made it clear to her that since I was not married, I should still have the freedom to socialize with other girls. In retrospect, even though I still had certain freedom to socialize, Pam was left with a lack of lasting assurance that ultimately I would be faithful to her. We were not engaged and had made no verbal commitments to each other, except the strong bond of friendship we enjoyed. Actually, we shared an unspoken understanding that we were committed to each other.

But I was wrong. My lack of directness left the door open to unsuspecting mischief. The chief of which was the questioning of my motive in openly pursuing these friendships with other attractive girls and, even worse, the attitude of these girls regarding our friendship. One of the girls had indicated to Pam that she could take me away from her, if she chose to do so. Since this and other emotional wars were confined to the girls' dormitory, I remained oblivious to their depreciating effect until our confrontation during the first few weeks of our marriage.

Needless to say, I reacted with surprise both that the girls had used our innocent friendship to undermine my relationship with Pam and that Pam had taken them seriously. Obviously, my youthful inexperience did not allow me the necessary prudence to avoid such a painful problem. So now I had to face my wife's emotional reaction. Quite likely, she may have been only seeking assurance that my friendship with the girls was only innocent campus connection, without any subtle subversive sabotage. Again, I failed to respond with understanding. Instead, I responded with impatience, using harsh words. Pam was very hurt and angry. But the incident awakened me to the need for an irreversible resolution never to engage in aggressive physical contact in an attempt to resolve any misunderstanding in our marriage. That decision has proved to be lasting.

> But the incident awakened me to the need for an irreversible resolution never to engage in aggressive physical contact in an attempt to resolve any misunderstanding in our marriage. That decision proved to be lasting.

Differences

Our differences have been the cause of many of our conflicts. Although we shared common views regarding several aspects of our lives, there remained sufficient differences that may be regarded as necessary to make our lives interesting or as a source of constant irritation. Fortunately for us, we have learned to be patient with each other even though those differences, though diminished, have not disappeared. Pam is generally gracious, patient, and gentle in manner and speech. I am aggressive, impatient, and loud. Pam has tried to change me during all these years with only limited success. For instance, when caught in traffic, invariably I will seek an alternative route, even if it eventually takes longer. I prefer to keep moving. Pam prefers the beaten path and is inclined to wait it out regardless of the length of time. I will then irritate her by saying: "That's why I could never be a slave; I just wouldn't live under restriction for long without reacting." Often my normal voice tone gives her the impression that I am upset. She has never gotten adjusted to that and my attempts to change permanently have attained only limited success. I would tell her: "My voice is an advantage in my profession." Pam usually thinks I'm shouting or quarreling, even if I think that I am speaking normally. It would appear that some habits are hard to break. Let's take a look at other points of view on the subject of conflict.

Predicting Outcomes

The opening statement in the book, *Seven Basic Quarrels*, reveals a reality that so many newly married couples tend to overlook: "Falling in love makes a man and a woman discover how much they have in common. Living together makes lovers realize how many things there are to divide them."[1] Regrettably, after the entrancing romance leading up to the honeymoon, a couple must face the harsh day-to-day reality of a normal life. How we wish that honeymoon would last forever! Yet this person you love deeply and to whom you vowed to be faithful throughout all of life's struggles or triumphs soon appears to be the source of your greatest irritation. "It is as though some powerful, subterranean current takes hold of you both and leads you down a path of negative thinking, destructive feelings, painful action and reaction, drifting toward isolation and loneliness."[2]

Bill Knott, in an editorial for the *Advent Review*, related an experience on visiting an old graveyard, which lies near the Vermont/Massachusetts border. He observed graves with obelisks of white marble from the 1830s and slate and granite stones from the Revolutionary War as well as more recent memorials from the Vietnam War. On one gravestone were the shocking words: "Captain John Parker, 43, July 25, 1786. Accidentally shot by one of his own men."[3] When we are with friends and family, we should feel safe. How tragic then that frequently spouses give way to anger and injure the person they claim to love dearly.

The early excitement of love soon dissipates for many couples and is replaced by anger, resentment, and conflict. Are there certain trends in a relationship or certain predictable behaviors that, if detected and corrected, may help prevent the failure of a marriage? Dr. John Gottman says there are. After decades of scientific research on what makes a marriage last, he has developed a system to predict—with 94 percent accuracy—which marriages will succeed or fail. Consequently, the use of this information could prevent marital failure. Gottman claimed that prior to his scientific approach there were a plethora of psychological theories about how to solve marital problems. Some of these theories were misguided or dead wrong. They were based mainly on psychologists' beliefs developed through intuition and experience with their clients. Psychologists and social scientists posited theories for marital breakdown such as the shift from a family farm economy to factories, relaxation of divorce laws, the emerging financial independence of women, and the increase of violence in our society. Due to a lack of scientific research on marriage, popular myths and misconceptions found a place with marriage counselors. Such notions as financial difficulties, lack of communication, sexual disagreements, and incompatibility were cited as reasons for divorce. These issues are valid contributors to the weakening of the social threads and interpersonal bonds that keep marriages together. But they do not explain the reason some marriages last while others fail, when facing the same pressures. Furthermore, newly married couples and those couples undergoing stress need to have a more precise understanding of issues they should deal with in order to ensure their success.

Furthermore, newly married couples and those couples undergoing stress need to have a more precise understanding of issues they should deal with in order to ensure their success.

Previous researchers, such as David H. Olson, professor of family social science at the University of Minnesota, developed premarital prediction tests to determine areas of conflict in marriage. "What [their] evaluation could not predict, however, was which among the many dissatisfied couples—were destined to stay married and which were headed for a fall. This is the crucial question. After all, many marriages that are basically stable go through occasional periods of dissatisfaction."[4] Previous studies led marriage counselors to assume that a similarity of opinions safeguards against divorce. Gottman observed that several couples with initial disagreements survived if they found ways to work out their differences. Some even fared better in the long run if they had early disagreements. "Clearly, marital bliss and perfect compatibility are not the only glue that holds couples together—and may not even be the most important glue."[5] In order to discover the crucial ingredients for a successful marriage, Dr. Gottman took to the lab. He engaged the husbands and wives in conversation, probing for elements of anger and frustration and isolating the elements that allowed some couples to stay together and others to divorce. He also used machines similar to a polygraph to probe for relevant information. Let's review his findings. Gottman's underlying research finding is that conflicts in marriage are inevitable. Successful couples develop mechanisms to resolve these conflicts when they arise.

Gottman's underlying research finding is that conflicts in marriage are inevitable. Successful couples develop mechanisms to resolve these conflicts when they arise.

Many psychologists assume that conflict avoidance and volatile marriages are destructive. Some couples believe that never having a fight is a sign of a successful relationship and that it leads to happiness. John Gottman's research has shown otherwise. "When I started the research I assumed, like most researchers and clinicians, that anger was destructive if there was 'too much' of it. But when I looked at what predicted divorce or separation, I found that anger only has negative effects in marriage if it is expressed along with criticism or contempt, or if it is defensive."[6] According to Gottman, the four destructive interactions that tend to cause a downward spiral in a couple's relationship are *criticism, contempt, defensiveness,* and *withdrawal.*

> According to Dr. Gottman, the four destructive interactions that tend to cause a downward spiral in a couple's relationship are *criticism, contempt, defensiveness,* and *withdrawal.*

Most couples could benefit greatly from Dr. Gottman's research regarding the five marriage styles. Two of them are negative and three are positive. The two types that lead marriage into a "free fall toward destruction" are *hostile/engaged* and *hostile/detached* couples. Couples facing a "marital meltdown" may argue frequently and hotly, using name-calling, insults, putdowns, and sarcasm (hostile/engaged), or they may ignore each other, fail to pay attention to what the other person is saying but occasionally attack each other or become defensive (hostile/detached.) The successful marriages resolve their conflicts in one of three ways. "In a *validating marriage* couples compromise often and calmly work out their problems to mutual satisfaction as they arise. In a *conflict-avoiding marriage* couples agree to disagree, rarely confronting their differences head-on. And finally, in a *volatile marriage* conflicts erupt often, resulting in passionate disputes."[7] Volatile couples were less extreme in expressing their anger and frustration. They complained, got angry but were not overly critical, defensive, or contemptuous. They remain engaged listeners. Successful couples retained love and respect.

> Another important predictor is how they relate their history. When the marriage is breaking down, they put a negative spin on their past experience together.

Of great significance to the marriage is the positive-to-negative equilibrium Gottman developed through a scientific methodology. The magic formula is a

5: 1 ratio. As long as the interactions and positive feelings between husband and wife are five times more than the negative ones, the marriage is likely to succeed.[8] Another important predictor is how they relate their history. When the marriage is breaking down, they put a negative spin on their past experience together. This is an early sign that the marriage is in a downward spiral. What you think of your spouse affects your attitude toward him/her.

William Betcher, a clinical fellow in psychiatry at Harvard Medical School and a psychotherapist, coauthored *The Seven Basic Quarrels of Marriage* with Robie Macauley. They concluded that there are seven basic recurring themes in marital battles. Obviously, there are other issues, but these seven represent the general areas of disagreements for most married couples.

> The magic formula is a 5: 1 ratio. As long as the interactions and positive feelings between husband and wife are five times more than the negative ones, the marriage is likely to succeed.

These seven truly basic subjects of quarreling are *gender, loyalties, money, power, sex, privacy,* and *children*. These recurring themes "are singled out again and again in therapy practice as the most common, the most emotion-filled, and the most deeply rooted of our conflicts."[9]

The basic quarrels are mostly invisible. Marriage is based on a system that is improvised by two people. They usually do not think through the process logically. Most people understand the daily functioning of their relationship, but only a few couples have a clear concept of the invisible system that guides it.

> During early marriage, the discords spring from passion and inexperience; in middle life, there are economic burdens and family obligations; and finally come the disappointments and physical aches of age. The basic quarrel may shift with a new stage of life, or it may arise out of the change. Since people who have been together for a long time tend to assume that they know each other very well, they are surprised when a new basic quarrel materializes in a new season of life.[10]

The authors may have surprised us when they announced (like John Gottman) that quarrels are necessary for marriages to succeed. "These quarrels are necessary because they are rooted in profound differences the man and woman understand only dimly. Only by having the quarrel in a new way—without destructive tactics and with a willingness to learn what lies beneath the surface—can it ever be solved."[11] They believed that real differences between people can be changed. If approached correctly, basic quarrels can be overcome. The greatest barrier to conflict resolution is "rigid thinking—one's conviction either that the spouse is a hopeless case or that one can't help reacting intolerantly. People tend to blame their own flawed behavior on circumstances beyond their control and their partner's sins on defects of character."[12]

The seven basic quarrels refer to a kind of ongoing battle between the parties rather than temporary fallout. It is the kind of problem that recurs, casting a bleak and hostile cloud over the marriage. Betcher and Macauley argued that whereas friction occurs in a marriage, a basic quarrel is not inevitable or incurable. It can be anticipated, understood, and resolved. "Overcoming it is a triumph that actually strengthens a marriage."[13]

Conflict Resolution

Catherine and Joseph Garcia-Pratts emphasized the need for identifying and acknowledging the problem. In many relationships only one spouse feels there is a problem. When problems arise, some couples just hope and pray that the problem will go away. But their attitude in dealing with problems in their relationship will become either a stumbling block or a stepping-stone. Acknowledging that a problem exists is a major hurdle that must be overcome for resolution to occur. Some spouses often opt for avoidance in order to elude pain, hurt feelings, retaliation, or an angry reaction from the spouse.

> Acknowledging that a problem exists is a major hurdle that must be overcome for resolution to occur. Some spouses often opt for avoidance in order to elude pain, hurt feelings, retaliation, or an angry reaction from the spouse.

Several therapists and marriage counselors have emphasized compromise as a way of solving conflicts. A study by Dr. Samuel Vuchinich revealed that conflicts ended in compromise only 14 percent of the time. The majority of the time (61 percent), the couple ended the quarrel in a standoff, both spouses maintaining their own views. Twenty-one percent of the time the argument stopped when one conceded and a mere 4 percent of the time the matter ended with one of the parties walking out of the room.[14] More than compromise is needed to resolve most of the disputes. It is obvious that other approaches are also needed.

Wallerstein and Blakeslee recommend *establishing a safety zone*. Good marriages provide a "holding environment for aggression." This is an understanding that anger and disagreements may be expressed freely without fear that the fight will fracture the marriage. Such reinforcement is crucial if one or both spouses are insecure or were abandoned as a child. The couple should have the assurance that their "love and friendship, the togetherness they have built, their shared interest and history, including the children, all combine to provide the overall structure that contains the aggression. The ties that unite them are far stronger than the forces that divide them. Their awareness of this strength acts as a powerful deterrent to letting things fly out of control. It enables one person to interrupt the anger out of concern for the other and for the marriage."[15] Couples must function within absolute boundaries. One such limit is physical violence. Even during times of anger, restraint and boundaries must be respected.

> Couples must function within absolute boundaries. One such limit is physical violence. Even during times of anger, restraint and boundaries must be respected.

Charlie Shedd proposed seven rules for a good fight. Using the illustration of two quiet streams creating wild commotion at the point of converging, then flowing gently as it meanders downstream, Shedd pointed to eruptions of conflict that take place in some loving relationships: "Personalities rush against each other. Preferences clash. Ideas contend for power and habits vie for position. Sometimes, like the waves, they throw up a spray that leaves you breathless and makes you wonder where the loveliness has gone."[16] The seven rules established between him and his wife are as follows:

1. Before the fight begins, you must both agree the time is right.

2. The only aim is deeper understanding.

3. Check your weapons often to see that they are not deadly.

4. Lower your voices one notch rather than raising them two.

5. Never quarrel or reveal private matters in public.

6. Discuss an armistice when one calls "halt."

7. Upon coming to terms, put it away until you agree it needs more discussing.

Husbands and wives should learn to say, "I am sorry." They should forgive each other and try to forget. There should be no concern for winning the argument. If the matter is settled amicably, both win.

Husbands and wives should learn to say, "I am sorry." They should forgive each other and try to forget. There should be no concern for winning the argument. If the matter is settled amicably, both win.

Dr. John Gottman gave advice to both wife and husband. His advice to men was as follows:

> Embrace her anger. Do not try to avoid conflict. Sidestepping a problem will not solve it. Rather, it may cause greater problems since your wife may think she is being ignored. Staying and listening to her may be unpleasant, but she is working to keep the marriage healthy.
>
> Try to remember that her goal is not to attack you personally, even though it may seem so at times if frustration causes her to couch her complaint in contempt and sarcasm. If you stay with her through this discomfort and listen to her criticisms rather than insisting that she is exaggerating or getting hysterical over nothing, she will calm down. If you stonewall and refuse to listen, she'll be edgy and may escalate the conflict, making it more likely that you will wind up feeling flooded.[17]

Getting defensive will ruin the chances of resolving the conflict. Remember to respect her opinion.

Gottman's advice to women includes:

> Confront him gently. In order to break the vicious cycle of demand/withdrawal, the wife needs to remember that you are emotionally from different planets. Approach him calmly and gently or he may try to withdraw. When you do criticize your husband, remember to tell him you love him and that you just want to change a certain behavior. Try very hard not to slip from complain to criticism and then to contempt. He will easily get flooded and

then the conflict can quickly escalate. It will be much easier for him to stay engaged if you let him know that talking together about what's bothering you is a way to keep the love between you alive.[18]

Both spouses should always take into account that biological and cultural differences can hinder complete understanding. Every effort should be made to resolve your problems together. The subtitle for the book *Seven Basic Quarrels of Marriage* states succinctly the process for dealing with conflict: *recognize, defuse, negotiate, and resolve*. Booth Tarkington is credited with the words of wisdom:

"An ideal wife is any woman who has an ideal husband."

Family Interview

Taking into account that both of you are very self-confident and hold very strong opinions, how do you deal with conflicts in your marriage?

It appears evident that conflicts are inevitable in a marriage. Conflict naturally exists by virtue of the differences in gender, personality, upbringing, values, perspective, life experiences, and decision-making styles. Conflict can be positive if it creates a forum for communication, information about your spouse, and an opportunity to build a stronger relationship. However, if conflicts aren't resolved, deep chasms can be created in the relationship and drive partners apart.

There are several avenues in which conflict can impact a marriage and serve to challenge its homeostasis. One important approach to resolving conflict is to identify its underlying source. Conflict in the marriage may stem from several sources including limited financial resources, competition, belief systems (values), power dynamics, or communication styles (personality clashes). Once a couple determines the underlying reason for conflicts, they will be a step closer to resolving them.

To illustrate how conflict has impacted our marriage, we will share a specific situation. First, I would like to explore the issue of physical distance. Several years ago, Frank was offered an opportunity to work abroad during parts of the year. He had a business in Manhattan at the time and felt this opportunity would enhance his financial options. We had been dating for five years and were very committed to our relationship. Frank felt, and I agreed, that this was a good business opportunity.

The first couple of years, he traveled only at Christmas and part of the summer. Two years later, we married, and our daughter was born. We were at a crossroad. With a new addition to our family, I reluctantly agreed that he would work abroad for two years. We lived apart but maintained a semblance of family as best as we could. As time went on, other issues crept into our relationship. Frank felt the pressures of maintaining the household, and I felt the pressures of raising our daughter alone. My feelings of abandonment in the marriage and Frank's resentment surfaced. I decided to leave my job and familiar surroundings to venture abroad with him. At the time, I felt that it was important to establish myself in my career field. I knew that living as a family in one locale was the healthiest decision, so I moved with our daughter abroad. By this time feelings of hurt and disappointment had already "nestled" in the marriage.

We did not anticipate these dramatic life changes. As a result, we were not fully prepared and equipped to handle them. The physical distance had exacerbated these conflicts; we did not have the "luxury" to nurture and rely on each other for physical comfort. Much transpired in the succeeding years. Needless to say, we survived them. Frank now resides in New York, but the task of rebuilding and negotiating conflicts is ongoing.

In order to resolve conflicts, one must first anticipate conflict events, identify their source, and choose the best approach to resolving them. The most effective method for resolving conflict is to solve the conflict collaboratively, remembering that the relationship and the issue are both significant.

Contributed by Tamaylia and Frank

Tamaylia, our first daughter and second child, was born in the Bahamas but spent most of her early years in Montreal and Edmonton, Canada. While attending Columbia University in New York, she met Frank, a Guyanese, who with his parents and siblings moved to New York while he was in his teen years. Both of them have a passion for each other and New York City. Frank was an outstanding athlete during his college years and traveled extensively to participate in competitions. He has transferred his passion for physical fitness into his career as a physical trainer. Tamaylia is director of a remedial educational program for youth in New York. They have one daughter.

4

Control

Early in our relationship much of our conflict was caused by the tendency to control. This does not mean malicious intent. To the contrary, this attitude emerged because our desire to assist each other to make the best choices motivated us to attempt to control the other. Since I understand my motives more clearly, I have chosen to use illustrations from my experience rather than Pam's. Although I convinced myself that as husband I had the right or duty to lead in the decision-making process, my own actions must have caused Pam much frustration. If I thought that we should follow a particular direction as a family, I would pursue that course single-mindedly. Frequently, my enthusiasm completely displaced the need for dialogue.

During the first few years of our marriage, several areas of control were very evident. Without any specific discussion on the issue, I took for granted that Pam would take care of the meals and care for the home. That included cooking, washing the dishes, and doing all the house cleaning. She did so voluntarily. However, with Pam's automatically assuming the house duties came something subtler than an inexperienced young husband would readily comprehend. Pam assumed the role of furnishing and decorating the house. Later, I discovered that her claim on this aspect of our lives included the choice of the house we would purchase. Not understanding what was occurring and thinking I was in charge of all decisions, the struggle lasted for several years as I refused to relent. Usually, when I went away on a business trip, Pam would move around all the furniture, including those pieces in my study. This resulted in several weeks of trying to find the simplest item. Just as I would develop a routine locating items around the house, we would be due for another move. To make a little confession, the moves usually gave me a sense of renewal and pleasurable satisfaction, but I just couldn't comprehend the reason the furniture could not stay in the original position. The problem was that usually I didn't allow my positive impressions to prevail, thereby offering the well-deserved compliments. In fact, if I indulged myself slightly by asking her why she had to rearrange the furniture again, or simply ignored the changes, I was condemned to the task of redeeming myself. I had to find the right words or, more accurately, develop the right attitude to soothe the simmering situation stirred up by my attitude. A difficult task indeed!

Our vacations usually had trying times blended with the anticipated excitement. On one occasion when we went on a family vacation, we traveled by car from Montreal to Miami, en route to the Bahamas. Our spirits were dashed soon after arriving in New York. I had bought tickets for the family to attend the baseball game between the New York Mets and the Montreal Expos. Late that morning Pam informed me that she had an appointment at the hairdresser. Just imagine my frustration when I learned that this was in White Plains and we were in the Bronx at that time. The game began at one o'clock. One thing I have difficulty understanding is the reason women take so long to have their hair done. The family traveled to White Plains together so that after the hair appointment we could go directly to the ball game. Imagine my chagrin when several hours had passed and my wife was still in the hair salon. We watched anxiously as the time approached for the game to begin. The stadium was at least fifteen miles away. The game had already started when Pam left the salon. I was so flustered by then that I locked the car keys in the trunk. After a locksmith arrived and opened the door, we sped down the Sprain Parkway only to hear the sports commentator announce the seventh inning. We felt very dejected. As it turned out that was our only opportunity as a family to see a ball game in New York and we lost it. Our children were also devoted fans of the Montreal Expos and equally excited about the Mets and Yankees. Missing the game left me in a mood that cast its long gloomy shadow over much of the two-week vacation in Miami and the Bahamas. Fortunately for us, the mood began to dissipate as we arrived in Freeport, Grand Bahama, where Richard and Tamaylia were born. My hurt feelings combined with the lost opportunity to attend the game with the children, who were exceptionally enthusiastic about the event, crushed my spirit. Dealing with the disappointment promptly would have diffused the situation and revived our spirits. Instead, I blamed Pam for disrupting our plans, and I allowed my feeling to spread into other areas of our activities, resulting in pain for my wife, our four children, my nephew, Michael, then living with us, and myself.

Another serious conflict occurred in the summer of 1979. We were visiting relatives in New York when Pam announced that she wanted to visit a former boyfriend from her teen years who was residing in Maryland. Little did I realize how deeply I felt about my wife having a male friend in her teens, even though it had only been an innocent youthful encounter. At that time dating in families was very strict and I knew she had excellent parental supervision. That's clearly demonstrated by Pam's high moral principles. Nevertheless, I felt an undefined emotional unsettledness simmering deep within me. Appearing to be bold and considering this reunion to be an opportunity for her to put closure to a kind of youthful fantasy, I agreed. Our four children went with us.

At first the trip to Maryland appeared to be an adventure. Pam's friend, a medical doctor, and his wife resided in a gorgeous home, nestled in a delightful neighborhood. We received a friendly reception. Of course, it is unlikely his wife knew about their early friendship. Following several hours of pleasant dialogue and a delicious meal, the hosts invited us to stay for the night. It was then that it dawned on me that this should not have been an inviting situation for me. I was a stranger to this couple and suddenly, for an unexplained reason, I felt like an unwilling emotional rival. Rising very abruptly, I tried to hurry my family from their home during their attempts to extend their gracious invitation for us to stay. As we left I felt confused and distraught.

My feeling grew negative as the night wore on. This feeling was exacerbated by our failure to locate a reasonable priced hotel until after midnight. By that time everyone was exhausted. Unfortunately, my unpleasant feeling persisted, later flaring up into a full-scale resentment against my wife. Instead of a pleasant adventure, Pam felt crushed and humiliated. As a result of that fiasco, I had to confront my immaturity. Surprised by my own negative reaction, I began a transformation that led to mature responses to future difficult situations. Today, we can tease each other about that and similar past experiences without rancor or repercussion.

> As a result of that fiasco, I had to confront my immaturity. Surprised by my own negative reaction, I began a transformation that led to mature responses to future difficult situations.

Dominance: A Biblical View

Since our modern view of marriage is rooted in the Judeo-Christian tradition, I have chosen to include biblical references in our discussion. One of the many references that have influenced our understanding of marriage is recorded in Ephesians chapter 5. Until recently, most religious ceremonies included this reference. With the emergence of the women's movement in the past few decades, many ministers have had difficulty with the interpretation of this passage. The problematic passage states:

> Wives, be subject to your husbands, as to the Lord. For the husband is the head of the wife as Christ is the head of the church, his body, and is himself its savior. As the church is subject to Christ, so let wives be subject in everything to their husbands.[1]

The view concerning the roles of males and females in marriage, as expressed in this passage, has clearly influenced marriages for much of the past two millennia. In fact, Paul, by this declaration, mirrored the patriarchal Jewish society. Of course, the Jewish concept of marriage was based on the creation narrative. Regardless of one's interpretation of this passage, however, one's conclusion could be erroneous if the context of this passage was not taken into account.

> **The biblical reference to the man being the head has to refer more to function than status in the marital relationship.**

The previous verse states: "Be subject to one another—." Two texts in the passage, following the problematic declaration, help to further clarify its meaning. "Even so husbands should love their wives as their own bodies. For this reason a man shall leave his father and mother and be joined to his wife, and the two shall become one flesh." The King James Version of the Bible uses the word *submit* in place of "subject." If the Bible were directing the husband to dominate the wife, it would be inconsistent in commanding the husband to submit to his wife. Furthermore, how could a man be able to dominate a part of his own body? Becoming one body would imply mutuality, since the wife being a part of the body has the power to participate equally in carrying out the functions of the body. The biblical reference to the man being the head has to refer more to function than status in the marital relationship. In considering the metaphor further, how could the head (man) be more important than, let's say, the heart (wife)? The head is the seat of decision making but the heart keeps the body alive as it pumps the blood—the life-sustaining source—throughout the whole body, including the brain. When the heart stops functioning, the body dies. When the brain stops functioning, the body, including the heart, ceases to function purposefully. So, being the head does not grant status but a particular vital function.

The fact that for several millennia men in many societies dominated women does not make the practice right. Similarly, the fact that slavery existed for centuries, and still exists in some parts of the world, does not make it right. Every human being yearns for the freedom God has granted to him/her. I am amazed that it took that long for freedom to come to women in some countries, since, undeniably, freedom is a natural quest of the human spirit.

> One thing is certain; their function does not include dominance or control over each other. Rather, the biblical command requires submission to each other as they carry out their respective functions.

In the functioning of the family, men have a function or role, and so do women. One thing is certain; their function does not include dominance or control over each other. Rather, the biblical command requires submission to each other as they carry out their respective functions. The natural endowments of the male and the female should aid us in discovering the areas of functioning to which each is best suited. They should support each other as a team rather than as competitors. The latter is the modern legacy of the women's movement, as helpful as it has been in aiding the freedom of women.

William Hulme, professor of Pastoral Counseling, made the questionable statement: "The woman's desire for masculine leadership is an expression of her femininity."[2] Since the context did not allow for full clarification, it is difficult to ascertain its precise meaning. However, depending on the interpretation, this statement contains elements of the negative view of women's role in our society, which was prevalent until the 1970s. It also could be interpreted positively. Rather than viewing the statement as women's naturally preferring men's dominance or control over them, I prefer to consider Hulme's statement to mean that women expect men to function as protector and provider for the family and to render exemplary leadership in spiritual matters. To his credit, Hulme expressed the functions of husband and wife this way: "If man's function in marriage is comparable in its leadership quality to the function of the head in the body, the organ most analogous to the feminine function represented by the church would be the heart."[3] He stated further that "the heart describes the nature of femininity as a complement to masculinity. No one would argue over whether the head or the heart is the more important for the life of the body. As with masculinity and femininity, the only issue regarding these organs is one of difference in equally important functions."[4]

Aggression and Anger

Men often use aggression to control women. Women are more likely to use it as a defense mechanism, possibly to retaliate. Male aggression as a weapon is particularly destructive because men have at least two decided advantages, their physical strength and their economic and social dominance over women in society. Anthropologists, psychologists, and sociologists have studied the behavior of the sexes to determine the reason they act so differently as males and females. Needless to say, they arrive at different conclusions. Dr. Neil Boyd, a professor of Criminology, tackled this difficult question of what causes these differences in behavior of male and female. Why do boys love to engage in rough sports and play while girls love to play with dolls and kitchen toys? Boyd concluded differently from some academics who claimed that the difference is due to socialization. Those on the side of cultural influence say boys are taught to be physically forceful and girls are trained to be quiet and cooperative. Boyd's research led him to the conclusion that the origin of sexually oriented behavior is in the genes. He stated that in study after study, even by feminists, the conclusion is the same. Children, including those, whose parents reject sexual stereotypes, were consistent in choosing boy toys and games for boys and girl toys and games for girls. "In the late 1980s researcher Diane McGuinness and her students watched thirty-eight boys and thirty-eight girls, ages 3 to 5, play without supervision in their preschool. Even at that young age girls participated in only half as many physical activities as boys, and boys were much more likely than girls to hit or push another child and to use a toy for some other purpose than that for which it was designed."[5] Some scholars insist that despite the evidence that genes play a role in the difference between the sexes, children could pick up cultural signals that could influence them toward aggression or passivity and cooperation. Scientific research has not been able to negate these findings.

Deborah Blum, in her book *Sex on the Brain*, concurs that "most scientists agree that the gender difference in aggression begins in Biology."[6] One person put it succinctly: "Men are simply more naturally inclined to gamble with lives—history is really the story of Biology." While we may agree with research finding that genes do play a vital role in the way male and female behave, the influence of culture should be given some importance. Dr. Anne Campbell, psychologist and criminologist, has researched this subject extensively and gave significant weight to the influence of environment. Campbell believed that mothers, unlike fathers, steer both sexes equally away from aggression. As they mature, boys and girls enter a different cultural experience. Campbell stated:

> "Whereas a boy moves away from his mother's condemnatory, expressive view of aggression into a world of men, where its instrumental value is understood, the girl makes no such change. She remains selectively tuned into a female wavelength, searching for clues to femininity and to aggression—. The most remarkable thing about the socialization of aggression in girls is it's absent."[7]

Campbell explained that girls do not develop the right way to express aggression; they learn to suppress it. Men are more inclined to use aggression to dominate. The difference between male and female aggression may be found in the two schools of thought regarding aggression: *expressive* and *instrumental*. Expressive theorists, such as Sigmund Freud and Dr. Benjamin Spock, who influenced several generations of child training, posited the view that aggression results from a buildup and release of frustration. "In an expressive representation, anger is tinged with fear. It feels like a rising crescendo of imminent chaos culminating in an abandonment of reason and control."[8] Spock advocated restraint. Females are more likely to fall into this category. Males, on the other hand, are more inclined to fall in the second category (i.e., instrumental), which uses aggression to humiliate, control, and conquer. How do these theories affect the married couple?

I believe that since men and women interpret aggression differently, the way aggression is used and interpreted by the sexes could lead to greater stresses and strains within the marriage. Both men and women "rely on these views not only to interpret past events but to guide their behavior. People who believe that aggression is a loss of control will express anger in a different manner from those who believe it to be a way of exerting control."[9] Whereas both sexes see a connection between aggression and control, "for women aggression is the failure of self-control, while for men it is the imposing of control over others."[10] In determining how social talk translates into social action regarding aggression, scientific studies have been able to ascertain predictable patterns of behavior. The critical difference between men and women does not reside so much in their personalities as in their thinking. Their differing beliefs about anger and hostility are manifested in different types of social action, particularly toward their spouse. It is doubtful whether men's anger is more intense than women's, but studies have shown that unlike men, women's anger lasts longer the more intense it gets. Women's anger is more likely to be out of proportion to the cause.

> The critical difference between men and women does not reside so much in their personalities as in their thinking. Their differing beliefs about anger and hostility are manifested in different types of social action, particularly toward their spouse.

Dr. Campbell made the point that men are more likely to use aggression without anger. Either way, men use aggression to instill fear and to gain control over another person. They use it strategically to gain power. Women are more likely to use aggression as a signal of emotional upset. Men are more likely to move quickly from verbal abuse to physical aggression. In one study, husbands moved from verbal to physical aggression twice as much as wives, when they were at a low level of anger. However, when exhibiting a high level of anger, wives escalated to violence 150 percent to that of their husbands. Marital violence studies show that when intensely angry, men and women express their anger much differently. Men usually push, grab, and shove. Women push, grab, shove, slap, kick, bite, hit, or throw things.[11] Men consider this behavior senseless since it does little to gain control over another person. Women's feelings at that time may be to be left alone rather than a desire to gain control.

According to Anne Campbell, the biggest sex difference in response to anger is that the women cry. Some men consider this as women's tactical weapon. Campbell disagrees by citing the study of psychologist Robert Averill, who concluded that 78 percent of women who cry during fights do so out of frustration. They rarely use it to end a fight since 80 percent of the time they cry at the beginning, middle, or when alone afterward.[12] "One route is open to women for releasing frustration without physical injury and without public condemnation. Crying, completely feminine and completely victimless, is the line of least resistance in discharging tension."[13]

The Passive-Aggressive Person

Although some women display passive-aggressive behaviors, men use this behavior more commonly against women and in a far more destructive way. Passive-aggressive behavior may be found in the workplace as well as in romantic relationships.[14] Psychologist Scott Wetzer wrote a book on how to cope with the passive-aggressive man. This term was coined during World War II to describe the behavior of men who felt powerless under the authoritarian army rules. It described soldiers who, in an attempt to cope with the lack of opportunity for personal choice, "resisted, ignored orders, withdrew or simply wanted to flee."[15] The passive-aggressive behavior is an attempt by someone who lacks empowerment to challenge the threat indirectly and covertly.

Scott Wetzer stated: "The tragedy of passive-aggression today is that the passive-aggressive man misconstrues personal relationships as being struggles for power, and sees himself as powerless."[16] This problem with men has escalated since the assertion of women's rights in our society, particularly in the workplace and in the family. "In relationships, these passive-aggressive men deny a woman's needs and feelings. They close off opportunities to address issues, and they focus on how they can get their own way. Therein lies the dilemma: it seems futile to confront them and infuriating to accept their behavior."[17] Wetzer claimed that the way to deal with the passive-aggressive man is to correct his misconceptions and help him feel more empowered.

The paradox of the passive-aggressive man is that he does not necessarily display passive and aggressive behaviors alternatively; rather he displays both attitudes simultaneously. He will deny his behavior while he is displaying it. This attitude will destroy a relationship that might otherwise succeed. "The truth is that the passive-aggressive man doesn't ride an emotional seesaw (although he may put you on one); he's not passive today and aggressive tomorrow, depending on the circumstances. Rather, the passive-aggressive man is simultaneously passive and aggressive. The paradox reigns because he renounces his aggression as it is happening."[18] His ambivalence will result in a contradiction between his pretense and his actions. His mixed messages will draw you in and let you down. He tells a woman that he can't live without her, but he won't commit. He appears charming, but when you get close to him he displays aggression. He leaves you feeling confused and guilty that you did something wrong to hurt him.

Some women have a low tolerance for dealing with the passive-aggressive man, but others are drawn in with the hope of changing him. To protect yourself or to determine his level of commitment, you must set limits and hold to them. Wetzer stated the obvious: that a person with power is not about to relinquish it. "The passive-aggressive man has an unerring instinct for tapping the weak spot in your willpower, will exploit any hesitation on your part and will constantly challenge your resolve."[19] By being firm, you will avoid an emotional ride between passion and panic, fun and frustration, commitment and confusion.

Sex and Control

Using sex to control one's partner is a double-edged sword. It may succeed in drawing the necessary attention to the present concern of the aggrieved spouse, but hurt feelings caused by rejection will most likely result in retaliation. Both husband and wife may be guilty of using sex in their quest for control. It may help a spouse assert a position of power over the other person, but it will likely result in resentment. Despite the assertion of women's autonomy in today's society, many men still feel that they are in control. When it comes to marriage, however, they find that to gain a successful relationship, they need to exchange their dominance for emotional equality. By so doing, they make themselves vulnerable. In the hands of untrustworthy wives, they may be humiliated. Men are concerned that their wives may interpret their surrender to intimacy to be a sign of weakness. Some women do.

> Using sex to control one's partner is a double-edged sword. It may succeed in drawing the necessary attention to the present concern of the aggrieved spouse, but hurt feelings caused by rejection will most likely result in retaliation.

Abusive husbands, who may feel threatened by their vulnerability, retreat and resort to verbal and physical abuse in their quest to regain control. They feel that intimacy allows women to gain control. If they think they are losing control and the women assert control, even temporarily in the case of withholding sex, they may abandon their feeling of closeness and loving concern for the familiar feeling of power, competition, and control. Consequently, they will no longer feel powerless and at the mercy of their wives. Here lies a fertile ground for serious misinterpretation of the spouses' feelings, actions, and intent. By withholding sex, women may be signaling their need for intimacy or a demonstration of affection prior to sex. Men may interpret that as rejection and thereby seek to retaliate.

> By withholding sex, women may be signaling their need for intimacy or a demonstration of affection prior to sex. Men may interpret that as rejection and thereby seek to retaliate.

Family Interview

Why do you think people attempt to control their spouses, and how do you deal with the issue of control in your marriage?

As the author posits, control can be the main cause of conflict in a marital relationship. The need/desire to control, gain power, and compete are certainly corrosive elements. Both men and women can have the need/desire to control their spouse. One of the most difficult things to do is allow your partner/spouse to control you. A common fear may be that by allowing the spouse to take "control," you give up your independence and individuality. On the contrary, to allow your spouse to manage a necessary element that may be an area of weakness for you could result in improving the relationship. To borrow a phrase: "Two heads are better than one." It might also be that people who battle for control may, in fact, be fighting not to lose control of their lives. They want to be seen as productive, competent individuals by their spouses and by the rest of the world. I would like to use an example to highlight this assertion.

It is uncanny that the same scenario and accompanying feelings of displacement experienced by my father also occurred in our marriage. When Frank went away on business trips, he returned home to discover that some things (furniture or personal items) were moved from where he put them. My attempts at decorating and rearranging our beautiful, but increasingly cramped, apartment were purely for aesthetic purposes. Frank viewed these changes as a loss of control and felt that having his and/or our things moved represented instability. When he returned from a trip to see a new arrangement, he felt resentful and annoyed. However minor, these changes represented a loss of control over his "sanctuary" and he felt excluded from decisions concerning it.

Control may be exerted in a more dramatic way. One spouse may feel responsible for making decisions in the household. He/she may consider himself/herself to be in the leadership role. However, if the other spouse does not agree or "buy into" the "chosen" leader, then undercurrents of criticism, sarcasm, and mistrust may surface. The other spouse may perceive this as lack of support. Frank and I have had power struggles for several years, in part, because we view ourselves in the leadership role. We have attempted to address this by assigning specific responsibilities. For example, Frank is in charge of health/wellness such as planning and preparing family meals. I am in charge of our daughter's education and religious growth. We share the expenses proportionate to our salaries.

Ultimately, faith and trust in your partner's ability to "manage" the designated areas of your family's needs are crucial for success. Mutual respect and cooperation, not control, aid in building the foundation for a healthy marriage.

Contributed by Tamaylia and Frank

5

Compromise

Since human nature may be considered selfish, self-centered, and self-preserving, our quest for compromise over very personal issues did not occur automatically. In fact, it took years before we began to operate our lives with concern for compromise. Even though we loved each other, my desire was to win over my spouse to my point of view rather than surrendering to hers. This does not imply passing judgment on her views in order to determine wrong or right. Rather, my desire to steer the family in a particular direction remained a strong motivation. After the early thrill of marriage settled into a state of normalcy or routine, there was less and less desire to compromise. In those early years, cooperation or lack of cooperation appeared to be somewhat spontaneous and caused little concern. However, as the years increased, the differences regarding our choices became more and more transparent and troubling. Pam slowly but surely matured in her decision-making process, thereby resulting in her assertiveness.

Viewing this from hindsight, Pam's assertive attitude was a natural consequence of her transformation from college girl to wife, mother, and professional. She never lost her calm, graceful, endearing demeanor. But she appeared to be strong and determined. Instead of giving in, my strong will resisted compromise. Without recognizing it, I was becoming more individualistic and even a bit authoritarian. I used to refer to myself jokingly as a democratic autocrat. Before long, our wills began to clash, consequently creating the need for compromise.

Considering the significant number of differences between us, we could have drifted apart emotionally and eventually physically. But we didn't. Determining the exact time (not date) I changed my direction in my marriage is not difficult to recall since it was not a linear experience. This change occurred at a time when other crises were occurring.

In November 1981, the family moved from Montreal, Quebec, to Edmonton, Alberta. Pam had to add a few college credits in order to obtain her teaching license for the Province of Alberta. This reduced our income substantially. Our four children had to adjust to their new high school and junior high school curricula. I was just recovering from pastoral burnout syndrome, and contrary to my expectation, the members of my new congregation—including youth and adults—proved to be radical in their views concerning pastoral leadership, moral conduct, and financial projects. They expressed little regard for pastoral authority, believing that pastor and parishioners had equal say. The youth placed no distinction between the sexes in their close physical contacts. Some of the girls became pregnant long before any commitment for marriage and were strongly defended by even adult church members. They rationalized their questionable conduct by claiming "we are all sinners." Some overly enthusiastic members had generated interest in a million-dollar worship and recreational complex even though the budget was in the red. These and other situations resulted in significant stress on my family.

It was during this time that I developed a new direction in my marriage and my ministry. As the year 1984 came to a close, I realized that my family was unhappy. While the children were affected indirectly, the lack of harmony between Pam and me robbed us all of the rich family fellowship we had enjoyed over the years. My New Year's resolutions for 1985 focused fully on my attitude.

My approach might be considered a "no-fault" marriage relationship. This means that whatever happened between us, I would consider only my part and how I could resolve the conflict or misunderstanding.

My approach might be considered a "no fault" marriage relationship. This means that whatever happened between us, I would consider only my part and how I could resolve the conflict or misunderstanding. Before this time, I was completely focused on what Pam or the children said or did to cause the problem. What I found to be the most difficult problem for me was to accept blame without considering my wife's fault in the matter. It took several years and much internal struggle before I felt comfortable to apologize to my wife regardless of who was responsible. My reasoning was simple. Whatever the sacrifice in surrendering my cherished feeling of being right, I was doing it for my wife. What I found was that the more I made an effort to take the humble role in order to please my wife, the easier it became to heal bruised feelings.

Another outcome was Pam's reaction. She felt she also surrendered her rights. Regardless of who made the sacrifices, this approach resulted in unquestioned success. We would enjoy extended periods, even years, without any serious conflicts. Eventually, periods of unpleasantness were either short-lived or did not occur at all.

> For me, compromise did not mean a surrender or abandonment of my position. Rather, compromise meant a conscious accommodation of my wife's opinions.

Much of the success in our marriage should be credited to an ongoing willingness to compromise. As was mentioned earlier, Pam and I started our marriage with significant differences. We felt certain, however, that the fundamental factors for a successful marriage were in place. For me, compromise did not mean a surrender or abandonment of my position. Rather, it meant a conscious accommodation of my wife's opinions.

Radical Styles

During the mid-sixties when we were newlyweds, women's hairstyles and dress styles caused much concern for the more conservative people in our Western society, particularly those who were members of conservative religious Christian denominations. This was before the revolution against authority and society's folkways and mores. Women who wore very short skirts, called miniskirts, were considered outrageous. Of course, today, decades after the cultural revolution, anything goes. Today, many people in our society are immune to shocking behaviors or styles of any kind.

When we began our lives together, I believed my wife to be stable and consistent. It was not long before she started to change her hairstyles drastically. At one time she even cut her hair very short, similar to a man's hairstyle. These changes were too much for me to accept easily. Pam's dress styles also changed significantly. At first, we shopped together for her dresses. When the changes began, I found it difficult to go with her to the store. But she always persuaded me to help her choose her dresses. After many years of bewilderment, I learned to accept her choices. I also learned that the idea men cherish that women dress for them is a fallacy. In my opinion, most women dress for themselves but seek men's approval. They may feel rejected if they fail to obtain it. Sometimes, some women may even make temporary changes to please their dissatisfied husbands, but their basic instinct is to retreat to their personal satisfaction with their appearance. In our case, I believe Pam respects my opinion, but generally she makes her own choices regarding dress and appearance. She expects me to respect and accept her choices. For instance, Pam loves to wear jeans. I do not. She wears them anyway, and I just try to admire her in them.

Need for Transparency

Perhaps the strongest aspect of my compromise has been in the area of relationships with other women. I would not consider my wife to be overly jealous. However, she seemed to express the normal caution and concern for my relationships with women quite strongly. In other words, she expressed care and caution, especially since my duties took me into my parishioners' homes day or night. Although she rarely expressed her views overtly, I got the impression that in order to provide her with reasonable assurance that I was honest in my relationships, my activities had to be transparent.

> Although she rarely expressed her views overtly, I got the impression that in order to provide her with reasonable assurance that I was honest in my relationships, my activities had to be transparent.

During the fall of 1973, I made contact with a lady who was very distraught about her recent traumatic divorce. She appeared desperate for someone's support to help her through this crisis in her life. I was an associate pastor for a church, located in West Toronto, when she telephoned the church for assistance. My family was living in Windsor, Ontario, because Pam was teaching there. I commuted weekly. After visiting and counseling her, I thought it would help her if I took her to meet my wife. That proved to be an error in judgment since Pam did not understand my concern for her. It took some effort on my part to disabuse her mind of any emotional attachment between us. Another incident in Montreal about two years later indicated to me that there was still need for me to deal with Pam's feelings regarding the way I dealt with other women.

A large number of visitors had entered Canada to take advantage of the new immigration law enacted by the new Liberal Government led by Prime Minister Pierre Elliott Trudeau. The law, enacted in the late 1960s, permitted visitors to Canada to apply for landed status while remaining in the country. The applicant was required to pass an interview with an immigration officer. The interview was to ascertain whether the person met a certain predetermined standard to be eligible to receive permanent immigration status. A young lady from the Caribbean who arrived in Canada as a visitor became pregnant out of wedlock and sought my assistance. After reviewing her situation, I realized she was facing other personal crises and needed much support. In order to help her, I had to spend much time with her, including taking her to the immigration office to appeal for exemption so she could remain in the country. She was able to remain until her baby was born, but she was eventually deported since she did not meet the predetermined set of requirements to obtain landed status. The problem for me was explaining to my wife the reason for spending so much time with one lady. I am not sure if I satisfied her curiosity in that particular case.

To be very candid and completely honest, I have never even been tempted to be unfaithful to my wife except in two cases. Before relating these two incidents, let me explain. This statement does not imply that I did not admire other women. The truth is that I did. I always enjoyed their company. However, at age eighteen, I arrived at two vital character-transforming conclusions.

First, that several great leaders in history reduced their impact, negated their success, or ruined their lives and careers by succumbing to improper sexual conduct, acquiring and using power inappropriately, and/or developing an insatiable desire for money. Second, the decision of a moment can change the destiny of a lifetime. I concluded on October 21, 1957, that I needed the help of a supreme power in order to avoid these serious pitfalls. The philosophy by which I lived was to predetermine my response to certain inevitable stimuli or temptations in order to avoid debating my course of action at the time a temptation presented itself, regardless of the garb in which it was clothed, whether it was overt or covert. Therefore, I never allowed myself to be tempted by women, power, or money without being armed with a predetermined response. I knew that the decision of one moment might well determine the entire course of my life.

> **The decision of a moment can change the destiny of a lifetime.**

Let me add one illustration to underscore these extremely vital points. While serving as a pastor in Montreal, two very promising youth of the church approached me for counsel. They were in the early stages of their friendship when the young man invited his new girlfriend to his home. Before the visit was over, they had a sexual encounter on the sofa. She became pregnant. Since he was getting ready to begin training for the ministry, he was devastated. She was fearful and anxious. I reviewed their options with them, and they felt it would be best if they got married. They contemplated the disadvantages but felt they loved each other enough to get married. Unfortunately, their marriage never survived. I felt drawn to them as though they were my own children. As I observed their struggle over the years, I contemplated how different their lives could have been if they had not made that fateful error of judgment and engaged in one hasty act.

Now back to the matter of my relationship with other women. During my first year of marriage, I had opportunity to test my theory. I accepted an appointment as principal of the Grand Bahama Central Academy in 1964. Since the school was located on Grand Bahama Island, we had to travel to Nassau, capital of the Bahamas, to deal with matters such as certification and curriculum with the Ministry of Education. Bernice, a young teacher, and I traveled by plane to Nassau to meet with the Ministry of Education personnel. We did not complete our business as expected and realized at the end of the day that we needed to stay overnight. To our surprise, we could find only one vacant hotel room. Both of us had to share the same room. She slept on the bed and I slept on the couch. Bernice was charming and we got along great. I was young and adventurous and would not deny that I was tempted sexually. When I awoke the next morning and realized the apparent compromising situation we had survived, I realized then that principle could triumph over pressure.

By far, my greatest challenge was one to which I voluntarily acquiesced experimentally. Before the age of forty, my contact with women in the course of my professional duties remained strictly professional. Even though I remained cordial, there was always a deliberate effort to keep space between the women and me while speaking to them. When greeting a woman, I would shake hands while remaining in an upright posture, neither hugging nor kissing. However, upon reaching forty years of age, I felt that my youthfulness had passed and my more senior status would grant me more flexibility with women without anyone thinking that I had another motive in mind. This worked fine for a while, until one Sunday after chairing a board meeting, a very attractive lady approached me and requested a meeting with me. In my position as pastor and family counselor, that request seemed quite normal. As soon as we were alone, she told me she was in love with me. Although this pronouncement was astonishingly direct, I felt so morally invincible at that time that, even though I was surprised, this did not cause me any great concern. As she continued to express herself, I felt as though this could be a very interesting challenge for me. Since I was already working with her on a few projects, I knew it would be difficult to avoid her.

At this point, I ended the visit. But I was still unsure of the best way to relate to her, especially since I felt confident that I would not yield to her in any way that would compromise my principles. However, since this issue led me into uncharted waters, I began to feel uneasy. At first, we spoke on the phone for long periods, exploring different subjects with no real barriers. This did not seem uncomfortable since I had many female friends in high school and college with whom I related very closely without any sexual involvement. While we had conversations, mainly for the purpose of exploring the male and female psyche or just plain friendship, the relationship remained healthy. There were no subtle pressures or unrevealed expectations.

> My openness provided her a measure of security in our relationship.

Before long, Pam felt that the relationship was transparent enough that she should get an explanation. For the first time, I felt that my wife did not need to know. Previously, whenever I felt someone displayed any behavior that raised my curiosity, I would mention it to Pam either in jest or in a serious discussion. My openness provided her a measure of security in our relationship. This time I felt that it would be difficult to explain. Furthermore, I would most certainly be misunderstood. Viewed by any casual observer, our frequent contact by phone and in person could leave the impression that we were engaged in an affair.

Since I knew my objective, I felt there would be no harm done to anyone.

As our relationship grew, it became more complex. We spoke more frequently on the phone, and we arranged to see each other more often. She would visit my office, and I would visit her workplace. Sometimes we would have lunch together. She was very talented and assisted me with several projects. Having developed a close relationship with my family, she visited our home. Considering her a special friend, I enjoyed her company. Because she was very creative and enjoyed stimulating intellectual discussions, we delved into various subjects, sometimes agreeing and at other times tenaciously holding on to opposite views. Despite our close relationship, I made it clear from the outset that I would not cross any boundaries that should be only the prerogative of our spouses. In other words, there would be no kissing, and sex would not even be contemplated.

As I view this experience in retrospect, my conclusion is unambiguous. There is absolutely no question in my mind that this relationship was an extremely risky venture. Here are some of my reasons. In this kind of relationship when both persons are attracted to each other, there is always a danger that one could step over the line of intimacy. Even though both may have the best intentions, sexual nature has a force that can overpower reason in an unguarded moment. An even greater danger is the unknown. A person can never be sure of the other person's motives nor can each have an accurate reading of the other person's strengths and weaknesses. Fortunately for me, this lady did not attempt to violate our understanding. For this I owe her my gratitude and I feel confident in her friendship. But in retrospect, I feel that I might not have been able to guarantee the outcome if an unfortunate set of circumstances had occurred. For the second time since my marriage, I felt a slight feeling of uncertainty, a sense of vulnerability. The usual feeling of being in total control gave way to sharing control. For that reason, I felt insecure. But I still held firm to my convictions. My settled predetermined commitment was to live up to the Christian values that had guided me from the age of eighteen years. Then, too, appearances could be misleading. In my case my wife had difficulty determining whether something sinister was simmering. It is not clear whether others also had suspicions. Another issue is the problem that arose when I began to limit my time with Pam because I spent some of my time with someone else. Since we were usually very busy, our time together was already restricted. Therefore, Pam had to be concerned not only with my special interest in this person but also the inadequate amount of time I spent with her.

One evening Pam reached the boiling point and exploded. The children and I were fearful and uncertain of the direction the conflict was leading. Since I felt self-righteous about my innocence, I shared little of her concern, neither was I empathetic with her for being angry. That attitude left her deeply hurt. In my opinion, not only was she distraught about the questionable relationship I wouldn't even discuss, she felt alone since my attitude indicated that I didn't care about her feelings. The incident ended without any physical harm, since we had eliminated that option in resolving conflicts from the outset of our marriage. The hurt took a long time to heal and an even longer time for me to truly understand my responsibility in protecting my wife from emotional hurt. Needless to say, we resolved the matter in a satisfactory manner and developed an even closer relationship. Compromise provided the key to resolution and reformation within our marriage. Pam suggested that we relocate. I agreed and we did. Let's take a look at how other marriage professionals view compromise within the marital relationship.

Differences between the Sexes

Psychologists and marriage counselors are constantly reminding us that men and women are inherently different. Although this fact is obvious, the more important matter that has researchers engaged in ongoing study is how to deal with this difference since both sexes are destined to share their lives together. Dr. James Dobson, the popular marriage and family lecturer, put the difference between male and female this way:

> When reduced to basics, women need men to be romantic, caring, and loving. Men need women to be respectful, supportive, and loyal.—Perhaps the fundamental problem is one of selfishness. We're so intent on satisfying our own desires that we fail to recognize the longings of our partners. The institution of marriage works best when we think less about ourselves and more about the ones we love.[1]

He stated further that men "want to know that they are respected and honored by their wives, just as their wives want to know that they are loved."[2] Since husbands and wives want different things, or more fundamentally, experience life much differently, what strategies are needed to ensure a successful relationship? Let's take a look.

The Bible vs. Bradshaw

In a college literature course, I discovered the Bible as literature. The books of Isaiah, Songs of Solomon, and the Psalms, for instance, have passages of rapturous beauty as well as depth of meaning. But how much more significant has been the contribution of Scripture to the history of the world and to those who have been subject to its impact in their lives. From the age of eighteen, I have relied upon its principles for guidance in my life. Its influence has been the undergirding for my marriage and the training of our children. Like the sun in its appointed circuit is the life guided by the principles of Scripture. Natural laws maintain the sun's constancy, and moral and spiritual laws are available to provide constancy in our human relationships. Ignore these laws and our destiny portends disaster. Therefore, I believe that the rich resource of the Bible should inform every couple desiring success in their marriage. These biblical counsels could prove invaluable even to those who do not adhere to Christianity. By reading the sayings of Confucius, the founder of the Chinese religion, Confucianism, for example, I found valuable ideas for life, including the saying: "Do not do to others what you would not desire yourself" (*The Sayings of Confucius*, XV. 24). Popularly known as the Golden Rule, this saying was spoken by Jesus in the positive: "And as you wish that men would do to you, do so to them." It is a popular saying of Jesus (Luke 6: 31), but Confucius said it some five hundred years before the birth of Christ. Therefore, we can learn from those who have a different cultural background or religious belief. Here is another universal principle that could guide us in considering resolving marital conflict. Paul appeals:

> —complete my joy by being of the same mind, having the same love, being in full accord and of one mind. Do nothing from selfishness and conceit, but in humility count others better than yourselves. Let each of you look not only to his own interests, but also to the interests of others. (Philippians 2: 1-4.)

> Therefore, I believe that the rich resource of the Bible should inform every couple desiring success in their marriage. These biblical counsels could prove invaluable even to those who do not adhere to Christianity.

Admittedly, this counsel is difficult to accept. It defies the human spirit. And many people who practice it do so for the wrong reasons. They may be doing an unselfish thing with a selfish motive. Men would be inclined to reject it because they are naturally motivated by achievement. Women would question it, even though naturally they are inclined to be caring. They may be inclined to reject it because of the strong influence of the women's movement, which has sought to free women from the domination of males. Some women find themselves in the throes of change from service and subservience to independence and self-assertiveness. John Bradshaw viewed this biblical counsel differently. He labeled this biblical call for surrendering to each other's interest out of love, codependency.

Codependency

John Bradshaw, in his *New York Times* bestseller, *Bradshaw On: The Family*, based on a nationally televised series, sought to inspire self-esteem. In doing so, he launched a tirade against codependency in the family, labeling it dysfunctional. Codependent children, he claimed, are negatively affected by codependent parents, thereby wrecking the family and, perhaps, through their "poisonous pedagogy" passing on this problem to society by "societal regression." What does Bradshaw consider to be codependency in the family relationship?

After berating those who believe in the "better half" concept of the husband and wife bond, he proceeded to point out that two incomplete people create a dysfunctional relationship in which each is convinced he/she cannot live without the other. This type of love can be viewed as addictive relationship.[3] Dennis and Barbara Rainey concurred: "When two people get married, they have high expectations about the relationship. An unspoken assumption by each one is that the other will 'meet me half-way.'—This concept sounds logical, but couples who use it are destined for disappointment and failure."[4] Bradshaw believed that this notion of love is reinforced by popular music, such as "You're the Sunshine of My Life," "Good-Hearted Woman," and "Lord, She Took Me in and Made Me Everything I Am Today." Bradshaw bemoaned the thought that millions of children have been robbed of their childhood "because they were enmeshed in their family system's intimacy vacuum."[5] He understood love as "an act of the will and a decision" rather than a feeling. He declared that true love has its beginning in self-love. By loving yourself, you gain the capacity to love others. Let us view a full passage to better understand his point.

> Our beliefs about marriage condition our notion of love. Our cultural beliefs about love are often forms of addiction.—Many religious preachers teach a form of passive-dependent love. They teach that the highest act of love is self-sacrifice. The highest love is to set aside one's own physical, emotional and intellectual needs to serve and take care of others. They teach long-suffering and martyrdom as two of the major ways to attain goodness. Acting good and acting righteous are more important than actually being good. Acting loving is more important than being loving.[6]

It is paradoxical to declare that I both agree and disagree with this passage. Perhaps the reason lies in my impression that he has so intricately intertwined two different elements. As presented earlier regarding my own experience, peace and sanity were brought into our marriage when I decided to avoid interfering with my wife's decisions with regard to shopping and other areas of decision-making. For several years, Pam protested against my view of giving our children freedom to make many decisions for themselves from the age of ten and most decisions by the age of seventeen, upon their graduation from high school. To my wife's credit, she allowed me significant latitude regarding my own decisions from the time of our marriage. So I can agree with that aspect of Bradshaw's opinion. The part that is troubling to me is the aspect that suggests complete independence of the family members and the idea that sacrificing or denying one's need in favor of his/her spouse and children leads to dysfunction in the family relationships. How does this clearly secularist view relate to the biblical admonition to husbands and wives: "Do nothing from selfishness—but in humility count others better than yourselves," and "Be subject to one another"? (Ephesians 5: 21). Clearly, both views are in contradistinction to the other.

Dr. Larry Crabb saw the issue differently from John Bradshaw. After relating the frustrating experiences of four couples, he concluded that their main problem was self-centeredness. "When self-interest continues as the dominant commitment of our lives, when we devote our energy to serving ourselves above all others, then we are wrongly self-centered, and this form of self-interest is a far more serious and dangerous problem than the words we suffer at the hands of others.—But few people notice their commitment to self-interest—."[7]

In her book, *Toward a New Psychology of Women*, Jean Baker Miller, a medical doctor, tackled the issue of women's desire for caring and service. She observed that in psychotherapy women spend much more time talking about giving than do men. Women constantly confront themselves about giving. "They wonder what would happen if they were to stop giving, to even consider not giving? The idea is frightening and the consequences too dire to consider. Outside of a clinical setting, most women do not even dare to suggest openly such a possibility."[8] In stark contrast to women's concerns for giving and caring are men's concerns. She pointed out that the question of whether he is giving enough does not enter a man's self-image. "Few men feel that giving is a primary issue in their struggles for identity. They are concerned much more about 'doing.'"[9] Dr. Miller believed that many men would like to give themselves, but they are hindered by the appearance of vulnerability and weakness. Giving comes after men have fulfilled their primary role of manhood—doing. She pointed out that despite the impact of the sexual revolution in our society, women "still feel deeply they are giving something to the man by having sexual relations with him."[10]

Interestingly enough, when my wife read this book (I pulled it from her library), she wrote comments in the margins. Beside the idea of women's desire to give, she wrote: "Concept getting outdated," and "especially the sex-partner relationship problem." Very revealing, I think! Miller was pointing to the new direction when she said that one form of sex therapy is to focus simultaneously on giving and taking by both partners. "That is, each person not only has to admit to her/his role as a giver, but also must accept her/his role as a receiver of pleasure."[11] Regrettably, the modern trend has led some women to participate in sex in a similar way as men. They begin to view sex as performance rather than sharing.

Toward a Balance: A Compromise

Based on the dichotomy of male and female differences and felt needs, it would seem that a compromise is needed so that both spouses may reach fulfillment. The path of self-interest may lead to one spouse being fulfilled and the other frustrated. In fact, many marriages operate on the basis of the man's innate tendency to dominate. However, sacrificing goals, ambitions, feelings, and that which enhances self-esteem in order to get along with a spouse would not be a wise option, except in extreme circumstances, such as serious illness.

Surrendering

Laura Doyle wrote the book, *The Surrendered Wife*, and subsequently became the catalyst for a movement in which other women join in to learn and practice her concept of developing harmony in marriage. She declared from the outset, in the introduction to the book, that surrendering to your husband does not mean returning to the status of a wife in the fifties, rebelling against the feminist movement or about subservience. Rather, she focused on relinquishing undue control over her husband, respecting his views, placing trust in him, and expressing her needs to him instead of nagging him. She aimed to make herself vulnerable with the view of attaining self-fulfillment. Doyle explained:

> When I was choosing to control over allowing myself to be vulnerable, I was doing it at the expense of intimacy. What I know now control and intimacy are opposites. If I want one, I can't have the other. Without being vulnerable, I can't have intimacy. Without intimacy, there can be no romance or emotional connection. When I am vulnerable with my husband, the intimacy, passion, and devotion seem to flow naturally. [12]

Laura Doyle wrote that before she developed this approach, as her therapist reminded her, she felt her chances for happiness would be better if she were divorced or with another man.[13] She felt that if she divorced and had a new start, she would have the chance to check up on everything. In other words, she would take control. "I was always on edge, so that the slightest problem seemed like reason to end this marriage and hope for a better one next time. At the time, I felt so pained and self-righteous that honoring my wedding vows seemed unimportant. Today my friends laugh at me when I tell them this because it seems so ridiculous that I was ready to toss out my perfectly wonderful husband."[14] Laura Doyle abandoned her unrealistic expectation of sharing responsibilities equally and functioned on the basis of her husband's strengths and weaknesses instead. She found the right equilibrium through compromise.

Laura Doyle abandoned her unrealistic expectation of sharing responsibilities equally and functioned on the basis of her husband's strengths and weaknesses instead. She found the right equilibrium through compromise.

Sharing

Judge Judy Sheindlin pointed out that some men develop a "learned helplessness" after marriage. Once some men get married, they suddenly forget all the house chores. According to her, "Suddenly, perfectly intelligent and capable males, who have been scrambling eggs and washing socks on their own for years, can't negotiate boiling water. The part of their brain that controls domestic chores has been wiped clean."[15] Some wives criticize their husband's attempts to do house chores. He retreats and leaves it to her. Soon problems develop as her burden increases.

The solution may be found in the advice given by Andrew Dubrin in *Sharing!* His view of the new husband is one who shares major and minor responsibilities with his wife. The new husband considers his role as part of a team, but he retains his responsibility for sharing in major decisions regarding the home. In the research Dubrin cited, more than 60 percent of the women polled said they preferred a husband who treats them as equals. In his own research, Dubrin found that an overwhelming number of new husbands preferred to share decisions with their wives.[16] "Sharing decision making, household tasks, and child rearing with their spouses," he reported, "tend to reduce a myriad of small tensions and potential feelings of resentment that often occur when these aspects of living are not shared."[17] Because these tensions have been reduced, sharing could lead to increased sexual enjoyment.

> Because these tensions have been reduced, sharing could lead to increased sexual enjoyment.

Nurturing

One theme in the book, *The Good Marriage,* is the importance of providing emotional nurturance. The point is made that "Our needs for comforting and encouragement are deep and lasting. A main task of every marriage from the early days of the relationship to its end is for each partner to nurture the other."[18] This idea may seem like codependency as John Bradshaw described it. But it is not. It is the building of a partnership, which provides a wellspring of support for each other. No one will deny that the most self-sufficient among us needs support in times of weakness, stress, or struggle. Marriage should provide mutual support, a kind of safety net when we fall. Wallerstein and Blakeslee saw this support as replenishing each other's emotional reserve. They stated that marriage "is to give comfort and encouragement in a relationship that is safe for dependency, failure, disappointment, mourning, illness, and aging—in short, for being a vulnerable human being."[19] Following the honeymoon, two different personalities must find a way to blend, not merely to survive in a relationship but to thrive in it and enjoy it. Should they allow their differences to emerge stronger than their mutual strengths, tragedy will strike. We have already established that serious effort is needed. But strategies must be used to propel the couple in the right direction.

> No one will deny that the most self-sufficient among us needs support in times of weakness, stress, or struggle. Marriage should provide mutual support, a kind of safety net when we fall.

Maturing

The book, *The Good Marriage*, points to nine strategies or tasks for couples to employ in this process. The task of building togetherness and creating autonomy illustrates well the need for compromise throughout the marriage experience. It is an ongoing process of discovering your spouse's likes and dislikes and finding agreeable ways to deal with them.

Quite revealingly, Dr. Judith Wallerstein, a clinical psychologist, who was married for nearly fifty years when she published the book, *The Good Marriage*, revealed to us that she and her husband found life after getting married radically different from their passionate love affair before marriage. "But our relationship changed dramatically when we got married. Suddenly our free and easy lives ended, and the rigid roles of husband and wife took over."[20] They soon discovered that there was no set formula for conducting their marriage. What was exciting about marriage was the early discovery and adjustment phase, even as hidden aspects of each person's personality rose to the surface. But this is precisely when unsuspecting spouses, who want to retain the image of their partners in the romantic phase of their relationship, seek to abandon the marriage. Bear in mind as well that everyone matures and is changed by life's experiences. Some couples find the discovery and adjustment challenging, yet positive. Others find this process unmanageable. Wallerstein revealed that she and her husband were married for one year before they felt comfortable enough to expose their feelings. During the year after the wedding, she made bacon and eggs for breakfast each morning. "Finally Bob felt secure enough to tell me that he hated bacon and eggs. So did I. It took two smart people a whole year to arrive at this candid confrontation."[21]

Negotiating

Learning to negotiate fairly when one partner is dissatisfied holds the key to survival as well as happiness in the marriage relationship. To succeed, a couple must find creative ways to build togetherness and simultaneously foster autonomy. Wallerstein said that the sense of being a part of a couple is the ingredient that consolidates marriages. Whereas, they may not have control over many forces in society around them, they can control their marriage. "A marriage that commands loyalty and is worth defending, requires each partner to relinquish self-centeredness and to sacrifice a portion of his or her autonomy.—In a good marriage the new identity is built on solid foundation of love and empathy. Each partner must learn to identify with the other, and both together to identify with the marriage."[22] Being married means forming a team that works harmoniously together toward a common goal, a common purpose.

Through their seminars and therapy sessions, Dr. William Glasser and his wife, Carleen, emphasize the importance of reaching resolution of marital conflict through negotiation. They documented their strategies in *Getting Together and Staying Together: Solving the Mystery of Marriage.* They advance the view that couples should learn to negotiate using caring language and the language of choice theory. Choice theory is based on the understanding that we can control only our own behavior. Rather than pressuring your partner with external controls (such as nagging, blaming, and criticizing), you should offer your solution to help solve the problem, thereby allowing your partner to do the same.

> Rather than pressuring your partner with external controls (such as nagging, blaming, and criticizing), you should offer your solution to help solve the problem, thereby allowing your partner to do the same.

Family Interview

How can a couple compromise when they have conflicting feelings about an issue? How would you illustrate compromise in your marriage?

Compromise in marriage is when either spouse makes adjustments to accommodate each other's needs. The ability to accommodate your spouse's needs is based on your understanding of what those needs are—being able to identify them through dialogue or observations. You will be sensitive to your spouse's need for privacy, expression of opinions, the right to experience mood change, feelings of peevishness, or the desire to be alone sometimes.

The ability to compromise is embedded in an understanding of one's self and an understanding of human behavior. For example: Your spouse plans with you in advance an evening out together. You plan to have dinner and attend a concert. At the last minute, the wife realizes that she is feeling drained and weary. She shares her feeling with her husband. How will he react? Will he feel offended and ruin the evening, or will he try to understand and adjust to the sudden change? How can both compromise? They may plan to go out for dinner and postpone the concert for another time, or they may postpone the evening out for another date. The husband may even go a step further and prepare dinner at home. This would allow his wife time to relax and feel that he truly understands.

Avoid indulging in behavior patterns that may fulfill only your needs without consideration for your spouse's needs or desires. Be sensitive to each other's needs. Learning how to compromise and make adjustments will encourage a healthy and successful marriage.

Contributed by Pamela

Pamela, my wife, provided significant support for me, as well as our four children and several relatives, during our forty-year marriage. She enjoys her profession as a special education teacher for grades kindergarten through twelve. She is also qualified to teach regular education and English literature. Pam is devoted to her four children and six grandchildren, but she still finds time to write poetry, travel extensively with me, and publish articles. She is currently completing a book of poems, which she expects to publish this year. Pam studied in three countries and taught in four countries. She attended

West Indies College, Andrews University, McGill University, and University of Alberta, where she obtained a Master of Education degree. She is currently pursuing a doctor's degree in education.

6

Cash

Money, Pam, and Me

Undoubtedly, money played a prominent role in the functioning of our family. However, money had a less important role in the relationship between Pam and me. In many people's lives, money is a crucial factor in their relationships. With us, money was viewed strictly in an economic sense. To us, money was a medium of exchange for goods and services. At no time was it considered essential to enhance our relationship. Pam took the lead early in our friendship, explaining that her attitude toward me would not be affected by whether I had money or not. Many people repeat this line to their lover and even begin their relationship with the intention of leaving money out of the equation only to recapitulate when reality strikes.

As her husband for more than four decades, I can state unequivocally that Pam has never elevated money to a status where it affected our marriage in any noticeable way. I consider this attitude to be remarkable since so many people in American society consider money of paramount importance. Money (disagreements over the lack of it or the use of it) is one of the leading causes of divorce. Because Pam did not place serious emphasis on money in our marriage, I had exceptional flexibility not merely in spending the cash we earned but also in my approach to earning it. Nevertheless, Pam always showed interest in seeing that our financial obligations were met. She always objected to her name being attached to any loan or legal document without careful scrutiny. When her signature was needed for executing a transaction—they were many over the years—Pam would most likely cooperate, albeit cautiously.

From the outset, during courtship, I made it abundantly clear that there would be no limitations placed on her. She would have the freedom to work or not to work: That would be completely her choice. Pam chose to work as a teacher. Regarding her pregnancy, she decided when to stop working and when to return to work. Of course, I made suggestions, but the decision was always hers. We maintained this approach even when we were facing difficult financial times. At such times, it was difficult to keep her from working. Similarly, Pam gave me the freedom to choose where I preferred to work. Consequently, we have lived and worked in four countries and have relocated several times without any complaints or objections. Of course, I considered the suitability of those situations for the family. This flexibility allowed me to work in three different professions—education, business administration, and ministry. I also worked with several language and cultural groups with her full cooperation. Because we supported each other's profession, I was able to study for a Ph.D. while working full-time. This kind of freedom in our marriage proved invaluable.

For the first six years of marriage, we had few concerns about financial issues. We operated mainly on a cash budget. The only items we bought on payment were a car and a house. Everything else was paid strictly by cash. Most of the items we owned were simple and inexpensive. What we found was that due to our inexperience about durability of household items and our rapidly changing view of home decoration, we replaced our furniture and other items frequently. As our need for more expensive items increased and our children approached their teen years, the desire to purchase more expensive items and provide more adequately for the children developed. Because certain immediate perceived needs were met as soon as they arose, we developed the practice of credit purchasing, which eventually ruined our finances. By choosing the plan to buy now and pay later, I surrendered present and future control of the family budget. We never stopped to consider the eventual outcome of this practice since this lifestyle seemed far more like a blessing than a curse. No thought was given to the present or future impact of credit purchasing on our finances.

In 1981 we were compelled to review the family budgeting system we were using. While we lived in Montreal, everything appeared to be normal. Bills were paid without a thought since both our salaries, a total of about $90,000 annually, were adequate to sustain our lifestyle. However, when we moved to Edmonton, more than a year elapsed before both of us received full salaries. By that time our finances had collapsed and we had to sell much of our belongings to survive. The recently acquired new luxury Ford Marquis was the first to go. The house we had bought in Edmonton subject to selling our house in Montreal now became a financial burden since the depressed housing market at the time contributed to the Montreal house remaining on the market for more than a year. Because we were determined to pay our bills regardless of the circumstances, our limited finances had to make room for two mortgages. Little remained to cover the other living expenses. We surrendered the house to the builder, sold the house in Montreal at a loss, and rented a small apartment. Still lacking the needed funds to cover our budget, we sold some of our furniture and other valuable items. These transactions caused a net loss of assets amounting to an estimated seventy-five thousand dollars.

Despite our limited finances, we decided to send two of our children, Richard and Tamaylia, to Andrews University, a Christian boarding university in Berrien Springs, Michigan. This proved to be an excellent decision since that experience gave them the privilege of exposure to a campus with students from several countries. These young people brought their rich cultural and linguistic diversity to enrich the college experience. Our children were also much more motivated to learn. The financial demand then and later, when all four children were in college at the same time, created additional stress for us. Pam did not allow financial struggles to affect our relationship directly. As I recall, I became very impatient and short-tempered. Whenever there was a problem that proved difficult to solve, I became restless, impatient, perturbed, and preoccupied. Pam was usually sensitive to my mood changes. Even though I emphasized strongly that she was not responsible for my negative attitude, she subconsciously reflected my mood, thereby resulting in a downward spiral in our relationship until a correction took place. Frequently, my mood did not change until I found a solution to the prevailing problem. Fortunately, although the problem would linger until it was resolved, I usually developed a strategy very quickly to deal with the situation. That was often accomplished by staying up late at night to focus on the issue and/or taking long walks to provide undisturbed moments to concentrate intensely until a workable strategy emerged.

Financial Frustrations

As I indicated earlier in this chapter, the first few years of our marriage had no financial difficulties since we bought everything by cash. The first nine years were spent in the Bahamas, Michigan, Jamaica, and Windsor, Canada. Upon arriving in Montreal in 1973, our differences over spending began to widen. Pam began to exercise her talent for home decoration. Considering our limited income and large resettling expenses, I sought a more conservative approach to setting up our home. Unfortunately, I failed to make room in my thinking for my wife's desire to decorate and furnish the house according to a woman's style and taste. Regardless of what I suggested, be it color, style, or positioning of items in the rooms, I was denied my views, albeit gracefully. Finding myself being shut out from that kind of decision making, I launched my defense by objecting to her choices. My approach was doomed to failure. Our arguments became increasingly intense. One day as Pam and I were driving toward downtown Montreal from Pointe Claire (a township on the western outskirts of the city where we had just purchased a house), I stopped the car abruptly to settle the matter we were discussing. Pam wanted me to take her to buy new furniture for our bedroom. My view was that we could live with the furniture we'd bought on sale in Windsor, the previous year. We had paid less than $500 for furniture to furnish our living room. I believe we spent even less to furnish our bedrooms. What I didn't know was that women have a keener sense of shades of color, matching furniture style, and use of space than most men even imagine. It was there, near the shopping center in Dorval (near the Montreal airport) that I became convinced that a special sensitivity was needed to cope with my wife's need to set up a home for the family. Until that time, I was completely oblivious to her basic female instinct. I decided then not to interfere but try to understand and cooperate with her.

> Unfortunately, I failed to make room in my thinking for my wife's desire to decorate and furnish the house according to a woman's style and taste.

Since the time of my "enlightenment," I decided that such decisions as the choice of house, furnishings, and color scheme would be solely the domain of my wife. Although I still share my opinions, I cherish no illusion that Pam would accept them as final. Nevertheless, Pam has sought my opinion before nearly every decision relating to the home. Not only did I learn to be her partner in the area of homemaking, I also learned to enjoy the process as well as the finished product. (*Finished* should be understood in this context as meaning until next time.) I should confess that I still find it difficult to accept the rearranging of the home, especially my study, without even a slight protest.

Since Pam and our daughter Sherine, with whom she frequently collaborates for redecorating the home, have proved to be very creative, I usually find myself expressing my surprise and appreciation at the changes rather than opposing them.

> **Not only did I learn to be her partner in the area of homemaking, I also learned to enjoy the process as well as the finished product.**

In August 1997, we experienced one of those creative changes. We purchased a new house in Antioch (a township in the southeastern section of Nashville, Tennessee). This area, called October Woods, was a beautiful new development. We had selected the design of the house, including the color scheme, carpets, cupboards, bathroom fixtures, and so on. Needless to say, the property was very expensive and since we were moving from a four-bedroom house in another part of the city, I hoped we would not need additional furniture. A serious surprise was awaiting me. Only a few items from the former residence were selected. As I recall, all that survived were Sherine's bedroom set (which she later moved into her own home after her marriage) and a few other items. All the other furniture and a variety of other household items were donated to the Salvation Army. Their truck made three trips to haul off the several items of previously prized household items. The reason was simple. I was told that they did not fit the décor of this new house. Contemporary style and southern style, cherry wood and oak wood didn't mix well, they said. When it came to my cherished wall unit in my study, I simply declared that regardless of what mixed well or didn't mix well it should be placed in my study. They relented and solved the problem by choosing accessories to complement it. What took place in the process of transforming this house into a pleasant, pleasing home several thousand dollars and some months later literally amazed me. We certainly enjoyed living in that home for the next several years.

Because Pam loved her teaching profession, she worked most of the time during our marriage. Occasionally, she would choose to stay home for a year or a few months at a time. I have not spent the time to analyze the reasons our financial budget worked well during those times she stayed home. But it did. My recollection is that we were more pleasant and we had less financial pressure. The main causes could be that the pace of our lives slowed drastically enabling us to spend more quality time together. Pam was more rested and relaxed, and we expected less from our financial budget and spent less.

Credit Card Crunch

Among the many difficult lessons we have learned is that a credit card is a potential curse. Over the years, we have used it like an asset. The available credit was treated as though we had that money. The reality is that it represents a debt the moment we spend it. No matter the limit allowed, the tendency was to spend it all. The result was the alarming unsuspected accumulation of expensive debt that may never be fully paid since it is revolving. At least it will never be paid without a resolve to abandon credit purchases. The philosophy of credit card purchases is fundamentally flawed. It represents convenience for those who really do not need it and an unexpected burden to those who really cannot afford to use it without paying a heavy price. Using Visa or MasterCard (debit/credit) on one's bank account is likely the best choice. For nearly a decade now, Pam and I have given up credit cards, and I doubt seriously that I will ever use one again. We encouraged our children to abandon their use as well, and although they may not be fully convinced, they are attempting to adjust their lives accordingly.

> The philosophy of credit card purchases is fundamentally flawed. It represents convenience for those who really do not need it and an unexpected burden to those who really cannot afford to use it without paying a heavy price.

The Value of Money

It is difficult for me to comprehend the extent to which money has increased in importance during the second half of the twentieth century. This is not to say money was not important prior to this, it was always important in some sectors of society and in most countries. However, today, the excessive regard for money appears to be universally pervasive. Obviously, some people will consider my concern incredulous because they cannot conceive of a time and place in which money was not central to people's lives. However, as recently as my childhood, my grandparents had very little money and didn't seem to care much for it. Their lives were fulfilled by providing for themselves in ways that did not require money to provide them a sense of well-being. I still believe that the happiest period of my life was between ten and fourteen years of age. I don't recall having any money at any time (well, except Christmas time or rare special occasions). I did not even get an allowance. There was no need. My friends and I created our own toys or games and had innocent fun. Those days were memorable because of fun, friends, and family. Many people in the community lived in a similar manner. They went to the store on rare occasions to buy a few necessary items. Clothes were purchased mainly once per year, at Christmastime. No one in our community gave money much importance in the overall running of their lives. They even built houses by community cooperation and selected lumber from the woods on their property. Cedar, oak, and other valuable trees were usually available.

Today, money has a completely different value. Recently, I was in negotiation with a gentleman whose family loaned money privately to investors. Our family real estate investment business had obtained a private mortgage loan through the family investment business he managed. I don't recall what I said, but it was related to the fact that I didn't consider money central to my life. Of course, I am totally committed to honoring my obligations, whether financial or otherwise. However, he became greatly upset that I did not value money in the same way he did. It took me several minutes to calm him enough to clarify what I meant. I have never considered money central to my life and have no desire to do so. As stated previously, I agree with the economic definition for money as a medium of exchange for goods and services. In our society, however, it is viewed much differently. "Those rectangles of printed paper we carry with us are daily life's most ordinary and ever present symbol. Worthless in itself, this arbitrary unit of exchange can be a bearer of almost any symbolic value we choose to put on it: Success, power, ability, worth, freedom, status, love, or security."[1]

Money and Prestige

In most modern marriages, money has an extremely high value. Referring to marriage, Dr. James Dobson called money "the great mischief maker."[2] Wallace Denton, associate professor of family life, Purdue University, pointed out that our possessions tend to develop a secondary or symbolic meaning. An automobile does not only serve as transportation but symbolizes prestige, freedom, independence, and even masculinity.[3] Clothes are used by both men and women to evoke a certain mood or feeling. The symbolic use of sex has led to widespread commercialization and romanticizing to such a bizarre extent that the real purpose and function of sex have been almost overshadowed. Similarly, money has developed a secondary meaning far greater than its real purpose. The emphasis on having money has shifted from its purpose of aiding us in providing what we need for our protection, comfort, security, and development to money for its own sake. To money has been attributed a false intrinsic value, a kind of power and prestige that tend to command us. So people will lie, cheat, steal, betray, and even kill or die in a relentless quest for it.

> To money has been attributed a false intrinsic value, a kind of power and prestige that tend to command us.

The class system in many societies is based on money and family tradition. There is no such thing as a poor person in the upper class, unless his/her true financial worth is disclosed for some reason. The upper class in most societies acquires that prestige because wealth has been passed down from generation to generation. Wealth acquired by someone who possessed only moderate means before acquiring riches rarely elevates him/her to the status of upper class. The wealth has to be seasoned. Regardless of the family inheritance, the acquisition of wealth usually gives an individual a special kind of prestige in the eyes of most people. This could result in scrutiny for the suitor. Some people may feel that the person may be after his/her would-be lover's money rather than the person. The person who falls in love with a wealthy person is immediately transformed into a person with prestige. As a result of associating with a person of wealth, one can change his/her social status immediately. Should problems develop in such a relationship, the difference between their financial resources prior to the marriage could cause greater friction. To respond to that problem, some couples use a marriage contract.

Money and Power

The use of money as a weapon has destroyed many marriages. One writer had this to say: "Money cannot buy love, but the longer I work with couples who have money problems, the more I realize that the capacity to manage both money and the emotions surrounding it is closely related to the capacity of love. This includes mature giving and receiving, the balancing of needs, and the ability to look at matters from another's viewpoint. A financially balanced budget and an emotionally balanced budget are great supports for each other."[4] Much of the power struggle is played out in the concept of the couple regarding earning power. If there is a feeling of rivalry between them for prestige and power, significant damage could be done to the relationship. During the early days of the women's movement, the conflict was more acute since the wife's quest for equality with her husband not only resulted in her competitiveness in the relationship but caused the man to seek to preserve what he considers his role as the family provider.

Sociologists and psychologists emphasize the difference between a dual-career couple and a dual-earner couple. Another set of terminology is breadwinning and employment. The differences provide clues to the type of psychological dynamic occurring in the marriage relationship. "Two special people are required to manage a dual-career family—a non-traditional wife and a new or liberated husband. Any family in which the husband and wife (or a live-together couple) both work is not necessarily a dual-career family."[5] Dubrin further explained that the difference lies between dual and career. "In this arrangement both the male and female have jobs into which each invests considerable time and emotional energy. Instead of just working for a living, each partner feels that he or she has a lifelong commitment to work—the difference between a job and a career. Duality is involved because both have approximately equal professions, in terms of status and/or income."[6] The dual-earner couple is the arrangement in which one person is the breadwinner or the one who is depended upon to provide the main source of income for the home. The other spouse is employed, but the income supplements the family budget.

In fairly recent research, Jean L. Potuchek, a sociologist, sought reactions of males and females to the two wage-earner family. Her interest in this subject developed when her students reported their findings on a questionnaire collecting data from their peers regarding their future plans to work. They were asked: "Assuming your spouse earns a sufficient income, would you expect to work?" More than 90 percent of both male and female students responded in the affirmative. But when asked: "Assuming that your spouse earns a sufficient income, would you expect your spouse to work?" the responses from were strikingly different. In the first instance, the women were more egalitarian in that they expected both spouses would combine families with careers. But in the second instance, whereas two-thirds of the males said that would be their spouse's decision, 80 percent of the females said that they would expect their husbands to work.[7] Potuchek's findings were similar to those of her students. "As I read the literature on wives' labor force participation, I began to find evidence that both women and men attach different meaning to the employment of wives than to the employment of husbands. Reports from men indicated that, even when their wives were employed, they still felt a special obligation to provide."[8] She pointed out that attitude surveys showed that both men and women generally attributed greater responsibility for family support to men than women.[9] Many career wives view their role as providing themselves financial independence and, consequently, a stronger voice in family purchases.

In a book published in 2002, Randi Minetor, after much research, confirmed the foregoing findings:

> I interviewed husbands and their breadwinner wives in households across America, expecting to find a shift in the balance of power. I thought that these women would manage the household finances, provide their husbands with allowances, demand that their husbands share in the housework and child care, make the major financial decisions, and, overall, play the role that traditional, breadwinning husbands have played for as long as most of us can recall. The fact is, very little of this is happening.
>
> Instead, I found a different kind of marital schematic—one that involves exactly the traits that now attract major corporations to female executives: collaboration, consensus-building, trust, and empathy. These marriages come closest the dream of a fifty-fifty split between husband and wife as any described by researchers and reporters. Within such marriages each spouse knows his or her responsibilities and takes these commitments seriously.[10]

This information is extremely valuable because we need to know how families are faring in the aftermath of the awkward relationships that emerged when the women's movement was in its heyday. Particularly during the seventies and eighties, many men and women were unsure what the opposite sex expected. With one-third of the married couples with wives earning more than their spouses, or about 10.5 million women by 1998, it would be logical to conclude that these women are assuming the role of breadwinner in the household. Consequently, women should appropriate the power that traditionally accompanies the position of head of the household. But according to Minetor's research findings, this has not occurred. Minetor's research did not seem to confirm the common concept emerging from the sixties that the one who controls the money controls the power. "Research by many venerable universities, psychologists, and sociologists have told us that the spouse who brings home the money is the spouse in charge."[11] Her findings revealed that the balance of power shifted from the husband's control of leadership in the home to a shared leadership. In some cases the roles are reversed. The man cares for the home and children while the wife is the breadwinner.

> **Minetor's research did not seem to confirm the common concept emerging from the sixties that the one who controls the money controls the power.**

This shift toward more women breadwinners has a profound impact on society. Even though breadwinner women have not generally acted as many predicted—that is, assuming the leadership role over their husbands—there still remain several other factors that create cause for concern. Randi Minetor mentioned the *Buck's Logic*. She coined this term after a brief discussion with a man she met at a conference, whom she named Buck. In attempting to share her idea about her book about women who make more money than their husbands, he interrupted her with the remark: "Oh, yeah? I've got the title of the first chapter for you. Chapter One: Marry a Loser."[12] Minetor considered her book a refutation of this "skewed logic." There should be no doubt that many men and women have to cope with issues arising from this reversal of society's expectation of the man as the breadwinner. There is also the idea to which some men still cling: that the wife is responsible for the care of the home. Some wives, after toiling all day, are expected to carry out their duties at home, while the husband still clings to his traditional idea of reading the paper or watching television while the exhausted wife prepares the meals and cares for the children. This attitude leads to conflict.

The power struggle may reveal itself in a competitive spirit. This unhealthy rivalry may cause self-esteem problems to surface. Since education is often related to earnings, there may be a desire by the man to be ahead of his wife in grades or level of education. If his wife surges ahead of him, he may become envious or discouraged. Consequently, some husbands may hinder or discourage their wives from pursuing a profession that will result in their wives' surpassing them. That attitude may cause the wife to develop a silent resentment. Fortunately, new husbands are learning to understand and respect the special needs and aspirations of their wives.

> Fortunately, new husbands are learning to understand and respect the special needs and aspirations of their wives.

Money and Security

Security, a key issue in the marital relationship, is emphasized by Laura Doyle, in her book, *The Surrendered Wife*. The spouse who handles the money usually feels that he/she has more power and control. The other spouse may feel less empowered and, consequently, less secure. Doyle has contended that by giving the financial control to her husband, the wife will trade security for intimacy. She wrote: "Giving up control of the money is scary because often we see money as giving us a sense of security."[13] She stated further: "The hardest part of relinquishing the finances was that I felt so vulnerable. When I considered whether it was worse to have the stress of the finances or to be that vulnerable, I had to keep reminding myself that the former has the added benefit of fostering intimacy."[14] If the funds are sufficient, the wife feels secure in the assurance that whenever financial demands arise she can handle it without depending on her husband. The opposite is also true. When there is not enough money to meet the expenses, there is stress. The husband may even accuse his wife of being a bad manager of the financial affairs of the home.

> Doyle has contended that by giving the financial control to her husband, the wife will trade security for intimacy.

Doyle expressed that when a man is in control of the finances, several benefits accrue to his wife. When the wife is in control of the finances, she spends according to her priorities. Even though the husband participates in the budget planning, he is powerless or "impotent" in the actual spending. This powerlessness is a damaging blow to his ego, since men carry a sense of responsibility for providing for the family. When he controls the finances, he feels a direct relationship between what he earns and providing for his family. Furthermore, if the funds are inadequate, rather than blaming his wife for failure to spend wisely, he would be motivated to earn more. Doyle wrote: "For a man, there's nothing more conducive to intimacy than feeling proud and masculine."[15] A loving husband will be more generous with gifts to his wife than she would be to herself when she is in control of the money.[16] Here is her stated concept: "There can be no intimacy unless there is vulnerability, and one of the ways wives avoid vulnerability (and therefore intimacy) is by controlling the family's cash flow. As an act of your faith in your husband's ability—ability to earn, spend, and manage money wisely—give him all the money you earn or receive from other sources."[17] Doyle cautioned that there is no need for panic. Trusting her husband does not mean she will be deprived, rather he will give her the cash she needs, thereby she ultimately gains the advantage. "Until you are willing to intertwine financially," she explained, "you will never be able to cross the chasm that keeps you from intertwining emotionally."[18] Ask your husband to give you your money in cash. This will help you avoid using credit cards or overspending. You will also avoid the problem of trying to figure out if there is money in the bank account.

In our marriage, Pam and I have had no conflict regarding control of money. After our marriage, we set up shared bank accounts. Control of the budget shifted back and forth over the years. The one in charge at the time took responsibility based on convenience or choice. We were careful though to give full control to the one doing the spending. Except for grocery shopping, Pam does a great job. Most of the time I do the grocery shopping because she seems to spend much more than I do. She does not seem to have the patience or interest to shop for items in season or on sale. For the past several years, we have set up personal accounts for personal purchases as well as for the payment of the budgeted items we assigned to each other. However, except for large amounts, we spent for each other with little accountability when the need arises. We keep in touch constantly about each other's need for assistance to cover unbudgeted expenditures.

Financial security is also an important goal for any family. Financial security will definitely lead to financial peace. Dave Ramsay is a Christian radio talk show host, whose program on WLAC, channel 99.7 based in Nashville, Tennessee, has, in a few years, achieved nationally syndicated status. He promotes his book *Financial Peace* and conducts seminars nationally. He has gained national attention because of his tenacious grip on the principle of "no debt." He advocates the immediate termination of the use of all credit cards and credit purchases. Families should start with an emergency fund and save rigorously to purchase items for cash by saving in envelopes labeled for the intended uses. Therefore, a family would not go out for dinner until there is enough money in that envelope marked for that purpose. A serious attempt should be made to set aside an emergency fund of one thousand dollars immediately. Selling any available assets, even the house, automobile, and furniture help achieve the goal of financial freedom. The money should be used to pay off as much of the debt as possible. Steps should be taken to downsize your house and automobile and put the debt liquidation plan in operation. Ramsay's plan is gaining great national support as more and more people discover "financial peace."[19] As a Christian, Ramsay advocates the strict adherence to financial contributions to the church in acknowledgment to God as the source of all we own. Liberal donations to worthy causes and those in need should be included in the family budget.

Dr. James Dobson also advocates giving to the church in the form of tithes (one-tenth of your income), offerings, and support for others in need. He, too, emphasized the need for restraint in spending. He wrote: "Since we have limited resources and limited choices, the only way to get ahead financially is to deny ourselves some of the things we want. If we don't have the discipline to do that, then we will always be in debt. Remember too that unless you spend less than you earn, no amount of income will be enough. That's why some people receive salary increases and soon find themselves even deeper in debt."[20] He enunciated the principle: "No amount of income will be sufficient if spending is not brought under control."[21]

Family Interview

How should a couple exercise proper management of family funds in today's commercialized society?

Although we have been married for ten years, this question has continually been a challenge in our household. The central issue has always been coordinating the use of our joint checking account when oftentimes we have entirely separate and busy schedules. Like many young couples with limited finances, we have often found ourselves trying to stretch the same modest dollars for an endless variety of competing needs. This, combined with the "easy-spend" temptation of the credit card, seemingly conspire to sink any attempt at maintaining a balanced budget. Quite often—especially in earlier years—it was almost impossible to stick to a budget when bills may exceed income. The emotional stress resulting from this financial insecurity can be overwhelming with conflict as the natural result.

In recent years we have become better at solving this common problem. It starts with better communication in setting joint priorities. It makes no sense to have opposite priorities if resources are limited. We contributed to our problems by assuming we would both agree on where funds would go only to find that we did not always see eye to eye. We have also learned that it is more effective for only one of us to be primarily responsible for the household bills, thereby producing a more coordinated approach to managing the family funds—especially when things get tight. Although we have been no better at adhering to budgets than most are with New Year's resolutions, we have been more successful with sticking to weekly personal "allowances." This strategy seems to limit unbudgeted spending. By following these few methods, we have managed to do much better at controlling cash flow—consequently reducing our finance-related stress.

Contributed by: Royland and Shawna-rika

Royland grew up in Montreal and Edmonton, Canada. He attended Atlantic Union College located in Massachusetts where he met Shawna-rika, a Bermudian. Although he left to complete his final year of undergraduate studies in upstate New York and later doctor of optometry at Ohio State University, distance could not quench their commitment to each other. Shawna-rika later moved to Ohio where she studied secretarial science. They were married soon after their graduation and moved to Bermuda where they now operate an optometry practice. Two children, a boy and a girl, have brought them the joy of parenthood.

7

Children

In recent years the practice of planning for the number of children a couple desires to have has become commonplace. In earlier decades, most families did not seriously discuss this topic before having children. The latter describes our situation. We did not plan or even discuss the number of children we wanted. That may seem strange especially in society today, but we felt comfortable with each other and took for granted that the future would take care of itself. It did. Our four children—two boys and two girls—were born in just over six years after we were married. And they came a boy, a girl, a boy, a girl. We could not have planned it any better. Because of health reasons, after the fourth child was born, the doctor advised my wife not to have any more children. At that point, we felt God had blessed us with the four children who would help us form a happy home. Pam often talked half seriously about wanting twelve children. I never challenged her about whether she was serious, even though she mentioned adopting children. To me, raising four children in North America is enough challenge.

When Pam gave birth to our first son, three days after our first wedding anniversary, our excitement was unspeakable. Obviously, having recently graduated from college and started on our first few months of employment we were broke, insecure, inexperienced, and strangers in a foreign country, the Bahamas. Accepting an invitation to teach at Grand Bahama Central Academy, we traveled from Edmonton, Alberta, by Greyhound bus to New York. Pam was nearly three months into her pregnancy. The trip lasted two days and two nights. It was frightening since we did not anticipate the extremely rough ride for much of the journey. We tried everything we could contrive to protect

Pam since she was in the delicate first trimester of pregnancy. We tried padding her seat with pillow, blankets, and anything we could find. Nothing satisfied us since the roads, particularly in Manitoba and Saskatchewan, were very rough. The chances of losing the baby loomed large in our minds. After arriving in New York, we decided to travel by train to Miami because we thought the ride would be smoother. We were wrong. The trip by train proved to be worse than the bus. When the coaches pulled apart in response to the sudden pull of the engine and then reconnected with a jolting force, nothing could prevent us from lurching forward and then suddenly back again. The thirty-hour journey caused us much anxiety. After traveling by air the rest of the way, we arrived safely in Freeport, Grand Bahama.

Even though the circumstances surrounding the birth of all our four children remain special in our memories, the birth of Richard was most prominent for two reasons. His birth created a high level of anxiety for us as most new parents' experience. Beyond that, however, at the time of his birth, Pam and I were separated by a series of circumstances. After taking her to the hospital about 3:00 A.M., I remained with her until bout 8:00 A.M. Being the school principal at that time, I hurriedly went to school to make sure there was proper supervision. While returning to the hospital, not one but two tires on my car blew out, leaving me stranded along a lonely section of the road leading from Eight-Mile Rock to Freeport. I didn't reach the hospital until 3:00 P.M. Richard had been born at ten o'clock that morning. Needless to say, I was deeply disappointed. However, the joy of seeing my wife and son completely dispelled the despair of the previous hours.

Pam and I took the responsibility of caring for our children very seriously from the beginning. Recognizing the need to prepare for the children's health before they were born, we made sure Pam had a well-balanced diet. In fact, she feasted on a wide variety of fruits during the summer while we were still residing in Alberta. Since our lifestyle excluded consumption of alcoholic beverages, non-prescription drugs, caffeine, and unhealthful foods, there was no sacrifice to continue that practice to give our children the best chance of getting a healthy start in life. As they grew up, our children were taught similar health principles. All four of them have adopted these principles and are practicing them in their adult years. We also made sure that they had regular medical and dental checkups as a preventive rather than curative approach to health.

> Since our lifestyle excluded consumption of alcoholic beverages, non-pre-scription drugs, caffeine, and unhealthful foods, there was no sacrifice to continue that practice to give our children the best chance of getting a healthy start in life.

An issue of great concern to many parents is discipline. Contrary to the popularly accepted view, I believe that children should not be shielded from conflicts. Although my wife did not necessarily share my views, we found a way to respect each other's position. However, my opinion on this matter does not include serious conflicts between spouses. Children should be shielded from that extreme conduct, and couples should avoid that level of conflict as well. My concern relates to unnecessarily trying to hide the fact that there is disagreement, even if it is regarding them. When parents lock themselves in a room or try to whisper while arguing, children who are sensitive usually detect that something is wrong and may feel excluded. They are left to speculate on the problems and the outcome. Another even more important issue relates to the fallout should a serious problem such as separation or divorce occur. Since the children would think that everything was normal in the relationship, the news that their parents are suddenly experiencing this level of conflict without their knowledge could be devastating. To the contrary, I believe that children should be exposed to real situations in the normal day-to-day interactions in the home. In that way they have a chance to adjust to the situations that arise from time to time. Later, even in their own experiences, they will not have unrealistic expectations about marriage.

Regarding the issue of corporal punishment, Pam and I differed somewhat. I drew the line at the age of ten. When children are small, they may need gentle physical corrective methods to help them realize that certain behaviors are unacceptable, especially if other more gentle methods fail. The wise man Solomon (of the Bible) eschewed this when he pronounced: "Don't spare the rod and spoil the child." To those who claim all forms of corporal punishment are bad, I would like to refer them to the outcome of the modern approach to child training. Because of certain overzealous legal protection, parents and teachers are afraid to discipline their children. Consequently, children feel empowered to defy those sources of their safeguard for proper upbringing. Understandably, there is a great need to protect children from abusive situations, but the law is so overprotective that children are using it to their advantage. Both teachers and parents are reluctant to use reasonable corrective measures to aid in the training of children. However, once the child can understand reason, about age ten, there remains no justifiable need for corporal punishment. Pam felt I should continue even when they were older. She tried it with our youngest at about age eleven. The process was fascinating to observe. Needless to say, I intervened to help calm the situation.

> Pam and I had frequent debates about the procedure, but never about the process for allowing the children to develop. We were united in the view that freedom is one of life's most precious gifts, which should not be denied to our children.

Pam and I also differed regarding the latitude we give the children to express themselves. Although our four children were much different in many respects, they responded to certain things fairly similarly. One of those things is parental authority. All four of them responded positively to discipline. Therefore, as each of them reached the age of ten, we began the process of giving them their freedom to make serious life choices. At that time, I discussed the topic of sex with them openly and thoroughly. I also presented each of them with a Christian-based book on sex, suitable for their age. The books I chose were *On Becoming a Man* and *On Becoming a Woman.*

Fortunately, all four children have pursued successful career paths, contributing positively to society. (Richard is an attorney, Tamaylia is a director for a youth counseling program, Royland is an optometrist, and Sherine is pursuing a career in vocal music). Pam and I had frequent debates about the procedure but never about the process for allowing the children freedom to develop. We were united in the view that freedom is one of life's most precious gifts, which should not be denied to our children. Freedom is divinely bestowed on every individual and should not be infringed without just cause. Unfortunately, history is replete with the record of those who use their position of authority, ill begotten or rightly bestowed, to restrict or even deny others the free exercise of their freedom.

We set in place a process that allowed our children freedom of choice incrementally in many areas of their day-to-day functioning as soon as they reached the age of responsibility. We began this process as soon as they began to transition into a responsible level of decision making and to realize that consequences are outcomes of certain behaviors. The objective of this process was to allow our children almost full autonomy in decision making by age eighteen or graduation from high school, whichever came first. This was explained to them in different ways from time to time. We also made it clear to them that although at age eighteen they would have full autonomy, they would have the option to stay home or live on their own. They may accept or reject our religion and choose a career and a life's partner without our interference. However, there were certain stipulations. We would not necessarily endorse their choices. In fact, we were forthright in giving our opinion on any of their important decisions, which required our guidance. In other words, while we allowed them their choices we would remain a part of their lives to render guidance, particularly in their transition years toward adulthood. We explained clearly that although college was their responsibility, we required that they get the minimum of a bachelor's degree before entering the job market. They were given our full support, which included financial assistance. We assisted them with their choices of which university to attend as well as their career choice.

> In other words, while we allowed them their choices we would remain a part of their lives to render guidance, particularly in their transition years toward adulthood.

We considered the education of our children to be very important. Our basic view of early-childhood education required us to provide a learning environment for our children in which negative forces would be minimized and character-building forces would be maximized. Our children did not need to confront destructive life choices at an age when they had few defenses. That meant choosing a house in a reasonably safe neighborhood and choosing a school, which respected and taught moral and religious values. We chose to live in Pointe Claire and later in Cote St Luc. Both were racially and culturally mixed neighborhoods. This provided us the opportunity to raise our children without concerns about strong negative forces influencing them or allowing them to be deprived of racial and cultural exposure. Those townships also provided or were close to wholesome activities and resources for children. For instance, a library and an indoor swimming pool were located about ten city blocks from our home. All our four children took swimming lessons at the recreational center and music lessons in a nearby township with Bob Laxton. Despite our very busy schedules, we found the time to take them to various activities.

The premise that the first few years of a child's education are fundamental since it is a time of character formation and provides significant patterns for future conduct played a vital role in our decision to pay for a Christian education. Fortunately, the level of education and the social environment were excellent because of the competence and commitment of Sylvia Greaves, the school principal and teacher. However, when they reached the senior high school level, we had to decide between sending them to a Christian boarding school and sending them to a public school nearby. We chose the latter. At that stage of the children's life, they needed close and keen parental oversight. The children understood that as parents we needed to know where they were at all times. They were not allowed to attend certain functions if the activities contravened the family rules of conduct. Sleeping over with friends was not allowed, even if their friends' parents had similar values. In short, we felt that they should be constantly under our supervision. We did not take a trip together and leave them with anyone, not even relatives. We did not take a vacation unless the whole family could travel together. While we recognized the importance of daycare, we never sent any of our children to daycare. Instead, we sacrificed to pay for a live-in helper even when both of us were attending Andrews University full-time. May I interject that Pam and I paid our university fees without the aid of bursary, student loan, or any outside financial assistance of any kind. I sold children's literature in the summer and worked in a factory in Benton Harbor during the school year. In 1975, my father came to live with us. His help in taking care of Sherine, our youngest child, during her travel to and from kindergarten a block away from the house, provided the necessary protection for her.

When the family moved to Edmonton, Alberta, in 1981, the ages of the children ranged from eleven to sixteen years. Less than three years later, they were all in their teens, the turbulent years. The youth with whom they associated had developed a pattern of conduct that did not appear to me to be immoral or deviant but uncontrolled. Although most of them were Christian youth from the West Edmonton Seventh-day Adventist Church, their conduct was questionable. The practice that affected our family soon after we arrived was the late-night get-togethers. Since they met in their friends' homes occasionally, we expected that there would have been a measure of adult supervision. Nevertheless, since we had no controlling influence during the very late gatherings, we had to enforce our family rule requiring our children to be home by midnight. On one occasion the children were not home by one o'clock in the morning. Pam insisted that none of us should go to bed before the children arrived. As I recall, I was very tired that night so I went to bed. Soon after I fell asleep, Pam awakened me insisting that I should go and find the children. We had the name of the person whose home they were visiting with a group of friends, but we did not have the address. Pam tried to reach them by phone with no results. We drove around for some time without any real plan just hoping to spot them or contact one of their friends who might know where they were. Finally, we gave up and returned home. Although I insisted that there was nothing we could do but wait, Pam declared that we must stay awake until they arrived. After they returned home about two o'clock in the morning, they were reminded sternly of the deadline for staying out at night. As I recall, they never stayed out late again, even though several of their friends considered it normal to stay out very late.

The only exception occurred one Saturday evening when Tamaylia attempted to leave home after ten o'clock to go out with her friends. This was particularly embarrassing since her friends accompanied her to our home to obtain our permission. We objected to her leaving so late, especially since she could not assure us that her friends would bring her home by midnight. Being a senior in high school at the time, Tamaylia felt she had the right to control such a decision. This resulted in a defiant confrontation. After reasoning with her and pointing out the dangers to which she could be exposing herself, she capitulated, albeit reluctantly. It would appear that our influence prevailed mainly because of our earlier parental discipline and guidance.

There were several rules and practices that helped in the smooth functioning of our home. These also aided us as parents to instill in our children the need for order, family unity, and character development. Let's have a look at a few of them. Apart from the duties that children usually perform at home, we assigned them specific duties, which earned them certain rewards. A list of these duties was posted on the refrigerator door. One type of reward was allowance for vacation. These duties with other matters were discussed at our family councils, which were held every Sunday morning at ten o'clock. During these councils we had the chance to discuss any matter of concern, particularly any issue that arose during the previous week. We practiced the rule of having one meal per day together as a family. Those occasions provided opportunities to discover anything unusual that may be occurring with any of the children.

We could also review certain rules or plans or just use the time for family fellowship.

We established and enforced bedtime, television time, and study time. Our children were not allowed to watch television during the week, only on Saturday nights and Sundays. We also gave them guidance in their choices of music, but we granted them some flexibility so they might express their freedom of choice within the established family guidelines.

Of course, views concerning child rearing are many and divergent. Let us look at some of these through the eyes of some professionals, who contemplated various aspects of family life. One writer has penned these poignant lines on children:

> Your children are not your children.
> They are the sons and daughters of Life's longing for itself.
> They come through you but not from you,
> And though they are with you yet they belong not to you.
> You may give them your love but not your thoughts,
> For they have their own thoughts.
> You may house their bodies but not their souls,
> For their souls dwell in the house of tomorrow, which
> you cannot visit, not even in your dreams.
> You may strive to be like them, but seek not to make
> them like you.[1]
>
> Khalil Gibran

Parents

There seems to be a universal yearning of parents for the survival and success of their children in life. I can still feel the challenge welling up in me as my father repeated his hope from time to time that he expected me to exceed his accomplishment in life. For much of my youth, he was a single parent. My mother, whom he loved dearly, died when I was only four years old. I remember my father refusing to eat for nine days after my mother's passing. His attempt at a second marriage failed. He worked hard as a truck driver for the government's Public Works Department. But he was a good father to me. He wanted me to excel in life and I wanted to please him. Perhaps, most parents want the same thing for their children, but many of them do not know the way to help them achieve it.

I doubt that there are many people who would argue against the importance of parents' influence on their children's upbringing. But there is much debate about the method. Unfortunately, new parents have very little experience of rearing children. It is a kind of on-the-job training. The problem is that when they get the experience, it may be too late to use it to help their children. If they have made grave mistakes, the effects could be devastating. Then, too, many parents have struggles of their own that limit their effectiveness in the child-training process. Obviously, there are various possible aberrations that could occur. One thing is certain: Children need guidance. Leslie Flynn, a clergyman, included a telling incident in an article on discipline. "A little boy refused to close a door that his father asked him to shut. A little girl who overheard was asked later what the little boy needed. She answered that instead of a whipping, he needed a father."[2]

The daily news, the talk shows, and the public in general are obsessed with the topic of the failing American educational system from the kindergarten to the high school level. Several theories are bandied about regarding the way to improve the system in order that children may have the opportunity to develop academically. Many of these ideas call for more money. My extensive experience in the field of education has provided me sufficient information to formulate and enunciate a bold statement concerning early-childhood education. I have served as high school and elementary school principal, superintendent of education for a private school system, and school board chairman for kindergarten through twelfth grade schools. I have also served on two college boards for seven years. In addition, I have lived with a master teacher, my wife, for forty years. My conclusion is neither new nor revolutionary. It is basic common sense. The key link in the education chain is the home. There are few, if any, viable substitutes for the role of parents in the process of educating the youth. Several people have said the same thing in different ways, but no daring policies have emerged to hold parents accountable for their children's education. Parents are fully, not partially, responsible for their children's learning. Educators and legislators are only paying lip service to this concept. Education in America needs a fundamental reorientation if significant results are to be achieved. Throwing money at the broken education system will not fix it. A strategy must precede the expenditure.

> The key link in the education chain is the home. There are few, if any, viable substitutes for the role of parents in the process of educating the youth.

Referring to the impact of parents on their children's development, John Bradshaw wrote: "The most dominant need that any child has is to gradually move from the complete environmental support of infancy and childhood to the self-support of maturity." He remarked also that "in order to grow, children need their parents' good modeling, attention, time, and teaching."[3] Oswald Hoffman, radio speaker for the Lutheran Hour, said that some parents have failed their children because they were too self-indulgent to pay attention to the real needs of their children. Others love their children and thought they were doing them a favor by allowing them "to do as they pleased without any consistent instruction, direction, or restraint."[4] He pointed to the grim harvest. "The results can be seen all around us in the price society has had to pay for the over permissiveness of a whole generation of parents."[5] "Over permissiveness is really a crime committed by parents against their children—a costly crime—costly not only to parents but also to children who deserve something better than this encouragement, this inducement, to underachievement at school, causing many young people to blow their opportunities for a genuine education and often for a satisfying life."[6] Parents can accomplish their role as successful parents in several ways. Brief mention will be made of only three of these important tasks: *discipline, dedication of time,* and *development of character*. One could point correctly to the hindrances to effective parenting, such as, poverty and single-parent homes. Would not government's increased expenditure on education be better utilized by targeting those areas of weakness in the education process rather than on experimental programs and bundling bureaucracy?

> Similarly, children left to their own devices without moral training and discipline will likely embarrass their parents, prey upon their neighbors, and wreck their own lives.

Discipline

Let me attempt to "paint the lily" by using an illustration. When we left Montreal in 1995, we decided to rent our house to a businessman. We had bought the newly built house seven years before, and my wife took great pride in landscaping the yard. We had a contract with a landscaping firm to care for the grass, and we planted a few pine trees on the front lawn. Upon signing the lease contract with the tenant, we expected the same lawn care to continue. Imagine our shock when we returned to Montreal a few months later to see a lawn overrun by weeds. My wife was particularly disturbed by the destruction of the beautiful decorative pine trees we planted on the front lawn. All this happened because of neglect, lack of regard for beauty, and lack of respect for the neighbors in the community. Nature has taught us that great care is needed to keep a lawn in good condition. Left neglected, it will be overrun by weeds. Similarly, children left to their own devices without moral training and discipline will likely embarrass their parents, prey upon their neighbors, and wreck their own lives.

Dr. James Dobson, who wrote a popular book on discipline (*Dare to Discipline*), also dealt with discipline in his book *Marriage and Family* in which he summarized his views in six points concerning disciplining a child.[7]

1. Define the rules before they are enforced. If you did not define the boundaries, don't enforce them.

2. Respond with confident decisiveness when your authority is met with defiance. The child should be held accountable.

3. Differentiate between willful defiance and childish irresponsibility. Children should not be punished for mere mistakes.

4. After a confrontation in which you assert your parental authority, follow up by reassuring and teaching. Express your love and concern for the child. "This moment of communication builds love, fidelity, and family unity."

5. Do not make a demand on a child that he/she cannot meet.

6. "Let love be your guide! A relationship that is characterized by genuine love and affection is likely to be a healthy one, even though some parental mistakes and errors are inevitable."

Dedication of Time

In order for children to develop normally and be prepared to take advantage of school, parents must spend time with them. Parents should in reality be their children's first teachers. If they lack the skills, they should either make the sacrifice to develop the necessary competence or get others, such as family members, to assist. There is no reasonable excuse for a child to complete grade three without developing basic reading skills. Public school teachers usually have large classes and cannot give careful attention to the slow learners. They need parental support. The problem remains that many parents do not consider teaching their children their responsibility; rather they believe it to be the teachers' task. Parents must at least pulverize the soil of the child's mind so that the teacher can sow the seeds, which will produce a bountiful harvest.

Development of Character

With the lack of character development lies the greatest tragedy of our postmodern age. Children at even an early age are bombarded with untold destructive forces within the society. I became more keenly aware of the impact of the media on the youth while watching television on April 11, 1993. The news broadcaster was reporting on a recent research that revealed that by age eighteen, a child would likely see on television 180,000 murders, 170,000 sexual references, and 70,000 beer and wine commercials. Now, more than a decade later, the problem is much worse. Without a direct intervention on the part of parents to limit those destructive assaults on a young child's mind and at the same time provide positive character-building reinforcement, the child would face life with a serious disadvantage. Oswald Hoffman pointed to one of the most destructive forces that attack our youth. He stated:

> Nowhere is the permissiveness of parents more evident today than the area of what some people are disposed to call "sexual freedom." Actually most of this sexual freedom is just plain, stupid misuse and abuse of one of the glorious powers given to man by God. All too often the result is a slave addiction which does not permit a man to be a real man or a girl to become a real

woman capable of the mature emotional attachments and downright physical enjoyment that make a marriage such a satisfying achievement—.[8]

Adults expose their children to a diet of instant gratification. This is
extended to social drugs, unrestrained passion, and violence. With a preponderance of behavior problems, teachers are unable to teach. Students are distracted and lack concentration necessary to learn. The society has to deal with
complex issues arising from undisciplined youth who mature into problem
adults. Fortunately, there are still principled parents who understand their
responsibility for the proper training of their children.

Family Interview

How have you disciplined your children and still maintain their confidence in your love for them?

Since I have published an article on that subject, entitled, "The Two Faces of
Mom," I will respond through the use of that article. (It was published in *Cel-
ebration* magazine, Review and Herald Publishing Association, Hagerstown,
Maryland, September 1994.)

Mom has the capacity to love and discipline in a maternal relationship.
These are the two faces of Mom. Discipline is training that is expected to produce a particular character or pattern of behavior. It is a systematic method of
obtaining obedience. Ephesians 6:1-3 (King James Version of the Bible)
relates to this concept:

"Children, obey your parents in the Lord: for this is right. Honor thy father
and mother; which is the first commandment with promise; that it may be
well with thee, and thou may live long on the earth."

In addition, Proverbs 22:6 counsels, "Train up a child in the way he should
go: and when he is old, he will not depart from it." How can a mother love and
discipline at the same time yet avoid sending mixed signals to her child? How
may a child develop the right understanding of Mom's discipline?

At a critical point your child becomes so confused that he/she is unable to
rummage through mixed signals to find the difference between your love and
your right to discipline. Little Johnny tells his sister a bad word, so he is forced
to stand in a corner for two hours. Mom lets him know that because he said a
bad word, she doesn't love him anymore. Your child might be genuinely con-

fused at this instance. It might have been better to tell Johnny that Mom disapproves of the wrong he did, but still loves him.

Although children can correctly interpret the expressions on an adult's face or judge intent in the sound of the voice, Johnny might not have been attending to any visual or psychological cues. Any mixed signals your child receives over a prolonged period of time are likely to create a dilemma that may lead to making wrong choices. This may appear to be a deliberate decision to challenge your authority.

Avoid Verbal Fights

Since verbal fights with many children are often about rules. Reevaluate the rules periodically to clarify any misunderstandings and to achieve a better relationship. Try the following:

1. Plan regular family meetings for discussions and an exchange of views. Make the sessions short to avoid boredom. Reevaluate the rules and check for an understanding of the consequences. It may be necessary to amend some rules, add new ones, or phase out others.

2. Give clear instructions, and be absolutely sure the instructions are understood.

3. Apply discipline only when it will help to change a specific behavior.

4. Affirm the parent-child love relationship. A simple hug, a well-deserved or long-awaited trip, a wished-for meal, a small gift, a walk in the park, or just a friendly chat can be effective.

5. If broken, insure that the parent-child bond is repaired within a reasonably short time. An open and honest dialogue is an excellent start.

6. Review with your child some of the desired values. Talk about changes needed in society to restore some of the good values. Brainstorming with your child is a great warmup exercise before a review of the rules or standards. Any material can be adapted, and a verbal conversation can be tailored or simplified to the level at which the child functions intellectually.

7. Teach your child to respect the environment and his or her school and church.

8. Be sensitive to your child's physical, intellectual, social, and emotional needs. Help your child to nurture a spiritual awareness. Learn to be a good listener and demonstrate proper judgment. When you make a mistake, admit it.

9. Do not underestimate children's ability to understand right from wrong. Encourage your children to communicate their feelings with you as a friend, and be a friend.

10. Learn more about your child by observing him or her at play, during homework and leisure activities, participation in outdoor life, and when interacting with adults in his or her life.

The concept of the two faces of Mom is derived from the experience and observations of those who have argued that while a mother nurtures and nourishes, loves and protects, she must also discipline and train the character. She needs a reward for her best efforts. A fountain that is not rejuvenated will lose its vigor; so children must be taught to give something back. On birthdays and special days a letter to Mom or Dad, a homemade card that simply reads, "I love you," brushing one's teeth, or taking a bath without being told are the kinds of surprises that show love and appreciation.

A mother will always be a mother, and the two faces of Mom must remain. How she deals with motherhood and the combination of love and discipline are her challenges. A Jewish proverb says that since God could not be everywhere, He made mothers.

Contributed by Pamela

8

Communication

Recently, my wife demonstrated vividly a practical lesson in communication. Something had occurred between us that caused us to lower our usual level of communication, that is, the disruption of our spontaneous spoken and unspoken sharing of our true feelings and thoughts with each other. This lasted about three days. Because we were still relating to each other in a polite way, neither of us attempted to break this mood. One morning Pam took me by surprise. Standing about six feet from me, she held out both hands toward me and in a gentle voice said: "Take two steps toward me." I hesitated and beckoned to her to come toward me. She stood firmly in her place and repeated the invitation for me to come toward her. Knowing how determined she is in such situations and feeling a strong impulse to respond favorably to my wife, I smiled and took the two small steps toward her. She took her two steps toward me. We found ourselves in a fond embrace, as we kissed each other as though we were newlyweds.

Communication has been a key component in our marriage. Communication between us has been both effortless and formidable. It was effortless in the area of sharing our thoughts, desires, and daily activities. It has been difficult when negative moods interfere.

From the beginning of our friendship, we enjoyed talking to each other. We shared much of our true feelings during our five years of friendship. Because I took courtship very seriously, I discussed with Pam anything I considered important. Early in our relationship, I spent much time with Pam's close family members for two main reasons. I enjoyed their company, and I wanted to learn as much as possible about Pam's background and influences in her life. I wanted to learn as much as I could about her before deciding to form a bond of friendship that could lead to marriage. Therefore, when we talked together, our communication was meaningful and substantive. Our marriage followed the same pattern. We talked about that which was meaningful to us. We found it easy to talk about our activities of the day. In fact, we have done that throughout our marriage. Every time we meet at the end of the day, we usually share our experiences. If sharing did not occur voluntarily, one of us would ask the other: "How did it go today?" Frequently, because my duties are confined to a pattern, Pam would prod me to remember some things she believed I forgot or she felt I was holding back. Sometimes this exchange would last for hours, especially if something important had occurred. I came to enjoy the long rides taking Pam to and from school, even though her car was parked in the driveway. This took several hours out of my day. At times, I bemoaned the loss of productive time from my program, but I have learned to value those precious moments. I also look forward to the pleasant exchanges during the long trips we take together occasionally.

> **Every time we meet at the end of the day, we usually share our experiences.**

Before acting on a major decision, our discussions would get very intense. Whenever Pam was skeptical about my intended action or if she lacked full information, we would engage in concentrated dialogue until we arrived at a mutual understanding. I rarely did anything significant if I thought Pam would not agree. That is not to say I did not take my chances and hoped for the best, especially if she was not available to render her opinion at the time. In such cases I made sure that the decision was reversible.

Many times in our marriage, difficulty arose when negative moods interrupted the communication process. This is difficult to explain because I have never truly understood it. There is an element embedded in human nature that appears to distort even our best intentions as we endeavor to communicate. We may use the choicest words, put on the most charming expression, and engage the purest motives as we speak to someone else and still the intended purpose of the communication could be thwarted or misdirected. Something negative could intervene and destroy the intent of communication. Sometimes the negative element could arise from an attitude displayed years before. It would surface to distort the communication at that particular time. It could be just a negative memory from that particular place where the communication is taking place. Regardless of the source of the negative element, if the mood of one of the persons communicating is changed sufficiently, communication could break down. And whenever that occurs with a married couple, it is difficult to predict the outcome. Without either of them being guilty of saying or doing anything wrong during that particular communication process, an external element could intervene and wreck their marriage permanently. Let me illustrate by revisiting an experience I presented in a previous chapter.

Soon after we were married, Pam and I had a very casual discussion about whether I was attracted to other women during our friendship. As the jovial exchange progressed, I mentioned that I liked Barbyra, one of our classmates and a coworker in the business office where we worked part-time. Not knowing that Barbyra had challenged Pam in the girls' dormitory by telling her that she could take me from her whenever she chose, I added that I admired her skin because it was like velvet. Pam responded cynically that I could not feel that way about her skin if I had not touched her affectionately. Regardless of my effort to explain that it was an innocent remark and should be taken only as mere observation since there was no contact or involvement of any kind between Barbyra and me, Pam remained unconvinced. Unfortunately, I became annoyed to such an extent that both of us developed negative moods and exchanged unpleasant words.

Common occurrences between us that resulted in a breakdown of communication were incidents arising from remarks made when my mood was less than pleasant, even though the issue at hand was completely unrelated to the cause of my state of mind at the time. For instance, after attending a difficult board meeting or a counseling session with a husband and wife who were having serious conflicts, if I met Pam at her work and she asked me certain personal questions, I had to be communicative. If my responses were not enthusiastic or I appeared less communicative than usual, Pam tended to feel that I was passing my problems from others to her. As we attempted to communicate, a further breakdown would occur since she began to take it personally. In the meantime, I struggled with my feelings but was unable to communicate them effectively. I proceeded to explain that there was no reason for her to think that she was the cause of my negative feeling or action. Oftentimes, the situation got worse before we realized that there was no substance to the cloud hanging over our feelings. The pleasantness would return and the matter would soon be forgotten.

There is a saying: "Experience is something you get when you are too old to use it." For us there is still time to learn from our mistakes and use them to benefit our marriage. For many couples, however, this saying is true. They do not stay in their marriage long enough to benefit from their experiences. When they move into another relationship, the experiences are different and the learning and, often the mistakes, begin all over again. The couples that do not stay together long enough to overcome the challenges they are destined to face are doomed to serve out their days alone or get trapped in the painful cycle of remarriage and divorce.

My reflection on these episodes is that I was frequently unreasonable in the communication process. I expected Pam to interpret my feelings without patiently letting her know how I felt so that she might have the opportunity to respond to me with knowledge and, if she chose, with empathy. Especially during her childbearing years, Pam complained that I was often impatient with her and abrasive. She observed that sometimes I would act in that manner publicly, embarrassing her. My memory may be selective so that I do not recall such incidents. However, I know my wife to be honest and would not charge me unfairly. I must, therefore, with great gratitude express my appreciation for her sacrifice in enduring such painful experience during my learning process. I trust she gives me a pass on my communication with her in recent years. One thing is certain, while I am still struggling to overcome lapses and limitations in our communication, I am very conscious of my role in the process, unlike our earlier years.

Our communication is constant. We are always in touch with each other. As a principle, we always know where the other is at all times. Whenever I leave home to meet any appointment, Pam has a general idea where I went and when I plan to return. If my plans change or I am unduly delayed, I keep her informed. This is done for two main reasons: communication prevents anxiety and offers security. Because we know where the other is at all times, should an accident occur, we would have fairly accurate indication of where we should be at a given time. We also do not have to wonder whether our spouse arrived safely at a destination, since we always communicate when we leave and when we arrive. My wife does not have to spend her energies wondering whether I was spending time with another person since I am open to questions at all times about where I was at any given moment. She is automatically secure in our openness. We feel free to question each other at any time about anything.

Our children were taught the same principles. We made sure that we knew where they were at all times. Even though they have left home, generally speaking, we still contact one another when we travel long distances. They know that we expect them to call when they leave home and when they arrive at their destination. We have an understanding that we should be able to contact each other at all times. Cell phones have made our task much easier nowadays. Communication is a crucial factor in any relationship. Good communication is indispensable for the success of family relationships. Let's spend some time exploring this vital subject to discover keys for improving any relationship, including our main focus: the marital relationship.

Toward a Definition

Communication is sending and receiving messages and information. The delivering and receiving of information is incomplete unless understanding occurs. The purpose of communication, as stated by Albert Ellis and Ted Crawford, is "mainly to influence others to give you more of what you want, and less of what you don't want."[1] However, unless serious concern is expressed for the other person's views and needs, the communication may prove to be fruitless. Generally, in a relationship this is done verbally or nonverbally. Regardless of the method used a marriage cannot survive without effective communication. Experts on marital relationships consider communication a key factor in successful marriages. The communication process in marital relationships is effective when "a couple can handle three principles consistently: (1) *when they can effectively utilize the fundamentals involved in speaking and listening, (2) when they can resolve conflicts through constructive methods, and (3) when they spend time on a daily basis in an intimate sharing of feelings.*"[2] *When two people get married, they expect a relationship that is personal, private, and intimate in order that they may relax and release their pent-up feelings freely and safely.* [3]

An important factor affecting communication between spouses is faulty expectations. A clinical psychologist said: "Whenever rational reality falls short of expectations, hopes are dashed, resentments flourish, blame is cast and the ensuing conflicts prove to be more than partners can bear...disillusion is almost always the precursor of dissolution."[4] Cohen and Sterling estimated that genuine satisfaction between partners ranges only between 2 and 10 percent.

Comparing the marriage contract to a purchase contract, they point out that it is not so much that the fine print is left out of the agreement; rather the agreement is left out of the communication.[5] Troubled couples often reach an impasse because their assumptions made when embarking on the marriage experience proved to be invalid.

> **Troubled couples often reach an impasse because their assumptions made when embarking on the marriage experience proved to be invalid.**

Differences in Gender

The literature dealing with married couples is replete with information concerning the differences in the way men and women communicate. Let's take a brief look at some of these differences.

Women and Communication

Nancy van Pelt claimed that she dealt with this issue in her seminars with women. There is much insight to be gained by knowing what women think about themselves. Van Pelt habitually asks her seminar attendees (women) the reason they attend her seminar. "The overwhelming answer has typically been their desire to understand men better."[6] Consequently, ten of her twelve-hour seminars deal with aspects of understanding the male temperament. The women were usually pleased. Interestingly enough, John Gray (author of *Men Are from Mars, Women Are from Venus*) said the same thing about men. Claire Etaugh and Judith Bridges, in their book, *The Psychology of Women*, pointed out that emotional expressiveness is very important for marital satisfaction. Spouses' expression of positive feelings does result in happier marriages. "Consistent with the social construction of females as emotionally expressive and concerned about the feelings of others, women are more involved than men in maintaining this important communication. They are more likely to think about marital interaction patterns and the quality of the relationship and are apt to try to listen to their spouses and make them feel loved."[7] They arrived at these opinions after reviewing several available studies. Whereas these popular views about women may be predictable, their conclusion concerning verbal communication of women may be less predictable. Referring to the best-selling book, *Men Are from Mars, Women Are from Venus* by John Gray, they said: "Stereotypes suggest that females are always talking, that they speak more than males do…here is evidence of a number of gender differences, and one of these is, indeed, talkativeness. However, interestingly, the talking behavior of females and males is opposite of the stereotype. In most situations examined by researchers males talk more than females; they speak more frequently and for longer periods of time."[8] John Gray found that communication by men and women is so different that it appears that they are speaking different languages. Women and men use language to make their point and solve their problems. However, women "also use talking as a way of discovering what they want to say; and sometimes they talk about their feelings in order to sort things out, as a means toward eventually feeling better. At other times, women feel a need to share and express their feelings, simply as a means to get closer, to experience greater intimacy."[9] *The Hite Report* confirmed the view that women want more verbal sharing. They want their partners to express their feelings more often.[10]

> *The Hite Report* confirmed the view that women want more verbal sharing.

Another popular view about women that may be difficult for men to comprehend is that much of the time women talk for reasons other than obtaining advice or solutions. "A man mistakenly assumes that when a woman talks about her feelings and problems his role as listener is to efficiently assist her in feeling better by offering her solutions. Like a fireman in an emergency situation, he is impatient to get to the fire and put it out as quickly as possible. When she is upset, he wants to put out the fire of her feelings by giving solutions."[11] It is difficult for men to listen patiently without listening passively. Those who develop this skill will benefit from an appreciative wife. "Lucky is the man who discovers that satisfying a woman's need to communicate and be heard is the most important requirement in making relationships loving and harmonious. When a man is a good listener, a woman can repeatedly find the place in her heart that is capable of loving him and embracing him just the way he is."[12] The problem with trying to solve a woman's problem without being asked to do so is that the man is risking being considered insensitive. Women sometimes assume that their spouse did not really listen in order to respond to the real need—that is, to be understood.

In five salient points, Barbara DeAngelis summarized the secrets of the way women communicate.[13]

1. *Women love to talk because it creates connection.* They talk to make loving connection with someone close to them. Their purpose is in the process.

2. *Women express their thinking and feeling process out loud.* Women are process-oriented. They find meaning in the process not only in the specific objective. It is like sharing a private place together through words rather than with bodies.

3. *Women communicate details.* Many men listen impatiently to their spouse relate their experience in detail. They often cut her off in an attempt to get to the bottom line or remind her that they've heard it before.

4. *Women use talking as a way to release tension.* When women talk about the same problems over and over again, they feel better in the process. "Men, however, don't always understand this secret about women. That's because they have a very different way of handling their tension. *Whereas women externalize our worries, men internalize theirs.* We spiral through ours out loud; men keep theirs to themselves. And so, guys, when your partner repeatedly talks about her worries or anxieties, you make the mistake of concluding that we are more upset than we actually are."[14]

5. *Women minimize how upset they are.* Women prefer to create harmony with the man they love. Consequently, they prefer to communicate in order to clear things up so that the relationship with the one they love will work. That helps to explain the reason men misjudge women's feelings. Her instinctive need to foster harmony tends to conceal her true feelings. Husbands are advised to consider their wives as more upset than they appear to be. I believe this also casts light on the difficult issue for men who have dealt with women's constant expectation that their husbands should know what they want without expressing it verbally. My wife actually tells me that directly. She frequently expects me to know how she feels and what I did to cause her to feel that way without verbalizing her feelings. At such times I seek for wisdom, patience, and grace.

> The problem with trying to solve a woman's problem without being asked to do so is that the man is risking being considered insensitive.

Men and Communication

What Nancy Van Pelt found out about women's interests in her seminars, John Gray found to be a similar attitude by men. Gray reported: "After men read my books or watch the videos of my seminars, many of them comment on one thing. For them, the most helpful insight involves discovering how women communicate for different reasons than men do."[15] It is obvious, therefore, that men and women communicate differently. Wisdom and patience are needed in order for effective communication to occur between the sexes. Van Pelt told the story about a salesman who was being undermined by his wife's lack of support and understanding. Arriving at home after a hard day at work selling a product he believed in, his wife would make sly remarks disparaging his efforts. Despite her constant sneers, he advanced to become an executive of his nationally recognized firm. Then he left her for another woman who gave him the affectionate support his wife denied him. Obviously, his wife was flabbergasted.

> Men need someone with whom they can share their challenges and successes.

Men need someone with whom they can share their challenges and successes. Men prefer a spouse with whom they can unveil their anxieties without their spirit being crushed before they are able to explain all the aspects of a delicate problem. His wife's intentions may be excellent, but in order to render appropriate advice she should first listen and try to understand the problem. Because men carry the reputation of being strong, oftentimes their wives do not consider that they are also sensitive. Paul Tournier, M.D., who has written on psychological-spiritual problems, explained that if a man feels his wife is criticizing him, he puts an end to the conversation by using sharp and cutting words in an authoritarian manner. He may seek to have the last word or resort to anger or obstinate silence. Tournier stated: "Often men are easily hurt as women, even though they hide it. They are afraid of being hurt by advice just as much as criticism. They resent it every bit as much. A woman for whom everything seems clear-cut, who confidently tells her husband how he must act in order to do the right things, no matter what the problem may be—such a woman gives her husband the impression that she thinks him incompetent."[16]

Barbara DeAngelis also shared her opinions about men as she did about women. She highlighted men's communication habits in a list of ten "habits that drive women crazy." Dr. DeAngelis arrived at this list after research, surveys, and responses in seminars from thousands of women.

1. Men are vague--*Mystery Man*

2. Men avoid discussing things----------------------------*Slippery Man*

3. Men withdraw into silence-------------------------------*Invisible Man*

4. Men don't tell us what they want and need--------------------*Secret Man*

5. Men bottle up feelings and then explode--------------------*Volcano Man*

6. Men walk out in the middle of a discussion--------------*Vanishing Man*

7. Men order us around-------------------------------*Commando Man*

8. Men make fun of how we feel-------------------------*Sarcastic Man*

9. Men lie to avoid dealing with something unpleasant-------*Chicken Man*

10. Men anticipate the worst and get reactive----------------*Reacto Man*[17]

Men are usually goal- or result-oriented. This is revealed in their communication. That's the reason they get annoyed when women express themselves without an aim to resolving a problem. Men will internalize their concerns until they need help to arrive at a solution or they know the purpose of the discussion. That frustrates women, who prefer to share the process as well as the results.

Negative Communication

In 1988, I was watching television when I heard something that taught me a lesson in proper communication. The Chevrolet Nova had recently been released in the U.S. automobile market and was gaining a solid market share. However, its sale in Mexico had been unexpectedly disappointing. The marketing experts were baffled until someone figured out that "Nova" in Spanish conveys the meaning of "no go." Whenever there is an underlying problem with the communication process, the results will be "no go" despite genuine effort and good intentions.

Communication is the ingredient that provides the basis for love and commitment to thrive. It is vital, therefore, for every couple to develop effective communication skills. This does not need to be a sophisticated process; rather, a system should be devised that provides a comfortable and meaningful pattern of mutual exchange between the two parties. We have heard couples or individuals say concerning their relationship: "We do not communicate." That remark is inaccurate since on some level everyone communicates. Michael Broder pointed out that "even 'the silent treatment' is a powerful form of communication. So what they're talking about is the quality of the communication. Is it superb, merely adequate, or just plain abysmal? To the extent that you and your partner spend time together, communication goes on constantly."[18] The concern should be whether the means of communication are adequate and effective. Could you, in fact, be communicating negatively without your knowledge? What negative outcomes might have occurred? Let me digress for a brief period to illustrate the gravity of inaccurate communication or the significant effect of radically different interpretations of the same words.

Two Biblical Illustrations

Two major divergent doctrines have emerged mainly over the interpretation of two biblical passages. The first is found in Matthew 16:18. Jesus asked his disciples: "Who do men say that the son of man is?" Peter replied: "You are the Christ the son of the living God." After commending Peter, Jesus said: "And I tell you, you are Peter, and on this rock I will build my church, and the powers of death shall not prevail against it." Based mainly on the belief that Jesus designated Peter as the foundation of the Christian church, the doctrine of the papal succession was established in the Roman Catholic Church. That is, the popes are Peter's successors. Protestants disagree with this interpretation. After considering my cursory comments on the two interpretations of the remarks Jesus made to Peter, you may choose to take a closer view. If anyone should ever doubt that words are important, this alone should remove that doubt.

By saying those words, did Jesus actually designate Peter as the foundation of the church as the Roman Catholic Church teaches or was He commending Peter for recognizing that He (Christ) was the rock on which the church would be built? The interpretation is crucial. Without delving into doctrine and remaining relevant to the purpose of this book, let's look at what should be obvious nuances. Protestants believe that at the beginning of the response, Jesus called Peter by his real name, Simon Bar-jona. Addressing him, Jesus said, "You are *petros* (which, in Greek, means a stone) and on this *petra* (which, in Greek, means a rock) I will build my church." (The Revised Standard Version of the Bible and most Bible commentaries record the two separate Greek words to alert the observant reader to the intended interpretation). The context of the passage reveals that Jesus was referring to Peter's confession obtained by divine revelation confirming him (Christ) as the rock on which the church would be built. He might have pointed to Peter as the little stone then to himself as the rock. Other passages of the Bible point to Christ symbolically as a rock but no other passage designates Peter in that manner. Should we still believe that the church was built on Peter and the papal succession? That depends on which interpretation you accept.

Here is another illustration, found in Luke 23:39-43. Jesus was on the cross hanging between two thieves. One of them derided him and the other begged for mercy, saying: "Jesus remember me when you come into your kingdom." Jesus replied: "Truly, I say to you, today you will be with me in Paradise." Bear in mind that the original language did not have the punctuations we observe in this and other passages. The translators of the Bible supplied the punctuation at their discretion. In doing so it is likely that the translators were influenced by their theological persuasion. With that in mind, just remove the comma before "today" and place it immediately after it. (Truly, I say to you today, you will be with me in Paradise.) (This appears to be the correct interpretation.) The position of that comma and the inflection of the voice determined the intended meaning. However, two radically different doctrines were derived: one mainly Protestant, the other Roman Catholic. The Roman Catholic Church teaches that at death a person either goes directly to Purgatory or Paradise depending on the life they lived. The story of the thief on the cross, combined with the parable of Dives and Lazarus told by Jesus, spurred the whole concept of penance to avoid Purgatory. It was the doctrine of Purgatory that ignited Martin Luther's passion to bring about the Protestant Reformation. Protestant meant protesting against the Catholic doctrines. If you are tempted to ignore the meaning and importance of language and communication, just consider what one comma has created. By the way, the other interpretation with the comma after "today" implies that Jesus was affirming that day (at that instant) that the thief would be in Paradise at the designated time, that is, the resurrection. ("Truly, I say to you today, (pause) you will be with me in Paradise.) This agrees with the doctrine of the second return of Jesus, which is embraced by most Protestant churches.

This was a digression to emphasize a point, the importance of correct communication. In these instances, the theological backgrounds of the interpreters of the passages influenced the vastly different meaning they derived. Now, back to the subject at hand.

The Revolving Ledger

Some years ago, I read an article in *Psychology Today* magazine concerning a concept the writer termed "the revolving ledger." This concept refers to the intentional or unintentional storing of negative experiences. Whenever we face a negative comment or incident brought on by a spouse or someone else, although completely unrelated at that time, it may trigger that previously negative experience and create a much greater conflict. Many marriages suffer greatly from this problem. Just as the previous illustrations indicate, our prior experiences could predispose us to react or interpret that which is said to us in a particular way. The supercharged racial issue in America is a valuable point of reference for this idea.

There are some words a black person may use to another black person and they find them funny. The same words said by a white person to a black person could escalate into serious consequences in today's sensitive society. A person who was sexually abused, for instance, may exhibit negative attitudes toward his/her spouse without either of them realizing the reason for the apparently uncalled-for reaction on the part of the abused person. A spouse may be upset when the other spouse spends money freely merely because of his/her earlier negative experience with spending, such as getting into burdensome debt. This experience was stored away in his/her memory. Some spouses carry to their marriage negative attitudes they developed in a previous friendship, marriage, or even work. One innocent remark made by a spouse could start a negative reaction that may develop into serious conflict. In such cases it may be difficult to determine what is the real problem. I have counseled couples that have serious conflicts and are ready to seek a divorce but cannot articulate the specific reasons.

> Blaming each other and pointing fingers rank high among destructive attitudes in a relationship.

The Healthy Marriage Handbook records a question from a wife whose husband is constantly expressing a bad mood. She asked: "My husband is under a lot of pressure at work—facing deadlines and dealing with sticky personal issues. Four out of five nights he comes home grouchy and stays like that most of the evening. His moods are beginning to affect the entire family. I want to be sympathetic to his problems, but at the same time I want to tell him he needs to temper his reactions. Is there a gentle way I can do that?"[19] (Suggestions in succeeding paragraphs will offer suggestions for solutions to this question.) The authors stated that "husbands and wives both go through times at work or home that create pressures and problems that carry over into their relational life."[20] Blaming each other and pointing fingers rank high among destructive attitudes in a relationship.

Kathy Dawson mentioned that as a youngster the blame technique may have worked, but it will not succeed in a marriage. "As soon as you point a finger at your partner, an invisible but no less impermeable barricade immediately rises between you. Even if your partner is guilty of your accusation, blaming will do nothing but put your mate on the defensive in preparation for an assured argument."[21] She pointed to another important negative communication—silence! Silence is not always golden. Silence is golden when the goal is peace, but when spouses retreat into silence indefinitely, their "wordlessness becomes the silent killer" of their relationship. "Zipping your lips shut may feel peaceful at the time of anger, but sweeping your problems under the proverbial rug only adds another layer of resentment to your already growing heap of relationship complaints."[22] The sharp sword of sarcasm is often used to wound one's spouse. Whether it is used intentionally, inadvertently, or in jest, sarcasm destroys even an otherwise good relationship and eventually undermines the marriage.

> Couples should be constantly aware of the feelings of their partner.

Insensitivity and defensiveness are also significant agents of negative communication. Couples should be constantly aware of the feelings of their partner. It is necessary to consider the appropriate time for gaining your partner's attention for discussing an important matter. Because the issue is important to you does not mean that it is equally important to your spouse. Timing and setting are vital if an important matter needs to be discussed. Some people are extremely sensitive and will react negatively at the slightest hint of blame. In such cases, patience and tack are needed to provide peaceful dialogue.

Deep Listening

On their list of "Ten New Laws of Love," Maurice Taylor and Seana McGee included "deep listening." They incorporated the following lines taken from a poem by an anonymous author.

> When I asked you to listen to me and you start giving me advice,
> You have not done what I asked.
> When I asked you to listen to me
> And you begin to tell me why I shouldn't feel that way,
> You are trampling on my feelings.
> When I asked you to listen to me
> And you feel you have to do something to solve my problem,
> You have failed me, strange as it may seem.
> Listen! All I asked was that you listen!
> Not talk or do—just hear me.[23]

Listening from the heart or deep listening with emotional integrity is the essence of emotional support.

"It is different from the everyday sort of listening in that it offers no advice or judgment, nor does it attempt to fix anything. The silence it entails opens a delicious space, one that invites our beloved to go really deep, to contact and express the purest forms of his or her feelings, whatever they may be."[24] This type of listening is not just to learn about the story, rather it is to relate to the feelings our spouse is having about the story. The modern electronic age is creating barriers to effective listening. People talk to each other while watching the television or being occupied with some other gadget. Deep listening is the way to build trust. You can be vulnerable as you bare your soul, knowing that your partner will not criticize or demean you but will seek to understand and share your deepest thought. Michael Broder explained that you are really listening when you can share the spirit in which something is being said as well as hear the literal words.[25] He expressed that listening is taking place when you simply take in what your partner is saying, whether it seems to be rational or irrational or something you want to hear or don't want to hear. The deep listener will try to ask questions or make comments only to qualify what the speaker is saying.[26] The basic aspect of listening is to make certain you know what the person is saying.

> Listening from the heart or deep listening with emotional integrity is the essence of emotional support.

Toward Better Communication

Professionals who deal with marital relationships usually consider communication to be among the leading causes for marital failure or success. Several consider it the most important ingredient. I consider that top spot to be commitment with communication next to it. Kathy Dawson, who conducts marriage seminars, is one of those who believe that communication is the most important element in a marriage relationship. She wrote: "Communication, whether it be verbal or nonverbal, is what I consider to be the most important element in any relationship, especially between husband and wife. Words, gestures, facial expressions, tone of voice, and touch are the connective tissue between you and your partner."[27] She expressed the view that if men and women make one mistake in their relationship, it is that they underestimate the importance of maintaining a vital connection between them. It does not matter whether you are wealthy or married by the pope, "if you and your mate don't have a functional system for communicating with each other, your relationship hasn't a chance of lasting a lifetime."[28] Differing opinions are good for a marriage. What is bad is if one spouse does not allow his/her mate to have different opinions. Of course, the fundamental values of the couple should be preserved in order for harmony to prevail, especially if the particular core value helped to form the relationship in the first place.

Changing your expectation about your marriage, according to Steve and Cathy Brody, may improve your chances to develop better communication. Programmed by cultural myths, mistaken beliefs, and false assumptions, we develop unrealistic expectations about relationships. Several of these expectations seep into our consciousness from childhood. One of these is that when we find the right partner, we live happily ever after. The romantic courtship in which communication is generally on the first or second level does nothing to dispel this faulty notion. During courtship, many couples dwell on small talk, factual information, and romantic niceties. After the wedding and honeymoon phases are over and the real face-to-face with life's issues begin, the couple must deal with a deeper level of communication, such as sharing opinions, feelings, and emotions. You allow yourself to be vulnerable as you seek to develop real intimacy. You now feel free to verbalize feelings of frustration, anger, and resentment as well as pleasure and happiness. Insights into each other's personality will lead to greater understanding, depth, and emotional satisfaction. "Communication about such experiences often makes a deep impression on both parties and enriches the relationship. Mutual sharing of personal ideas and feelings is the ultimate goal in marital communication."[29] Before you can listen effectively, Steve and Cathy Brody informed us, you need to be prepared in three key areas: *prioritizing your relationship, quieting your mind,* and *ceasing to say and do things that frustrate your partner.*[30] This means that you place a priority on communication in your marriage, you calm down when you are frustrated, busy, or angry and avoid the comments and attitudes that turn off your mate. They cautioned against using "stoppers." These are remarks that belittle and annoy the person such as lecturing, judging, analyzing, threatening, moralizing, criticizing, denying, interpreting, and name calling, to name a few. These block the channel of effective communication and create hostility.

Wives should get what they want from their husbands by being understanding and strategic. After deciding what you want, you should tell your husband, whether it's a time for yourself, new furniture, jewelry, or anything that you desire him to do. It's a more workable strategy for a wife to tell her husband what she wants without pressuring him. Without the controlling element, he will feel that he has the opportunity to please his wife rather than being pressured. Laura Doyle has pointed out that when women say out loud what they want they have a better chance their husbands will respond and that will enhance intimacy. I enjoy finding out what Pam wants and then obtaining it for her or doing something she would like to be done. She feels special and I feel satisfied that she is pleased. When Pam makes demands of me, I tend to feel resentful and controlled. When I feel pressured, I hesitate to respond in a timely manner. I am tempted to do it later rather than sooner. Both of us benefit greatly whenever she lets me know how she feels and allows me to respond in my own way and in my own time.

Admiration and Acceptance

Praising your mate works wonders, especially if it's done sincerely. Admiration—the opposite of contempt, which is one of the most destructive forces in a marriage—should elicit positive responses. Dwelling on what is negative in your marriage could cause you to lose sight of the positive. You must control your thoughts. You can focus on irritation, hurt, disappointment, and contempt or train your mind to focus on what is right in your marriage. When you praise or compliment your spouse, he/she will be less defensive and more agreeable. This approach will work magic in the relationship, since everyone enjoys being complimented and admired. Sometimes couples are so distracted by the practical issues of everyday life and bombarded with various problems that they pass on this mood to their mates. This behavior will most likely cause your spouse to react negatively rather than to share your pain. Couples should resist passing their negative mood on to their spouses. By being open with your spouse about your feeling, you may gain empathy and support. Even in those difficult times, you will improve your chances of finding your spouse to be an ally if you find something positive to say. Some therapists know that it is difficult for change to occur without a climate of acceptance. People tend to respond positively to those who show them respect, admiration, praise, and value. This approach will lower your spouse's defensiveness and allow for better communication. It is crucial that your compliments are genuine.

> People tend to respond positively to those who show them respect, admiration, praise, and value.

Reason vs. Emotion

An attorney found an interesting strategy for effective communication in the practice of law. Robert Cohen, a top matrimonial lawyer who adapted the legal method in presenting seven ways to help married couples remain together, named communication second on his list. He related an episode in the experience of another attorney. He was putting the finishing touches on an opening statement while working in his office at home. As he thought of a brilliant ending, his wife burst into his office upset because he had not answered the phone. She had to interrupt her shower to do so. He lost his trend of thought, causing him to be upset. Just before expressing himself in an emotional outburst at his wife who was visibly angry, he thought of a solution. He was preparing his opening statement before the court, which would be based on logic rather than emotion to make his argument more persuasive. What if he tried the same strategy in his marriage? He did. The result was positive. His wife understood his side of the frustrating episode and empathized.[31]

When used correctly, this strategy could prove very beneficial in the communication process. Cohen remarked: "Truth and justice play as important a role in a marriage as they do in the courtroom. In court, you have to back up your arguments with cold, hard facts or suffer the consequences of defeat; the only thing that matters is what you can prove and how you go about proving it. The same thing goes for your marriage. It is very important how you present your case to your partner.[32] It is important to remember that both in marriage and in the legal system, a willingness to settle could prove more valuable than holding on to your opinion that you are right. To use a pun, in an automobile accident you could be "dead right." Being right doesn't matter anymore. It would be much better to yield your right to the other driver and save your life. Doing this in your marriage may lead to a happier experience with your spouse.

> It is important to remember that both in marriage and in the legal system, a willingness to settle could prove more valuable than holding on to your opinion that you are right.

Family Interview

So what's so important about communication?

Anyone who has been in a male-female relationship could certainly attest to the importance of free-flowing communication. We have found it to be the single most important human factor in the success of our marriage. We have also found it to be our greatest weakness and the source of many difficulties. Most of our greatest battles have been as a result of failing to communicate plainly when things became emotional. Typically, we would fail to clearly state our intent or feelings. This would result in a communication gap that would be promptly filled by erroneous assumptions.

Any man can bear witness to the frustration that results when a woman expects you to "read," interpret, and respond to the unspoken inferences in her body language or indirect dialogue. Likewise, most men have been guilty of simply failing to communicate verbally or otherwise. A great number of women have experienced this wall of silence. Such a breakdown in true communication or dialogue can only become a barrier to resolving disagreement. Just as electronic communication requires a common standard, we need to find ways of speaking the same language. Talking through problems openly, honestly, and straightforwardly while listening empathetically can go a long way to diffusing potential conflict.

Contributed by Royland and Shawna-rika

9

Sex

Treating the topic of sex between two married partners could threaten the privacy of sexual intimacy between them. However, the purpose of this book is primarily to use our own experience as a backdrop for practical discussion on marriage and family relationships, not the least of which is sexual intimacy. My approach is to look critically, analytically, and incisively at our own experience and cull out certain issues, principles and practices that may be beneficial to the experiences of others who desire to make progress in their own relationships. While endeavoring to maintain our privacy, I will be as open as is judicious in the present circumstances.

From our first contact, Pam and I were comfortable with the principle of reserving sexual relations until after marriage. I don't recall discussing the subject; we just had that understanding. In fact, we didn't even kiss during our five-year friendship until after our engagement in the summer of 1963, six months before our wedding. We felt that one thing would lead to another. We would be led down a precipitous path to a place we did not want to be prematurely. Much credit should be given to our parental upbringing. We enjoyed the advantage of fostering a normal friendship without the complexity of sexual involvement. We were in our mid-twenties when we got married and, naturally, we were ready to deal with sex in a responsible way.

> Therefore, it is likely that when a man is at his peak of sexual interest, his spouse may be in the process of rising or falling.

Perhaps, the most valuable counsel I received in my preparation for marriage was that given by the doctor who examined us in order to provide the medical clearance for our marriage license in the state of Michigan. The minister who performed our wedding didn't suggest marriage counseling and we didn't request it. In fact, the first time I met the minister, Pastor John Rhodes of the Andrews University Campus Church in Berrien Springs, Michigan, was at our wedding. Pam made all the arrangements, even ordering my tuxedo. She knew the minister. I did not. Although I did not consider the need for marriage counseling, soon after our wedding I realized that the doctor's unsolicited advice seemed like an oasis in the desert. He told me that the emotions of men and women follow different paths. Women have a slow rising emotional curve that peaks slowly and tapers off gradually. It remains in a valley before rising slowly again. With men it is different. Male emotions rise and fall rapidly and usually peak and fall more frequently than those of women. Therefore, it is likely that when a man is at his peak of sexual interest, his spouse may be in the process of rising or falling. The doctor explained that this phenomenon applies to monthly periods for women as well as during sexual encounters. In order for both partners to be satisfied sexually, there must be constant awareness of the other person's level of sexual response. The male, being more likely to respond quicker to sexual desire, may reach a peak of sexual intensity more rapidly than his wife. If he does not make an effort to wait for his wife to respond, he may leave her in midstream both physically and emotionally. If that happens frequently, difficulty in their relationship would most likely ensue.

Then, too, there is the issue of frequency. Generally, men may desire sex far more frequently than women. In fact, healthy men seem to respond to sexual impulses on an ongoing basis. When a couple is passing a group of attractive men and women, it is more likely that the man would stare at an attractive female than the woman would stare at a handsome male. The sexual experience needs patience, understanding, and love. Those instructions from the doctor proved to be invaluable, given my lack of exposure to sexual relationships, theoretically as well as practically. It didn't take me long to discover that Pam and I were very different in more ways than I anticipated. Soon after we were married, I found that the counsel the doctor gave was conceptually applicable without much difficulty but practically very difficult to implement. There were several factors affecting what theoretically appeared to be easily effected. I found that my natural instinct was to be very responsive to my wife in our private relationship. Even though I desired to wait on her, despite significant effort, very frequently I could not. Without thinking about it, we had embarked on a long journey of patient understanding in several aspects of our relationship, including sexual relations.

Pam was more patient and understanding than I. Perhaps, she was more naturally endowed with those gifts. She exercised them gracefully and rarely chided me for going off to sleep before she was satisfied. However, between ages thirty and forty, I had difficulty engaging in sex satisfactorily, mainly due to overwork. My level of sexual energy was seriously diminished because of my excessive workload. During that period I worked seven days per week, day and night. My task included administrative and pastoral assignments, which I performed without restraint. I was exhausted much of the time. So despite my best intentions, from time to time Pam had to question what was happening to me. Nevertheless, she was very understanding. We found that this effort to be patient and understanding with each other served to strengthen our bond of love.

When I realized that my excessive zeal to achieve extraordinary results in my profession had caused harm to my body and limited quality time with my family, I changed my work assignment in an effort to lessen my workload. Nevertheless, it was not until I had a burnout episode that I really came to terms with my mortality. Fortunately, it was not too late for my children or for my wife. Sometimes, when I expect more from Pam sexually than she is prepared to give, she will remind me of my "difficult days" when she had to be understanding and patient with me. After all, that's fair!

Sabbath and Sex

An issue that has never been quite resolved in the area of sex within our marriage is concerning sex on the Sabbath. The Bible does not specifically mandate the conduct of couples in this matter. General principles may be deduced from several biblical references. Pam and I have reached similar conclusions. In an attempt to limit this discussion, references will be made to only two biblical principles before stating our position on the issue. The Bible presents the Sabbath as sacred. It is reserved for worship of the Creator, reflection on His creative and redemptive acts, as well as fellowship with one another in a sacred setting. This rules out secular activities, which are performed on the other six days of the week. Similarly, the Bible refers to marriage as a sacred relationship. Several biblical passages, particularly in the books of Ephesians and Revelation, refer to marriage metaphorically as the experience between Christ and his church. Sex in marriage should be viewed as the physical fulfillment of the higher principle of love uniting two people as one. It should be viewed and expressed not merely as a physical act but rather an expression of the sacred bond of love between married partners. Placing both views together, we may conclude that sex within marriage as an expression of love would not violate the sacredness of the Sabbath. However, Pam and I believe that sex on the Sabbath should not become commonplace. Sex between couples is not always conducted as an expression of love. Consequently, we have concluded that sex during Sabbath hours should be avoided. I believe that this should be left to the conscience of the couple. Mutual agreement between the spouses is necessary in order to avoid resentment.

One of the most important lessons I have learned over the years is to be sensitive to my wife's feelings regarding sex. Her level of comfort, her mood, her wishes, and her readiness must all be taken into account. In our marriage, my wife's "no" really means no. Therefore, I do everything to avoid that irreversible negative. My overall view is that our private relationship has been very positive and we do enjoy healthy sexual experiences.

Let me add a special observation. A thought came to me recently that surprised me with its profound truth, yet with its unqualified simplicity. Although it is so obvious, I cannot recall discussing it or reading about it as plainly as I view it now. When it occurred to me, I asked my wife about it in this manner: "Lovie, what is the only essential biblical element in a marriage relationship that makes it a marriage?" She guessed various things: contract, love, commitment, and so on. I pointed out that all those things are duplicated in other relationships. Biblically, *sex* is the only element that truly creates a marriage. It may occur in other relationships, but you cannot have a complete marriage without it. Without sex you have a partnership not a marriage, even though all the other elements are in place. By sex I mean procreative sex, but not sex only for procreation. Sex cements the sacred bond that creates the biblical principle of "one flesh." Therefore, sex outside of marriage is an aberration or a distortion.

The secular view of sex is, obviously, in conflict with the biblical view. Although the author is sympathetic to other points of view, his experience upon which this work is based is a Christian one. However, in dealing with the research sections of each chapter, the author employs a more general perspective. Let's explore the subject of sex further as we evaluate the opinions of other professionals.

Sex: Simply Complex

Consider this comment about sex: "Sex comes with a big shiny bow wrapped around it: a present that promises the ultimate physical, mental, emotional, and spiritual fulfillment, but once the box is open, everything's in pieces and there are no instructions."[1] Despite the glamorizing of sex by Hollywood and the advertising media that permeate every corner of our society, sex still saturates our society with as much pain as pleasure. A 1994 study, which was based on the National Health and Social Life Survey, revealed that more than 40 percent of American women between the ages eighteen and fifty-nine don't enjoy sex. The study found that women had a greater variety of sexual difficulties than men do.[2] One would think that after the sexual revolution brought on by the women's movement of the sixties and seventies, men would be burdened with the greater sexual problems. One thing is certain, the subject of sex, which was so private in previous generations, has become commonplace in our generation. More knowledge, however, has not brought more wisdom.

Because of my upbringing and devotion to Christian principles, I viewed exploring knowledge about sex as a bit beyond the bounds of normalcy for a committed Christian. I felt the same way about viewing or participating in sports during a part of my adult life. I concluded erroneously at the time that Christians should use their time more productively. My attitude to sports changed a long time ago. I enjoyed watching the Montreal Expos, the Montreal Canadiens, the Edmonton Oilers, the New York Yankees, and the Tennessee Titans. I still enjoy watching a good game. However, my attitude toward sex did not change significantly. I limited my reading on the subject to preparation for lectures or counseling. When I began the preparation to write this book, I decided to explore the subject of sex as a part of my responsibility to be thorough. To my surprise, much of what I have learned about sex has caused me to think that many people who are married for several years, or even decades (as in my case), do not have sufficient knowledge about sex and intimacy to develop a meaningful sexual relationship with their partners. To my wife's credit, my limitations did not mortally wound our relationship. For many marriages, however, ignorance in the area of sex and intimacy has shipwrecked their dreams of a lasting happy relationship. In fact, their assumption about their level of understanding about sex and intimacy might have even helped to defeat their desire for a happy marriage.

> To my surprise, much of what I learned about sex has caused me to think that many people who are married for several years, or even decades (as in my case), do not have sufficient knowledge about sex and intimacy to develop a meaningful sexual relationship with their partners.

The Healthy Marriage Handbook has subscribed to this view in pointing out that: "In our sexually explicit society, it seems almost inconceivable that anyone could be uninformed about sex. Yet it happens all the time…Wives and husbands know they react differently to sexual drive and stimulation, but they don't understand the intricacies of their two very different systems."[3] Many married adults have a basic knowledge of the physiology of the reproductive system and no more.

Many adults have a view of sex they obtained from various sources, such as the movies, the Internet, novels, and childhood or teenage friends. Most of these sources are unreliable. Some people enter marriage with an unrealistic expectation of sex, as well as ignorance about it. They don't even talk about it to each other. As one person commented, they believe that sex should be in the dark, on the bed, under the covers with their eyes closed. Ignorance is certainly not bliss when applied to sex in marriage. Since so much of one's personality is wrapped up in the package of sexual closeness and meaningful sex, every effort should be made to understand the deep inner feelings of one's sexual partner.

> **Some people enter marriage with an unrealistic expectation as well as ignorance about sex. They don't even talk about it to each other… they believe that sex should be in the dark, on the bed, under the covers with eyes closed.**

Most women don't realize that testosterone creates a physiological drive in their husbands that demands expression every few days. Without that insistent testosterone, women experience little physical drive for sexual release. Rather, they desire the relational closeness that leads to sexual intimacy. Many husbands assume their wives will get aroused and reach a climax as quickly as they do. But most women are only in the early arousal stage when their husbands have their orgasm. This discrepancy often leaves a woman feeling cheated when her husband falls asleep just when she's getting interested. And her husband ends up feeling inadequate as a lover since he has failed to bring his wife to orgasm.[4]

In this chapter, we will explore this subject within morally acceptable boundaries in three aspects: *sexual inhibitions, sexual intimacy,* and *sexual knowledge.*

1. Sexual Inhibitions

Religion and Sensuality

Despite the explicitness with which sex is explored in our society, most married couples are still being influenced by the Judeo-Christian tradition, which informs our current sexual conduct. They may not go to the Bible for information, yet the biblical foundation concerning marriage is strongly entrenched in our culture and continues to influence our behavior patterns, even subconsciously. Several books have been written about marriage and sex from a biblical perspective. It does not mean one has to be a Christian to be happily married. But respect for the biblical principles on which marriage is based ensures a more favorable outcome. However, distorted views of biblical guidelines for marriage can create damaging results. This is most evident in dealing with sex, both within and outside the marriage relationship.

During the past few decades, Christians in our culture have been challenged to reinterpret the biblical view of sex. Until the first half of the past century, people accepted the puritanical view of sex and male-female relationships as the correct biblical view. With the sixties' rebellion against the establishment came a new sense of freedom to explore various aspects of our cultural beliefs. Sexual behavior did not escape this scrutiny. Now that the pendulum has swung completely to the other side—from prudishness to public display—what, then, should a reasonable person with moral principles consider acceptable or unacceptable regarding the subject of sex?

Linda Dillow and Lorraine Pintus are two Christian Bible teachers and lecturers who have dedicated themselves to the task of informing Christian women on the biblical view of sex. I listened to them being interviewed on the Family Today radio program. Subsequently, I read their book, *Intimate Issues,* which presents answers to twenty-one questions Christian women ask about sex, developed from a nationwide poll of more than one thousand women. I believe they are contributing positively to the correct biblical view of sex.

Before exploring what "God's voice declares," they reviewed the conflicting voices that have led to the confusion about sex that many people are experiencing. The Victorian voices said, "Don't talk about it." The Psychologists' voices (such as Sigmund Freud, Alfred Kinsey, William Masters, and Virginia Johnson) said, "Be sexual creatures." Church Fathers, such as Augustine, Aquinas, and Luther said, "Sex is good but passion and desire are sin," "Sex is acceptable as long as it is not enjoyed," and "Sexual intercourse is never without sin; but God excuses it by his grace because the estate of marriage is his work." Bombarded by the secularists and the church dogmatists as well as parents who are reluctant to discuss sex with their children, it should be no surprise that our attitude toward sex ranges from "ignorance is bliss" to explicit experimentation.

Billy Graham was forthright in declaring: "A book that has never gone out-of-date, the Bible could properly be called the world's most reliable textbook on sex. No book deals more forthrightly with the subject. As history, it records without distortion the sexual aberrations of its time. As biography, it refuses to gloss over the sex sins of its heroes, but details them and their consequences with straightforward explicitness. As philosophy, it sets forth the changeless standards of God."[5] Instead of condemning sex or rendering it undesirable, the Bible celebrates it. A whole book of the Bible is devoted to it. Consider this passage:

> How graceful are your feet in sandals,
> O queenly maiden!
> Your rounded thighs are like jewels, the work of a master hand.
> Your navel is a rounded bowl that never lacks mixed wine.
> Your belly is a heap of wheat, encircled with lilies.
> Your two breasts are like two fawns, twins of a gazelle.
> Your neck is like an ivory tower.
> Your eyes are pools of Heshbon, by the gate of Bath-rabbim.[6]

These lines seem to describe the author's undressed lover who appears to be sensuous in his presence. Billy Graham stated unequivocally that the Bible does not teach that sex is sinful. "Far from being prudish, the Bible celebrates sex and its proper use, presenting it as God-created, God-ordained, God-blessed. It makes plain that God Himself implanted the physical magnetism between the sexes for two reasons: for the propagation of the race, and for the

expression of that kind of love between man and wife that makes for true oneness."[7] Graham further stated that God's command to the first man and
woman to be "one flesh" was just as important as his command to "be fruitful
and multiply."

Scripture teaches that sex can be a wonderful servant but a terrible master.

Scripture teaches that sex can be a wonderful servant but a terrible master.
Paul, the most prolific writer of the New Testament, gave direct counsel concerning sexual relations between married couples. He saw the impending crisis
for families that would occur as a result of persecution and he advised those
who could remain single without submitting to having sex outside of marriage
to do so. To those who needed to get married, Paul permitted them to do so.
But as a true pastoral counselor, he admonished: "The husband should give to
his wife her conjugal rights (sexual relations), and likewise the wife to her husband. For the wife does not rule over her own body, but the husband does;
likewise the husband does not rule over his own body, but the wife does."[8] The
implications for marriage are profound. The principles of mutuality, equal
responsibility, equal authority, fidelity, and spontaneity in the matter of sex are
clearly enunciated here and elsewhere in Scripture. Similarly, the Bible condemns the wrong use of sex. Same-sex coupling and sex outside of marriage
are clearly and unequivocally labeled as sinful. Yet the Bible emphasizes one's
freedom of choice in his/her conduct. Many people in our modern society
strive to change the biblical teaching about the abuse of sex. It would be honest if they would acknowledge that they are supporting aberrant sexual conduct by their own standards rather than seeking biblical permission, which is
impossible to obtain without obvious distortions of clear biblical teachings.[9]

In the book, *Intimate Issues*, the authors emphasized the difference between
sensuous and sensual. The Bible condemns sensual behavior. This term has
negative implications, denoting unrestrained sexual conduct. To the contrary,
sensuous is positive, referring to being responsive to the pleasures to be
received through the senses. Some married persons, who spend years frustrating the proper expression of their sexuality whether through the pursuit of a
pious life or ignorance, may have unknowingly abused their spouse by denying
them the affection they deserve or properly expected from a normal relationship. They have confused sensual and sensuous. "Spiritual intimacy and
delight are not in opposition to sexual intimacy and delight. Spiritual intimacy

is actually found in the midst of the relational, fleshly delight of sexual union."[10]

Here are two illustrations that should help us focus more meaningfully on the artificial dichotomy between the spiritual and physical in relation to sex. One woman, finding herself passionate with spiritual things but passionless with her husband, described her concept this way: "The more I grow as a Christian, the less important the physical becomes. I want my emphasis to be on the spiritual."[11] She quoted from Colossians, chapter 3, and Galatians, chapter 5, to justify her view. Another woman put it this way: "It's as if I live in a two-story house. The top floor is my spirituality and the bottom floor, my sexuality. In between the two floors is a brick barrier separating my spiritual self from my sexual self. Because I want to be godly, I can't allow myself to be too earthly—and sex is definitely earthly. I allow myself to experience pleasure—but only so much. If I got really carried away, it would be 'too fleshly.'"[12]

Dillow and Pintus expressed their opinion this way: "No doubt about it, the Shulamith (as portrayed in Song of Solomon) was a sensuous, sexual woman and God describes her sensuousness in explicit and erotic terms. God wants us to understand the beauty and freedom of our sexuality. Through the young bride Shulamith, God unveils the portrait of a godly, sensuous wife, and because His blessing is upon her, we can follow her example with confidence."[13]

Nancy Van Pelt, a Christian writer and lecturer on marriage, was very direct in pointing out that a *Ladies' Home Journal* survey of more than four thousand men listed "unresponsive woman as the biggest turnoff and a cold, uninterested woman as what irritates men most during sex."[14] Here is a valuable point worth noting:

> The only portion of the sexual experience enjoyed by a man more than ejaculation is the satisfaction he derives from an amorous wife who finds him sexually stimulating. Sometimes, however, a Christian wife does not see creativity and responsiveness as part of a religious woman's demeanor. These women might be surprised to learn that 65% of their husbands wanted more interest, response, and creativity from their wives. Only 35 % felt satisfied with the status quo.[15]

Nancy Van Pelt conducted her survey and concluded that few husbands will complain about a passionate, creative wife who responds with enthusiasm to his advances. It is widely known that women are stimulated by experiencing the emotions of love. Men are stimulated more by sight. Men enjoy looking at their wives.

Yet one woman considered her husband to be "a dirty old man" because he became aroused when she undressed before him at night. She eventually found out that God designed his body that way. She also discovered the importance of dressing in appropriate ways to attract her husband.

The Janus Report on sexual behavior may give us some insight into how religious people think and behave regarding sex. For centuries religion has served both the religious and secular societies in regulating sexual behavior and moral conduct. Religious authority acted "as judges and sensors of all matters sexual;...and, for generations, had almost total control over the legal and social norms governing sexual practices. Their control has survived to a large degree in today's world, despite the sexual and social changes our society has undergone. The result has been a widespread discrepancy between preachment and practice, particularly within the more affluent segments of Western culture."[16] Based on the survey in *The Janus Report*, there is sufficient evidence to conclude that even very religious people in the American society are changing their attitude toward sex and may be less inhibited concerning sensuality or extramarital affairs.

Similar surveys of sexual attitudes by married couples were conducted by Tim and Beverly LaHaye and *Redbook*. The LaHaye's survey results have been published in *The Act of Marriage*. They concluded that spirit-filled Christians enjoy sex even more than the general population. *The Janus Report* asked whether they consider themselves romantic, 81 percent of the religious and 83 percent of the very religious categories responded "yes," compared to 69 percent of those considering themselves non-religious. The percentages are even higher when asked to respond to the statement "Sensually, I feel that sex is deliciously sensuous." In the top two categories, on a scale of 1 to 5, 89 percent of the very religious and 86 percent of the religious categories responded affirmatively. In response to the same question, 87 percent of Protestants, 90 percent of Catholics, 93 percent of Jews, and 88 percent of nonreligious agreed. However, 25 percent of the very religious and 22 percent of the religious compared to 15 percent of the not religious category considered themselves sexually inactive or below average. More frequently, Christians are disregarding the moral imperatives enunciated in Scripture. More than 70 percent of the very religious respondents had premarital sexual experience and more than 30 percent of them admitted to having extramarital sexual relations at least once.[17]

One may wonder about the extent to which guilt affects the relationships between those couples. The authors of *The Janus Report* postulated that the sexual scandals in which top religious leaders have been embroiled might have contributed to the loss of religion's spiritual and moral authority. "While primarily equally active on a broad range of sex practices, religious people have some difficulty enjoying their lives. There is a need to manifest a well-defined set of values for the public and for raising children, but many religious people live by another set of values privately."[18]

Affairs

Because trust is so important for a couple to build confidence in each other, an affair could drive a wedge between an otherwise good relationship. When this occurs, it is very difficult for the aggrieved party to rebuild confidence in his/her partner. As long as that lingering doubt remains, the couple may find that the lack of unhindered intimacy limits full participation in sex. About twenty-five years ago, I counseled a couple that had fractured their relationship because the husband had an affair. They were facing a difficult crisis since his wife asked him to leave the home. At that time they had two young daughters and the husband appeared to be genuinely sorry for his unfaithfulness. I advised the wife to forgive him, since I was convinced that they truly loved each other. She agreed to let him return home. However, he did not display the sensitivity to her feelings that she expected and she did not readily allow him back into her full confidence. Unfortunately, the breach was never healed. They later divorced. I was in contact with them for several years later and it was evident to me that they still loved each other, although the love was frustrated and thwarted. She never remarried and he remarried at least twice. This occurred in the early years of my experience in counseling couples and I learned many lessons from it. Here was a young loving family that was unsuccessful because of an unwise decision by the husband and their failure to reconcile their differences.

In giving counsel, I have always favored the survival of the marriage, unless there is violence or other types of problems that threaten the well-being of either spouse. Dr. James Dobson reminded us that the fastest horses do not always win the race, but we still bet on them and sometimes well-conditioned athletes drop dead from a heart attack. Therefore, mistakes can be made in marriage and one may err in deciding to break up. He claimed that there is nothing risky about "treating oneself with greater respect, exhibiting confidence and poise, pulling backward, and releasing the door on the romantic trap. The positive benefits of that approach are often immediate and dramatic. Loving self-respect virtually never fails to have a salutary effect on a drifting lover, unless there is not the tiniest spark left to fan."[19] Dobson added that when explosive individuals are involved in a midlife turmoil or a passionate fling with a new lover, competent counseling should be sought before, during, and after the confrontation. Tact and wisdom should be preferred over ultimatums and deadlines. A "tough love" approach is sometimes needed. There are times when confrontation and ultimatum may risk the sudden demise of a relationship. However, in such a case facing a crisis could be preferred to a much higher probability of a slow lingering death.

"Instead of bringing the matter to a head while there is a chance for healing, the alternative is to stand by while the marriage dies with a whimper."[20] *The Healthy Marriage Handbook* added its words of wisdom in response to a wife who is dealing with a husband who had an affair. It recorded this confession:

> My husband was involved in an affair. We have worked through some of our problems, and I believe he now intends to be faithful. But the memory of his affair freezes me up whenever we try to make love. I can't help but wonder if he's thinking about this other woman, and if he would secretly rather be with her. What can we do to get our love life back on track?"[21]

The response is included the following comments. The key elements in the response were forgiveness and communication. This person had gotten over the initial feelings of shock, hurt, betrayal, rejection, and anger. Many wives would end the relationship at that point. She had even started to trust her husband again. What she needed now was to go through the difficult process of forgiveness. If a Christian, she could rely on her faith in God to help her. The Lord's Prayer offers a good beginning: "Forgive us our debts as we forgive our debtors." Communication is vital. She should let her husband know how she feels and give him a chance to respond. This is best done when both are not distracted and not having sex. The affair may have occurred for reasons other than competing sexual preferences such as low self-esteem or sexual additive tendencies. During sex, you should find ways of communicating to allow yourself to share your concerns with your spouse as they surface. This will give him the opportunity to adjust and respond to your concerns. The response also suggested that affairs may occur from failure to take precaution to affair-proof your marriage. No one is exempt from temptation. Because two people are in love does not mean that one would not be attracted to another person. "When response to someone other than our spouse suddenly shocks us and we haven't safeguarded our relationship against such temptation, we don't have the tools needed to strengthen our resistance."[22]

After working through the issues of forgiveness together and finding ways to communicate effectively, make a commitment to each other to start your sexual relationship as if it were new. This approach will help the rebuilding process to getting back on track sexually and emotionally.

Inadequacy

No attempt will be made to deal with this complex subject comprehensively. That information is best handled by sex therapists and other related professionals. I will only touch on relevant aspects of this topic. In fact, I will avoid the medical aspect of this subject as beyond the scope of this book.

Sexual dysfunctions are sexual problems that interfere with sexual satisfaction. Fortunately, with the current wealth of knowledge in medicine and therapy, most sexual dysfunctions can be treated and corrected. Four of the main types are sexual desire disorders, sexual arousal disorders, orgasm disorders, and sexual pain disorders.[23]

Perhaps the leading sexual problem for women is a lack of desire. One study concluded that one in four women have this inhibited desire for sex.[24] About one in seven women have female orgasmic disorder. They experience the excitement phase but do not reach orgasm. Seven percent of women report painful intercourse. Physical and emotional problems may cause men and women to develop sexual problems or lack of interest in sex. Women have frequently used headaches and being upset as reasons for putting off sex. Men have their problems too. In the Health and Fitness column of the *Paducah Sun* newspaper (Kentucky), an article entitled: "Men's sex lives aided by exercise," pointed out that researchers linked exercise to potency.[25] The article stated that men over fifty who kept physically active had a 30 percent chance over those who were inactive in lowering their risk of impotence.

The article quoted researcher Eric B. Rimm, associate professor at the Harvard School of Public Health, as saying: "One could postulate that it would at least add years to your ability to have and maintain an erection."

They also found another fascinating connection: Lack of potency may precede a heart attack. Rimm stated:

> Being a vigorous exerciser and adding other healthy lifestyle factors such as not smoking, staying lean, and drinking only moderately had the effect of adding ten years to a man's sexual status. Exercise seems to benefit the small arteries that control erections, much as exercise benefits other arteries, such as those that feed the heart. Thus what happens to the penis may be an early warning of what could happen to the heart, such as a heart attack.

Researchers have also determined that age, marital status, ethnicity, education, and economic status are related to sexual dysfunctions. Etaugh and Bridges wrote:

> For women, the prevalence of sexual problems declines as they get older, except for those who report having trouble lubricating. Men, on the other hand, have more problems with age, such as trouble achieving and maintaining an erection and lack of interest in sex. Single, divorced, separated, and widowed individuals show an elevated risk of sexual problems. Formerly married women, for example, are roughly one and one-half times more than married women to experience sexual anxiety and trouble reaching orgasm. Ethnicity also is associated with sexual problems. White women are more likely to have sexual pain, while Black women more often experience low levels of desire and pleasure. Latinos, on the other hand, report lower rate of sexual problems than other women.[26]

Anxiety is another factor affecting sexual inadequacy. Masters and Johnson regarded fear of inadequacy as the "greatest known deterrent to effective sexual functioning, simply because it so completely distracts the fearful individual from his or her natural responsivity by blocking reception of sexual stimuli either created by or reflected from the sexual partner."[27] The husband whose wife is nonorgasmic is more anxious about his inability to fulfill her than she is about being fulfilled. In order for a natural experience to occur, both partners need to eliminate their goal-oriented approach to sex.

> **In order for a natural experience to occur, both partners need to eliminate their goal-oriented approach to sex.**

Andrew Dubrin associated power and control with the ability of some men to perform sexually. Some men, in order to feel masculine, must be allowed to wield most of the power and control in the relationship. A man who equates masculinity with power often feels "unmasculine" when he has to share important decision making with his wife. Such men need the feeling of being in a commanding position. Otherwise, he is rendered incapable of pleasing his partner sexually. Dubrin pointed out that the new husbands who have developed an egalitarian relationship in decision-making, house chores, and raising the children are not trapped by the psychological link between power and sex. Sharing these responsibilities tend to reduce friction and tension and prepare the way for better sexual relations.[28]

Age and Sex

Until very recent decades, the general view of sex was that the young should not have it and the old cannot have it. The culture in which I grew up gave me the impression that after midlife people could expect to be beset by pain and various physical problems. Sexual activity was gradually eliminated. In fact, I expected sexual interest to be diminished drastically after age forty and it nearly became a self-fulfilling prophecy when I had symptoms of burnout at age forty. Dr. Phillip Moore, my father's physician, taught me a valuable lesson, which prepared me to deal with the problem. While my father (at about age seventy) was living with us, he developed a nagging back pain. During conversation with his doctor, I mentioned that pain at his age should be expected. Dr. Moore corrected me immediately with the remark that older people do not have to suffer from aches and pains. These can be relieved. Even though my father had been treated unsuccessfully by previous doctors, Dr. Moore found the cause and effected a cure.

Similarly, the idea that older people should expect to lose their desire for sex because of age has proved to be invalid. The study done by Samuel and Cynthia Janus disproved the concept that old age eliminates the desire for sex. In the research regarding frequency of sexual activity in the category of daily to weekly, the frequency of the over sixty-five-year-olds was men 69 percent and women 74 percent. By comparison, the eighteen to twenty-six year-old category was men 72 percent and women 68 percent. Both categories (old and young) are on a similar level of frequency of sexual activity. A similar percentage of males and females in both categories said they had sex at least once per week.[29] "Our research findings indicated that, among respondents over age sixty-five, 93 percent of the men and 50 percent of the women often or always have orgasms when they have sex."[30]

When asked if it is inevitable that sexual desire must diminish after the fifth decade of life, Dr. James Dobson replied that there is no organic basis for those who are healthy after the fifth decade of life to experience less sexual desire. He stated: "The sexual appetite depends more on a state of mind and emotional attitudes than on one's chronological age. If a husband and a wife see themselves as old and unattractive, they might lose interest in sex for reasons only secondary to their age. But from a physical point of view, it is a myth that men and women must be sexually apathetic unless there are disease processes or physical malfunctions to be considered."[31] David Schnarch, in his book, *Passionate Marriage,* made a bold claim that: "If you're interested in sex with intimacy, there isn't a seventeen year-old alive who can keep up with a healthy sixty-year-old!"[32] Schnarch further stated that most people never really reach their sexual prime and those who achieve it do so in their forties, fifties, and sixties. Profoundly meaningful sex has more to do with maturation than physical reflex.[33]

Several publications during the last two decades explore the subject of aging and sex. Among them is the book by Robert Butler, a Pulitzer Prize winner, and Myrna Lewis, entitled *Love and Sex After 60.* They point out that one in six people in the United States is sixty or older. Much ignorance existed about this subject until the 1970s, but since the 1980s society is opening up to receive this kind of information. They have found in their own research and confirmed by others such as those of gerontologists, Kinsey and Masters and Johnson, that relatively healthy older people who enjoy sex are capable of experiencing it until late in life.[34] The "dirty old man" attitude within the society toward older people having sex is no different from racism. Some attitudes may develop from associating aging with loss of strength. But sex and intimacy are not determined by whether one can run a mile or lift fifty pounds. Athletic ability is less important than experience and quality of the sexual experience.

Of course, various factors affect couples in later life that may have an impact on their sexual relationship. One of those is illness. Another is the decrease in hormones, such as the decrease of estrogen in women after menopause, resulting in various bodily changes. Still another is the lack of desire on the part of one partner and the desire to continue having sex by the other.

"In late life we find just as many complaints between partners about sexual incompatibilities as at any other time: interest on one side and disinterest on the other, or passivity, or rebuffs, or failure to agree on the frequency of love-making."[35] Butler and Lewis gave the illustration of the sixty-five-year-old man whose sixty-three-year-old wife granted him the favor of having sex with her on his sixty-third birthday and announced to him that he should forget about having sex with her in the future since they were too old for sex. Both of them were in reasonably good health at the time.[36] The normal physical changes that occur with aging do not necessarily interfere with sexual ability. Butler and Lewis concluded that the decline in women's sexual interest as they age appeared to be mainly psychologically defensive rather than physiological.

> Although still controversial, there is some evidence that regular sexual activity helps preserve functioning, especially lubricating ability, and may even stimulate estrogen production. Sexually active women also seem to have less vaginal atrophy. The regular muscle contractions during sexual activity and orgasm do maintain vaginal muscle tone, and it is thought that intercourse helps preserve the shape and size of the vaginal space.[37]

Statistics taken during the last decade showed that more than one million men were receiving treatment for impotence. That number should only indicate to us the much larger number with this condition who are not seeking treatment, especially with advent of the pills for male sexual dysfunction. Likely, a large number of these men accept this loss of sexual ability as natural, if this occurs after the age of forty. Doctors have been emphasizing that most of these conditions are curable. Sexual activity in later years may be significantly enhanced by the desire of both partners to continue this aspect of their relationship. Adopting an appropriate exercise pattern is vital for overall health, especially in the later years of life.

2. Sexual Intimacy

The Meaning of Sex and Intimacy

The Hite Report considered the term, "sex" as somewhat problematic because of language. It claims that our culture defines sex as an institution having only one form of expression, that of physical reproductive sexual contact. There is no separate institution for other erotic activity. Intimacy, for example, is a part of that definition. Our cultural definition is so rigid it does not allow us to imagine physical intimacy without sex. By age five or six, boys and girls are not allowed to touch their mothers, except their extremities. They are separated from bodily warmth. Nevertheless, physical affection does not mean sex. *The Hite Report* expressed the view that a problem with the institutionalization of human needs "is that the whole spectrum of physical affection is basically barred from acceptable behavior unless it is channeled into the area of "sex," meaning that one has to have "sex" in order to get affection and/or physical closeness."[38]

Intimacy and sexuality are frequently used interchangeably. Even *Webster's Dictionary* includes sexual intercourse as one of the definitions for intimacy.[39] However, they are distinct concepts. There can be intimate relationship without sex. The reverse is also true. There can be a sexual relationship without intimacy. As Catherine and Joseph Garcia-Pratts reminded us, a healthy marriage must have both. In marriage, sexuality and intimacy should be inseparable. "Intimacy is a couple's sharing of their thoughts, dreams, goals, and fears. Intimacy in a marriage is different from intimacy in other relationships because, in a marriage, intimacy also includes the sharing of oneself physically."[40] "We become complete in the total, committed giving of ourselves: emotionally, intellectually, and spiritually as well as physically."[41]

Masters and Johnson took a close look at the concept of intimacy and shared some of their views in their book on sex and human loving. They pointed out that the search for intimacy is familiar to most people, but finding and maintaining intimate relationships seem elusive to most people. Although desirable, intimacy is difficult to discover, understand, and establish.[42]

Intimate is derived from the Latin, *intimus*, meaning "inmost and deepest." The meaning of intimate, according to *Webster's Dictionary*, is pertaining or indicative of one's deepest nature. Masters and Johnson emphasized the importance of self-knowledge in the process of developing intimacy. Several psychologists have stressed that those who form intimate relationships usually have a reasonable degree of self-acceptance buttressed by a firm sense of self-knowledge. People who do not like themselves or are ashamed of who they are find it difficult to form intimate relationships since they are preoccupied with proving themselves to others. They may also seek security in superficial ways, such as taking drugs or engaging in promiscuous sex.

Barbara DeAngelis has found an effective way to illustrate the dynamic between sex and intimacy through a couple's experience as told in an interview. A couple that came for counseling claimed they were on the verge of divorce. The wife felt she couldn't stand the thought of having sex with her husband anymore. Her husband didn't seem to know what the problem was. "As she angrily shared her feelings, he sat there with a bewildered look on his

146   MAKING MARRIAGE MEANINGFUL

face as if he had no clue what she was talking about. I couldn't tell if he simply wasn't interested or if he truly didn't understand."[43] After quizzing her alone for some time, the therapist asked her to describe what happened in their last sexual encounter. She related this episode:

> I had just put our daughter to bed, and I was standing at the sink brushing my teeth, when my husband came up behind me and kind of grabbed me and started rubbing himself against me. I thought, 'I guess he wants to make love.' Then he started kissing my neck and acting all excited. He led me into the bedroom and took off my clothes. He was touching me, and he seemed very aroused. And then things progressed, and he was obviously getting more and more passionate and making all these sexual sounds, and I knew what he wanted, and I thought 'Let's get this over with.' Then he entered me and we had intercourse and he finished and it was over.

The therapist asked her to describe her feeling on a scale of one to ten, ten being the most satisfying. She chose three. The therapist invited her husband in and asked him the same question. He judged the same experience as a nine. When asked to describe what happened, he said this:

> My wife was standing at the sink brushing her teeth. She'd just put our daughter to bed. I saw her there, and felt turned on. I was in the mood to make love, so I started kissing her neck. Then we moved into the bedroom, and I took off her clothes. Then I was touching her—I guess you would call it foreplay—and in a little while, I entered her, and then soon it was over, and that was it. It was great—a nine!

The therapist was still unable to figure out why the wife was so angry that she reached the brink of divorce. The husband seemed like a "sweet, sincere guy" who is happy. The therapist asked the husband to describe how he felt inside while having this experience with his wife. After describing his loving feeling for her in detail, he said: "I love this woman so much! I worship her! How could I be this lucky?" At that point, his wife, who was listening intently with tears running down her cheeks, leaped off the couch, threw her arms around her husband, and cried: "That's a ten! That's a ten!" As Barbara DeAngelis correctly noted, this man loved his wife intently, but he was only doing something to her body but failed to connect intimately with her feeling. "Since she didn't know he was feeling all that love and intimacy, she presumed he just wanted sex, and that turned her off. As soon as she heard him describe how he was feeling, it drew her attention to his heart, and the fact that he really was making love to her, and not just having sex. And that's what made it a ten."[44] He was feeling the connection but she was not. "This is why it's called 'making love'—because when you truly come together in this most intimate way, you are making more love between the two of you, and that love will infuse every other part of your life with joy, sweetness, and contentment."[45]

Intimate Solutions

In the book, *Satisfaction*, Kim Cattrall and Mark Levinson emphasized the need for reciprocal intimacy that so many marriages lack. They claimed that the majority of women do not have satisfying sex lives. The main reason is that men do not understand women's sexual needs and sensitivities. "When he fulfills her, her passion will be released and she will be naturally motivated to fulfill him. Ultimately, both the man and the woman will benefit from increased desire as both enjoy satisfaction."[46]

Harville Hendrix based much of his marital therapy on the concept that early separation from or lack of parental affection develops into a kind of lingering longing that spouses seek to fulfill in the relationship with one another. His therapy is based to some extent on remediation of this problem through a strategy called the conscious marriage. Giving an overview of his methodology in resolving marriage problems, Hendrix considered that the first step is becoming more conscious of our old wounds. We look into the past to find evidence of "how we were denied adequate nurturing and how we repressed essential parts of our being." As we gather new insights, we should share our thoughts and feelings with our partners, who in turn listens with understanding and compassion and accepts this knowledge as a sacred trust.[47] In the atmosphere of safety and trust, we create a safe and nurturing environment and then begin to redesign our relationships to heal our wounds. Most people resist change. Therefore, the next step toward healing is the most difficult. A decision must be made to act on the information shared between the couple about their fears and weaknesses and critical illumination of each other's darkness. One partner acts as the other partner's healer. "We go against our instinct to focus on our own needs and make a conscious choice to focus on theirs. To do this, we conquer our fear of change.

As we respond to our partner's needs, we are surprised to discover that, in healing our partner, we are slowly reclaiming parts of our own lost selves. We are integrating parts of our being that were cut off from childhood."[48] This new self discovery will allow us to regain our capacity to think, feel, and become sexually and spiritually alive. The painful moments are, in fact, opportunities to grow and share intimately. The elements of marriage that were previously buried in the subconscious, such as the fears, anger, the childhood needs, and the pain, are brought to the surface to be accepted and resolved. Striving to create a more conscious marriage, according to Hendrix, is a very practical, daily struggle. Intimacy is often sabotaged when the early romances fade and the partners begin to think that the other partner has changed. But change is inevitable. The tragedy is when one partner does not grow with those changes.

While I agree with Dr. Hendrix regarding his strategy of probing into the past for problems that could help remediate the current problem, I believe that this approach could be overemphasized. It should not be considered a panecea.

Dr. Steve and Cathy Brody said it well. "We re-create dysfunctional relationships because our sense of familiarity often lulls us into feeling comfortable. We may also falsely believe that we'll finally get what we didn't as children."[49] Marriages are like an engine. If you move an important part, the whole thing changes. "Better to keep your partner abreast of your changing needs and directions rather than overwhelming him or her late in the game. If you're the other partner, be sensitive to cues along the way."[50]

Dr. David Schnarch analyzed intimacy through the concept of differentiation. He challenged the accepted theories that intimacy is when our partner validates us and good communication is being understood the way we want and getting the response we expect. We assume that intimacy depends on acceptance and validation from our partner without considering self-validated intimacy. This kind of intimacy is when we validate our own disclosures when our partner doesn't. "We're driven by something that makes us look like we crave intimacy, but in fact we're after something else: we want something else to make us feel acceptable and worthwhile. We've assigned the label 'intimacy' to what we want (validation and reciprocal disclosure) and develop pop psychologies that give to us, while keeping true intimacy away."[51]

Seeing sexual desire as a biological drive causes us to believe that we are automatically supposed to know how to have sex. Some therapists, Schnarch claimed, encourage embittered couples with low sexual desire to bypass or ignore their partner and fantasize about someone else in order to perform sexually. This may jump-start the arousal process but destroys intimacy. How will a woman react, for example, when she discovers that her husband is touching her and pretending she is someone else? She will not be filled with desire, to say the least.

Dr. Schnarch also criticized the "squeeze technique," which is widely advocated by sex therapists. This is when a man or his partner squeezes the portion of the penis just below the head with thumb and index finger above and below this area for a few seconds to prevent premature ejaculation. Obviously, he has to withdraw temporarily to do this. This interrupts intimacy. (This procedure may also be done before insertion of the penis.) The other procedure is for both partners to stop movements for a few moments just prior to the man's ejaculation. This is intended to relax the tension and retard the premature ejaculation. Schnarch said: "this approach has gone largely unchallenged because it teaches troubled couples the same intimacy-incongruent sexual lifestyles used by most people."[52]

"Until couples go beyond viewing sex as a biological drive, they presume sexual behavior is a good measure of sexual desire and orgasm always involves high arousal and satisfaction. Common experiences of married couples disprove both assumptions."[53] These distortions, he claimed, fuel the even higher divorce rate among second and third marriages. This is a source of misery for many couples. "We usually think problems with sex and intimacy are caused by how we're uniquely screwed up. I propose, instead, that they're often caused by being normal. If you're well-adjusted to ill fitting beliefs that permeate society, you're going to have trouble."[54] Schnarch opposed the view that childhood wounds drive marriages. "Passionate marriage is about resilience rather than damage, health rather than old wounds, and human potential rather than trauma."[55] His non-regressive approach does not deny the effects of the past, but one does not have to go back to them to achieve resolution.

David Schnarch has pioneered the field of using sexuality as a vehicle to promote human development. "Previously, sex therapy aimed mainly at curing dysfunction and low desire. Reducing sex to issues of performance-expressive misinformation, and inhibition destroys the possibility of using it to make yourself grow. Resolving common marital problems requires personal development rather than skills and techniques."[56] Integrity will develop when one partner places his/her goals on par with that of his/her spouse or delaying one's agenda in favor of one's partner's desires.

Dr. Schnarch's opinions have validity. However, what about a middle ground in dealing with concerns about inadequacy. This problem is real for many couples. Surely the couple can share the concern for each other's satisfaction during sex, which may include the squeeze technique or another mutually agreed upon approach without encroaching on intimacy. There is no reason for intimacy to be interrupted because both pause for a moment to give the husband time to regain control. He may even try the squeeze technique before entry. What is important is that both partners share the experience with mutual understanding, love, and concern.

Sexual Crucible

Dr. Schnarch developed a method he termed the "sexual crucible approach." One's spouse can pressure his/her partner to choose between keeping one's integrity and staying married or choosing between holding onto one's self and one's partner. The issue is about integrity. These integrity issues usually surface around sex and intimacy. It is about what the partners will and won't do together. Other issues, such as money, in-laws, and children also appeal to one's integrity.

Schnarch posited the view that differentiation—the development of core values in order to bolster the integrity of the self, a kind of individualism—and emotional fusion—the drive for togetherness—are not opposites; rather, they complement each other. Emotional fusion is operating out of one mind, which is dangerous for marriage. It is the surrendering of individuality. When you have a core of values and beliefs, you can change without losing your identity, even when your spouse attempts to pressure and manipulate. Decisions are made by soul searching rather than by adapting to situations and merely following the wishes of others.

Another vital concept enunciated by Schnarch is that foreplay is where we negotiate the levels of intimacy, eroticism, meaning, and emotional connection in terms of that which follows. The boring nature of sex arises from sameness of meaning rather than the same behavior. This concept is a radical departure from the approach of popular sex manuals and sex advisors such as Dr. Ruth.

The popular view is to treat low sexual desire with sex toys and provocative lingerie and sexual techniques. Schnarch disagreed. He wrote that "Low sexual desire is no fun, but it does have a purpose. It's part of marriage's intricate people-growing machine: it invites you to stretch yourself and your relationship."[57] It's your choice to do internal or external change. Isn't this the reason divorces occur? That's the reason sex manuals are lacking. The key is relationship not biology.[58]

As I see it, couples realize that foreplay is a negotiating process, which reflects the politics and power in the marital relationship. The success of foreplay may lead to an enjoyable experience and the failure may lead to alienation as the couple disconnects emotionally. The process begins long before you get into bed. Pastor Wayne Martin, a friend and fellow minister, and I have joked about the term "taking care of mama." Men need to pay more attention to the desires and concerns of their wives on an ongoing basis. But this in reality is what husbands need to do long before the time for sex. They should be concerned about caring for their wives' needs during the day, if they expect responsiveness at night.

> **Men need to pay more attention to the desires and concerns of their wives on an ongoing basis. They should be concerned about caring for their wives' needs during the day, if they expect responsiveness at night.**

The popular approach to sex today is sensation. This is the search for maximum pleasure. The idea is to get as much as you can, as often as you can, in as many ways as you can, and with whomever you can. There is a recent surge of advice by sex psychologists directed to even elementary school children to pleasure themselves sexually. This activity Schnarch termed "sensate sex." Focusing on sensations short-circuits the basic ingredient of true intimacy in favor of self-validated intimacy. Someone has put it cleverly: "Some people become sexual vegetarians in marriage but carnivorous in extramarital affairs." Stephen George remarked: "Marriage requires confronting one's own crucible. Develop some core principles and use them to advance personal growth. By so doing you will focus on your own development rather than focusing on what your spouse is doing or not doing and pressuring your spouse to change in conformity with your desires. Sex alone will not sustain a relationship: intimacy will."[59] "Ultimately, you can't have truly great sex if you don't know how to cultivate intimacy with a partner. Nor can you have great sex if your attitudes, your health, your life are in disarray."[60]

3. Sexual Knowledge

Barbara DeAngelis has detailed what she considered important sexual and emotional differences between men and women. Let's take a look at her findings as well as the findings of a few other writers on this topic. Here are some secrets that should enhance a couple's sexual relationship.

Men's Sexual Secrets

A man's wife begins to caress him. His nerve endings receive the information that he needs to be aroused sexually. The message is passed on to his genitals and in seconds blood flows to his penis and it becomes erect. He is ready to carry out the sexual act. Men can perform sexually even when facing distractions, such as work, children, financial concerns, and even stress. In fact, men use sex to relieve stress and tension. Perhaps one of the main challenges for men is their desire to reach a conclusion or release. Barbara DeAngelis observed:

> Part of the problem is that men have been taught that they need to release any sexual tension as soon as possible. So that they don't like getting turned on without being able to satisfy themselves. Guys, don't be in such a hurry to get rid of any little feeling of love or sexual energy by ejaculating immediately. Allow that energy to build in your body and learn to pull it up to your heart. You'll find love for your partner expanding, your desire deepening, and when you do finally make love, you'll experience new levels of joy and ecstasy you hadn't even imagined were possible.[61]

Dr. James Dobson responded to an inquiry concerning the felt need for sex in males and female. Regarding males, he explained that a man can come home from work in a bad mood, proceed to work in his garage or around his desk, and then watch the news and go into bed with his wife for a brief sexual encounter before going off to sleep. Although he had no special time with his wife during the whole evening, he is not bothered or inhibited sexually. As he sees her undressing to go to bed, sexual arousal occurs.

This illustrates the reason for the frustration between men and women regarding sexual feelings. As we will observe later in this chapter, women react much differently. Men are aroused much more quickly. "They may reach a point of finality before their mates get their minds off the evening meal and what the kids will wear tomorrow morning. It is a wise man who recognizes this feminine inertia, and brings his wife along at her own pace."[62] It is common knowledge, therefore, that men are primarily aroused by visual stimulation. Men are easily excited by feminine nudity. Perhaps that is the reason women have traditionally sought to gain men's attention by suggestive or revealing styles of dressing. There have been no few disagreements in bedrooms regarding the difference in preferences by men and women. He wants the lights on to see his wife unclothed; she may prefer to be caressed in the dark.

Dr. James Dobson emphasized that men are not discriminating with regard to the qualities of the person in a beautiful body. "A man can be walking down a street and be sexually stimulated by an approaching female, even though he knows nothing about her personality, her values, or her mental capacities. He is attracted by her beauty itself. Likewise, he can become almost as excited over a photograph of an unknown nude model as he can from a face-to-face encounter with someone he loves."[63] Women have complained that men consider them to be sex objects. Dobson expressed that this characteristic about men accounts for the much larger number of women than men who are prostitutes and that rape is mainly a crime of males against females.

Some men develop temporary sexual problems caused by factors such anxiety, fear, illness, tiredness, tension, drinking, fatigue, sadness, boredom, depression, or stress. Dr. Robert Butler explained that a major emotional problem for older men is the fear of sexual impotence. While some men suffer from actual impotence, many others have only a temporary condition brought on by a reversible cause. Nearly all men of all ages experience impotence occasionally at some time during their lifetime for a variety of reasons.[64] When the condition that caused it is reversed, potency usually returns. According to Dr. Butler, the sex organs function as a barometer of men's feelings and reflect their state of mind and current life experiences. "In fact, the nerve connections that control the penis are extremely sensitive to emotions. Anxiety, fear, and anger are the primary feelings that cause a man to lose an erection rapidly—or fail to achieve one in the first place. So a disturbance in sexual functioning is often one of the first indications of unusual stress or emotional problems."[65] The men who do not know about the physiological changes that occur to men's bodies as aging takes place may be alarmed when certain changes occur and they may assume falsely that impotence is occurring.

> The expectation of high performance, which is taught to males from childhood on through constant emphasis on competition and winning, leads many men to overemphasize the physical-performance aspect of their sexuality. They become focused on erections and ejaculations rather than on expressing their feelings. This makes impotence or even its threat greatly upsetting. Thus the very fear of impotence can cause impotence. The harder a man tries to have an erection, the less likely he is to succeed. Impotence does not respond to will power and force. And it is truly transitory, it is much more likely to improve with relaxation and freedom from pressure.[66]

An unresponsive partner may also be a cause of impotence. His partner may experience frustration from his lack of vigorous performance and, subsequently, become disinterested, thinking that he is no longer interested in her. She may even become impatient and demanding, resulting in even more severe problems. To prevent or minimize the effects of impotence, married partners should discuss their concerns openly to each other. The common problem of premature ejaculation, which according to Masters and Johnson occurs in 15 to 20 percent of American men, can be aided by the various remedies available. Masters and Johnson developed the "squeeze technique" (mentioned earlier) and the "stop-start procedure" or the control of the "point of no return" by cessation of motion each time the man approaches the critical point when ejaculation is inevitable. Motion by both partners may resume after the feeling of release has subsided.

Dillow and Pintus mentioned that "men are very vulnerable in the sexual area. You may think women are sensitive in this area, but men are even more sensitive. Remember their feelings about their masculinity are wrapped up in their prowess as a lover. Your husband feels emotionally rejected when you turn down his sexual advances. It is important that wives understand the vulnerability a man has in offering himself to her."[67] Valerie Raskin's advice may prove invaluable. Men should "ask for sex on the basis of desiring her, not desiring sex. Pay attention to the words you use and be clear that you are attracted to her."[68]

Women's Sexual Secrets

Someone has recorded this episode that clearly depicts one major difference between men and women concerning sexual matters. A therapist asked a husband and wife the same question regarding their sexual frequency. She replied: "Constantly, three times a week." He replied: "Never, three times a week." This attitude has led many women to believe that all men want is sex. Many men, on the other hand, question whether women are interested in sex.

Barbara DeAngelis has developed some salient pointers to help men understand women and develop a better relationship. She explained how a woman is different from a man in relation to sexual arousal. Imagine a man starts caressing his wife as they prepare for bed. Her nerve endings receive the information that he is in the mood for sex. Contrary to the way a man processes this information, her processing is relayed through the "Emotional Headquarters" in her brain. She explained:

So a message is relayed from the nerve endings the man is touching to the 'Supervisor of Sex and Intimacy' in his wife's head. Who's she, you may ask? She's the part of a woman who protects her from opening up sexually if she's not feeling safe. It is the job of the Supervisor of Sex and Intimacy to decide if the information being received by the woman's nerve endings will get transferred on to the erogenous zones in the form of arousal or not.

The Supervisor of Sex and Intimacy in this woman's brain checks all the latest reports that have been stored in her psyche: How's the balance in the woman's Love Bank? Hmm, it looks low. It seems she's been feeling neglected by this man. What's this? Some resentments have built up over the past week. She's been trying to talk to him about some decisions they need to make together, but he's been putting her off. Not good, not good at all.

The Supervisor of Sex and Intimacy in the brain makes a decision—it's not a good night for this woman to have sex. Maybe in a few days if he's nicer to her. She decides not to send the sensory information on to the woman's body. That means no matter what the man does to try to get his wife aroused, she won't feel turned on.[69]

When a woman does not feel the flow of affection toward a man, erotic touch "can actually be annoying instead of arousing." A man may do some things to a woman and get completely different reactions, depending on her mood and their relationship leading up to the lovemaking. Many men do not know that women process their reaction to sex through the additional step DeAngelis revealed. Many bitter marital disagreements have occurred because the couple failed to recognize the emotional differences between men and women. Women do not respond to touch and sight the same way men do. The stimulus passes through their hearts and heads before reaching their bodies. This helps to explain the reason they do not feel in the erotic mood as frequently as men. "When (men) learn how to fill a woman's heart with love, it will overflow into the rest of her body, and she will want (him)."[70] It seems necessary for men to keep their mates' hearts filled with desire by constantly showing affection. Little notes, flowers, hugs, cuddling, kind words, and considerate actions foster the flow of love through her heart and back to you. You must do the hard work of sowing before you can enjoy the sweets of reaping. Whereas the woman needs only one key (physical) to unlock the man's passions, "a man needs two keys to open the door to our body," says DeAngelis. He needs "the key of physical touch, and the key of love and intimacy; physical foreplay and emotional foreplay."[71]

With regard to sex, men are so responsive to what is happening in the present that they fail frequently to regard the fact that women's present response is based, to a large extent, on past actions of her lover toward her. DeAngelis stated succinctly: "When you let a woman get love-starved, you will end up sex-starved!"

Men are known to compartmentalize their activities. If he is not pleased with his wife, or had a frustrating day at work, he may still have a successful sexual relationship. Not so for most women! They usually need to be relaxed and free from distractions. In contrast to men, women get rid of their stress and tension before feeling in a passionate mood. Therefore, men need to pay more attention to women's need for relaxation and seduction. "Seducing the woman you love means letting her know, long before lovemaking begins, that you want her, that you are attracted to her, and that she turns you on. It means continuing to court her, even if you've been married for twenty years."[72] Women like to take things slow, gentle, and caring. James Dobson added: "When she makes love in the absence of that romantic closeness, she often feels used. In a sense, her husband has exploited her body to gratify himself—she may either refuse to participate, or she will yield with reluctance and resentment."[73] Dobson explained that most marital problems are not caused by sexual problems. To the contrary, most sexual problems are caused by marital difficulties. Couples with problems in bed usually have much greater problems during the rest of the day.[74]

Nancy Van Pelt admonished: "Men are the pursuers to a great extent, and women are the responders. But women must have something to respond to. Even an inhibited woman can be responsive if her husband woos her gently, slowly, patiently, and creatively. What could be more exciting or challenging for a man than improving his sex life? Any man can become a better lover or even a great one if he works at it."[75] Men should also remember that few things could be more damaging to a relationship than disrespecting their spouse. Her whole sense of well-being is linked to her self-esteem. Words, actions, and attitudes should display affection for her.

Regarding the importance of understanding your mate, Peter admonishes:

> Likewise, you husbands, dwell with them according to knowledge, giving honor unto the wife, as unto the weaker vessel, and as being heirs together of the grace of life; that your prayers be not hindered [76]

Family Interview

Should a married couple have sex when they are angry with each other?

We feel that sex is an expression of love. It is an unspoken rule that we abstain from sexual intimacy until we have resolved all conflicts. Some say that "angry sex" is exciting but we believe it to be a product of an unhealthy relationship. Sex is sacred and is meant to be enjoyed in harmony.

What is the relationship between sex and communication in a marriage?

While sex may not be the most important aspect of a marriage, it can certainly determine whether a marriage survives or fails. We pride ourselves in the friendship we have shared while dating and throughout our marriage. We like each other and love each other. But there have been times when we have not felt the closeness that a married couple should feel. Because we are constantly changing, as individuals, we stand the risk of not being "on the same page" at times. Since women and men view sex in significantly different ways, an imbalance in the emotional connection of a couple may lead to the obliteration of the sexual relationship. We have found that when there is a breakdown in our line of communication, our level of sexual intimacy is affected. There are some couples who believe in having sex whether or not they are connecting on an emotional level. For us, that is not the case.

Should Christian couples be sexually creative?

Although we come from two totally different backgrounds, we are fortunate in that we share the same Christian principles. This has made it easier for us to share various levels of intimacy without serious conflict. However, because we both have an innate sense of sexual conservatism, we have been challenged to release deep sexual passion without guilt. As a Christian youth, you are taught that sex before marriage is a moral sin, but you are not taught that sex after marriage is to be cherished and enjoyed. No one bothers to instruct the Christian youth on how to adapt to sex after marriage. Suddenly, on the wedding night, you are expected to release all inhibitions, tear down the protective barriers of modesty and virtue that you spent your entire life building up, and become a sexual goddess or champion. While we both enjoy sex and the closeness it creates between us, we have often found it difficult to initiate sex because of our feelings of uncertainty. We both desire a sex life filled with passion, eroticism, and excitement but oftentimes we fall short of our goal. It is a constant challenge to find new ways of creating sexual interest in order to keep our sexual relationship "alive." As we explore options, however, we have always adhered to the inferred Christian guidelines that discourage sexual acts that are by nature perverse or may lead to sexual deviance. We have discovered that there are healthy options that are both creative and morally sound. It is a personal determination for the Christian couple to make when deciding how creative is too creative. Because we are confident in our personal spiritual relationships, we feel secure that one, if not both of us, will know if a creative sexual act crosses the moral boundary.

Contributed by Sherine and Stephen

Sherine, our youngest child, met Stephen at Tennessee State University, where she studied music and political science and he studied engineering. Their love journey began when they happened to be the only ones who turned up for an English class that was canceled due to an unusually heavy snowfall. Although born in the United States, Stephen's background is Hispanic, with ties to Mexico and Spain. Sherine's exposure to West Indian, Canadian, and American cultures certainly creates an interesting international blend. They have two adorable daughters. Stephen has developed a successful career as an engineer and Sherine continues to pursue a vocal music career. Their hobby is home decorating.

10

Secrets

Sharing Secrets

Pam and I have enjoyed an open relationship. We usually share our private thoughts with each other. I would hope that only very private thoughts that do not affect our relationship have been undisclosed. Occasionally, Pam mentions that I am secretive, but I feel differently about that. Of course, my profession as a clergyman and function as administrator require that I keep confidential information received from my parishioners or staff. Certain information is necessary to disclose to my wife for security and other reasons. But she is aware that most of the information shared with me remains confidential. This is important, not only to preserve confidentiality but to prevent her from having to be insincere or untruthful. For instance, suppose I shared certain personal information from one of my parishioners with my wife and the person whose confidence is broken asks, "Mrs. Samms, didn't your husband mention that problem to you?" That would place Pam in an awkward position. She has also made me aware of another aspect of this issue. Should I share certain information with her and the person heard about it from another source, he or she could incorrectly assume that my wife was the talebearer. Especially since Pam abhors gossip, she would be gravely disappointed.

Apart from professional privacy, I believe we share our private experiences honestly. Our marriage has been secure enough for us to feel comfortable sharing our inner feelings. We also tease each other about things that would ordinarily be threatening. Sometimes this can be a little annoying. For instance, Pam has not kept up with most of her friends, but I have kept up

159

with most of mine. Several of my friends are women. When we are in a good mood, I tell her that I could have married any of those women. Before an inevitable questioning about my motives occurs, I add that I have chosen the best. I am very pleased with my choice. She understands that my continued friendship with my female friends remains as friendship. Some of these relationships were formed during my college years and others during my professional years, and they are important to me. My relationship with them is strictly open with no hidden motives. Fortunately, since we have passed into a mature phase of our marriage, Pam has related to all of them without any suspicion (at least, that is my hope). They have become her friends as well as mine. When I speak on the telephone with any of them, usually she shares in the conversation either directly on a shared line or indirectly through an update with me afterward. Occasionally, I invite her to speak to the person after I am through. Even though I am open with my relationship with female friends, I still need to be careful not to give the impression that I am concealing information that I should be sharing.

Pam has told me that I am secretive. In the past that remark has left me feeling uneasy about whether that meant that I was hiding a secret affection. More recently, that remark appears more innocent. I interpret it to mean that I do not like to share certain information that is deemed to be private or personal. In reality, most of the time, I just do not feel like talking at that time. In most of those situations, I share the information with her at a later date. To think of it, when I do share it at a later time rather than immediately, it could appear as if I did not want to share the information with her. Fortunately, there is sufficient trust between us to foster positive responses.

Secrecy vs. Privacy

The matter of secrecy in a marriage is complex and requires more than one point of view. Some think that no secret should be held from one's spouse. However, the better part of wisdom dictates that it is unwise to reveal everything, since some things are better left unspoken. Solomon, known as the wise man, admonishes us to be wise concerning this matter. He said that a fool utters all of his mind, but a wise man keeps some things until afterward.[1] At least, the passage suggests that if sensitive information is to be told, it should be done judiciously.

Marriage counselors have been cautious in their advice as well. One very direct caution was penned several years ago by Andrew Weiner in an article published in *Quest*, a Canadian magazine. The subtitle said it all: "Shut Up and Save Your Marriage: The dangerous myth of total communication." He claimed that "belief in the need to communicate is really more an article of faith left over from the utopian yearnings of the encounter movement, than a conclusion based upon hard empirical evidence. No one has actually proved that better communication guarantees better marriages."[2] The reverse may be more likely: "that open communication may instead prove the quickest possible route to the divorce court."[3] In his article "Should I Confess?" David Augsburger based his counsel on relief for the guilty partner rather than on openness. In response to a conscience-stricken husband inquiring whether he had to confess adultery to his wife in order to obtain forgiveness, Augsburger replied: "Well, that depends on you. If you can accept God's forgiveness and trust him with your guilt feelings, maybe you won't need to open it up with her to get relief."[4] In this case the man confessed to his wife and she forgave him. Augsburger emphasized the crucial necessity to confess and halt the deceit. Guilt wants to remain hidden. But it thrives in the dark and eats away at our personalities like termites. When we confess, guilt dries up and dies. The book *Staying Married* states that "both need to feel secure in the knowledge that your partner accepts the real you and is just as committed to that hidden self as to that self you present to the world."[5] No deep dark secrets should be kept, but "there are times when keeping quiet is the best idea." Dr. Laura Schlessinger considered withholding important information from your spouse as one of the ten stupid things married couples do.[6]

For Nancy Van Pelt, it depends on the nature of the secret and the reasons for disclosing it. "Certain things, however, should be confessed if they would affect the couple's future relationship, or, if found out later, would make for trouble in the marriage."[7] She suggested that anything that can be easily learned by a third party should be told. Secrets that could affect the decision-making during friendship or courtship should be revealed before the wedding.

I can recall being called to the home of one of my parishioners many years ago to assist the family in a crisis. After inadvertently coming across his wife's passport, her husband discovered that she was ten years older than she had told him before they were married. That information was shocking to him since that explained one important reason they did not have children. Despite her pleas, he broke up the marriage. I favor complete disclosure of anything that can adversely affect their relationship, if disclosed involuntarily. That is, should the spouse discover that secret from other sources. Trust in the spouse could be diminished. Van Pelt suggested that if someone is in doubt about whether to share a secret with one's spouse or friend, seeking the advice of a competent counselor or pastor is a wise course to follow. It is advisable to seek advice about something that may damage the relationship but when viewed more closely may not be very significant in the relationship. "Findings indicate that almost all engaged persons confess serious problems in their background. And it seems that when one breaks down and confesses things about the past, it very often prompts the other to tell things also. Only a minute portion of couples studied regret having told about the past."[8] Sharing secrets indicates that the couple has reached a level of intimacy in which they feel secure to reveal something very personal and private to their partner. This indicates a strong mutual trust.

> Sharing secrets indicates that the couple has reached a level of intimacy in which they feel secure to reveal something very personal and private to their partner.

Dr. William Betcher added another important aspect to the matter of secrecy. He pointed out that the line between privacy and secrecy is often blurred. People use these words interchangeably, but there are important differences. Privacy is usually "a neutral thing," which we would consider "that's my business." We hold it secret because of the possibility that it could, if revealed, prove detrimental to others or used as a disadvantage to ourselves. A secret, according to Betcher, "is usually provocative, kept a mystery because it might become part of someone else's business. Its content is usually not neutral. Those who share secrets are engaged in a conspiracy of silence, while those who share privacy simply deny intrusion into their closed world. It is possible, however, for something private to be transformed into a secret, and vice versa."[9] Most marriages have both. Successful marriages allow a maximum of privacy and difficult marriages have a predominance of individual secrets. "Unshared secrets in marriage may be indicators of guilt, distrust, or selfishness or signs of immaturity. The other side of that coin is the relentless need to know and the continual suspicion that the other person is holding back something."[10] In a *Redbook* article, "The Case Against Cheating in Marriage," the authors had this to say:

The unfaithful partner who pretends that by keeping his affairs a secret he protects his wife and safeguards his marriage, practices the deepest deception of all: self-deceit. Since the use of deceit transforms the person against whom it is used into an adversary, a self-deceived person is obviously his own worst enemy…It is when we feel we must lie to someone who trusts us and whom we love that we are trapped in what psychologists call a double bind. Whatever we do, we lose…This is the ultimate act of self-deception. Instead of resolving conflict, it perpetuates it; the deluded person lives the lie. He is sick and does not feel the fever.[11]

Openness in a relationship certainly fosters trust and understanding. However, the relationship should not be suffocated by intrusion into each other's privacy. Such things as private time, privacy in the bathroom, privacy with one's personal belongings, and privacy with one's mail are only a few personal items that should be respected by the other partner.

Family Interview

Should a husband and wife tell each other everything?

This is one issue that is definitely not black and white. While we both agree that sharing everything is ideal, some things are better kept secret. When something is in breach of the wedding vows, it should be disclosed. Holding these types of secrets can destroy a marriage even if the secret has never been revealed. However, there are some secrets that, if disclosed, could cause an unnecessary rift in the relationship.

A spouse may choose to keep a secret, not because he or she doesn't want to share everything, but because disclosing the information may be misinterpreted or could lead to angst, mistrust, or suspicion. When we started dating, we shared most everything. We agreed that open communication is the key to a successful relationship. After five years of marriage, we continue to hold to that principle.

However, open communication does not have to mean full disclosure. We respect each other's privacy and also understand that any secrets we may have are held not because of our failure to communicate but our understanding of what is important for the other to know. Because we respect each other and ourselves, we share those things that we know affect the health of our relationship. In a healthy relationship, withholding information cannot be used as a rationalization for avoiding confrontation. We have faced each other on difficult issues in the past.

At times, revealing our innermost feelings has proved painful, but we did so because we understood the significance of maintaining trust in our relationship. When full disclosure was necessary to maintain the integrity of our marriage, regardless of how difficult it was to share, we did so. But as we have matured, we have come to understand that not all secrets are equal.

Contributed by Sherine and Stephen

11

Security

The feeling of security in our marriage has been invaluable. I cannot imagine living in a marriage relationship in which I was unsure about its future. Although it is difficult for me to speak definitively about my wife's feelings, I do believe I have given her a sound basis for relying on me for the long term. Apart from the times we say or do things, which lead to feelings of disappointment in the relationship, we have felt secure throughout our marriage experience. We have tried to avoid doing anything to erode the foundation of our relationship. There have been many incidents, which created doubts, concerns, and questions. In such cases, we were patient with each other with the clear intention of resolving them. Of course, a rational process prevailed, following the feelings of frustration caused by unkind words or inconsiderate acts.

Emotional Security

One of the most significant pillars of our marriage has been emotional security. Most of the time we have enjoyed this important ingredient in our relationship. Traditionally, the element of emotional security has been relegated to a deep feminine need that a man should recognize and satisfy. To be fair, this has not been the case in our experience. Viewed cursorily, one may conclude that the demand has been more on my part to provide emotional security for Pam and to ensure that she is not left with doubts about my commitment to our marriage. Additionally, Pam has been far more overt in her demonstration of the need for security. Nevertheless, a closer look will reveal that there has been a commensurate desire on my part for emotional security. I did not express it overtly most of the time. Perhaps, I did not even appear to need that kind of support. It may be fair to say that I had an easier time fulfilling my need for emotional security since it may not have been as strong as Pam's. From my observation, Pam's need for emotional security had been evident even before marriage. While I felt confident and secure about her commitment to me during our college years, she was frequently concerned about my commitment to her since I appeared to be interested in other girls. It may be helpful to point out that Pam and I attended the same classes as high school seniors and college freshmen. Since it was a coeducational boarding school, we saw each other several times each day. During the weekends, we met together frequently at church, cafeteria, socials, and other planned or chance meetings. Whenever I spent time with any other girl, Pam would either see or hear about it.

During our marriage Pam would occasionally seek to assure herself that I was not romantically involved with another woman. She often expressed the view that men can be deceived easily by women, a view I did not accept as fact. I preferred to believe that some men choose to respond to the natural charm of women by fulfilling their sexual urges even at their peril. I tried in vain to assure her that moral restraint was more powerful than the apparently over-powering pleasure of sex. Nevertheless, I had to endure that scrutiny, and Pam had to deal with the emotional undulations.

My emotional insecurities arose from different issues. Some of them were related to or arose from sexual impulses. Maybe my maleness played tricks on me. Nevertheless, I was vulnerable. I used the past tense in this case because our marriage is in a mature phase, and our relationship is far more satisfying. When we express our love sexually, I believe that Pam's participation is usually influenced by her feeling about me at that particular time. She would with-draw or hesitate if I speak an ill-advised word or did or did not perform an act that cast a negative feeling over her. Even though Pam mentions the problem and I seek to remedy it, an emotional divide may develop between us. In our earlier experience, although this feeling was often very temporary, I harbored a lingering question about the depth of her love for me. Viewing the issue logi-cally, I knew that her feelings at that moment were not related to our long-term commitment, but for several years I could not separate the two issues. Consequently, I bore the emotional strain. Frequently, my wife was the object of my unresolved negative feeling toward her. To my dismay, she was always quick to notice and frequently responded in her own defense.

Upon reflection, I consider my insecurity to be the extension of this feeling of rejection, which resulted in a negative reaction to her for a brief period following an incident of failed sexual fulfillment. I took it personally as though any incident of rejection by my wife meant a rejection of me. I felt our love was diminished. I also felt that my wife's attitude arose from the lack of a deep loving relationship. I was wrong. More recently, I have found that the problem rested far more with my attitude than with hers. Since my negative reaction precipitated a negative response from Pam, I felt that it was my responsibility to change my attitude. This process of change proved to be extremely difficult. When an emotional reaction to an emotional stimulus, especially if it is sexual, is repeated over a long period the reaction becomes automatic. For me, there remained little mental control. Even though I observed a potential stressful situation emerging, I frequently gave way to my emotions. To my disappointment, I watched as we fell into the same conflict over and over again. What created an added problem for me was that I felt I was acting correctly and my wife was at fault. Furthermore, because I was functioning as a pastoral counselor, I could analyze the situations and determine that I should take the lead to rectify them. But for a long time my emotions prevailed. My reaction was to withdraw for a while until my courage to resolve the matter returned. Eventually prayer and my personal philosophy helped me break the cycle. As expressed earlier, during my sophomore year in college, I developed the belief that "the decision of a moment can change the destiny of a lifetime." I also believed—and still do—that the will is stronger than the passion. However, there is much empirical evidence to support the view that a large percentage of men allow their emotions—particularly sexual impulses—to prevail over reason.

My insecurities sometimes lead to resentment and even anger. Feeling that my wife did not care about me deeply, I would react in different but predictable ways. At times, I would go for a long walk or watch television late into the night. During this time, my main concern was not the activity in which I was engaged but rather the release of the built-up stress. My purpose was to take the time to think through a strategy to deal with my feelings. Fortunately, when the following morning arrived, I frequently felt better emotionally. By that time, I was armed with a strategy to deal with my relationship with Pam. Often, what I found was that because the process was introspective, it did not allow for reciprocity. Since Pam was not privy to my thinking during the night, she was suspicious of my motives. I had reached the solution phase while she was still in the problem phase. At times, it was difficult for me to accept her feelings. Why could she not accept at face value the solution or reconciliation I was offering? It soon became obvious that I had to revert to the problem phase, acknowledge my faults, tender my regrets, and then proceed with a possible solution. Since I had already dealt with the problem in my mind and developed a solution during the long hours of the night, it proved problematic to present them to Pam as a process rather than a solution.

> **It soon became obvious that I had to revert to the problem phase, acknowledge my faults, tender my regrets, and then proceed with a possible solution.**

Conversely, when Pam had a problem with me, she could not sleep until the matter was addressed. That meant that I could not go to bed before discussing it to her satisfaction. Often I tried to sleep only to be awakened by a vigorous shaking. Pam stood over me demanding that I address the concern she had. If I deemed the matter of little importance, I either tried to ignore her pleas or attempted to respond. In the latter case, hasty speech was accompanied by sharp words. Either approach was doomed to failure or an escalation of our emotional reactions. Unfortunately, for most of the early and even middle years of our marriage, I had not learned a few vital lessons. As painful as it was, I had to learn to admit my fault, real or perceived. This admission could not be diluted by any semblance of her guilt in the matter. Often that could be brought up later when emotions on both sides had given way to reason. My tone of voice had to be subdued, despite my tendency to speak with a strong voice even in normal conversation. I had to give her my undivided attention, even at two o'clock in the morning following hours of frustrating discussion. At such times, we had to say the right words in order to avoid compounding negative reactions.

The main problem I had during the turbulent years of our marriage was my failure to remain silent in a time of conflict or a simple misunderstanding. In fact, even if there was no known problem at that time, one could develop if I raised my voice or made a statement that could have a negative overtone. In an attempt to explain what I meant, Pam might emphasize the negative aspect, which to me appeared contrived but to her was logical. Let's look again at the Barbyra episode mentioned earlier. Many years ago, Pam and I were reflecting on our time at West Indies College. Remembering the girls I admired, I mentioned innocently that Barbyra's skin was like velvet. Thereupon, Pam wanted to know how I knew. She had difficulty believing that I meant by appearance and not by touch. Since Barbyra and I had worked in the business office and were in the same classes, it seemed logical that my admiration could have been expressed in a physical way. I was then drawn into a negative dialogue.

> I learned that my comments should not be crafted to correct a wrong impression of me. Rather, they should be positive and directed to dealing with my wife's feelings. Much of the solution during a conflict lies in being silent yet attentive.

What I did not know at the time was that Barbyra had challenged Pam for my friendship. I do not recall how the matter was resolved, or if it was resolved, but I know that I contributed to the escalation of the conflict by talking more than I should have. Several times I kept quiet and after listening to Pam say something that I thought was incorrect, I would make a comment that then became a new aspect for the frustrating fracas. I learned much later in our marriage that oftentimes "silence is golden." I learned that my comments should not be crafted to correct a wrong impression of me. Rather, they should be positive and directed to dealing with my wife's feelings. Much of the solution during a conflict lies in being silent yet attentive.

Financial Security

Although money was never a major factor in our relationship, it certainly had its place. As we approached the retirement years, we became more cautious about our attitude toward money. This has not changed our spending habits drastically. Both of us agree that we do not want to live with our children, even though we love them and are very close to them. This decision is more for them than for us. We prefer to see them pursue their own lives free from responsibility for their parents. Since we were committed to raising our family, especially giving them our support until not only college was completed but their careers were established, we did little to plan for our own financial future. For reasons unknown to us, we did not consider this issue a major concern. Our religious faith may have influenced us far more than we realized. Nevertheless, we feel confident about the future.

During the past few years, I have begun to think more deliberately about how my wife would provide for herself should she survive me. Because of the policies of my employing organization, when I retired from professional employment, my insurance policies were terminated. Due to my age, my new insurance policies are limited because of high premiums. Fortunately, our children have developed their own financial independence. We can now place more emphasis on providing for our own future financial needs. Fortunately, we are still in good health and can continue to make adequate provision for a more secure financial future.

Physical Security

Pam and I have always felt the need to protect our family from physical harm. Since we did not believe in perpetrating violence on anyone or be harmed, we chose to avoid risky situations that would bring us into conflict with others. We minimized our exposure after dark and taught our children to do the same. Unfortunately, our children chose to follow the more modern trend of increasing their social activities at night. While under our protection, we required their adherence to our rule to return home before midnight. As parents, we followed our own rule. After sunset, we would go out only for specific reasons. Our goal was to return home as soon as possible. We avoided nightclubs, theaters, and late-night parties. Whenever we attended functions, religious or secular, we went as a family, unless it was work related. Now that the children have left home, Pam and I attend symphony concerts, plays, or other functions. Sometimes we go out for dinner together, but we usually return before midnight.

Having moved to different locations frequently over the years, we chose to live in safe neighborhoods. This does not mean exclusive communities, rather our emphasis was on respect for one's neighbors. We had no plans to disrupt the lives of our neighbors. Similarly, we did not choose to live in a community where the residents or their visitors disrespected our property or the peaceful enjoyment of our home. Therefore, we chose communities where our neighbors were most likely to share our view of respect and concern for others.

There was always a constant concern for each other's safety on the road or when any family member traveled away from home. As previously indicated, we developed a practice to call a family member upon arrival when traveling far from home and before departing to return home. Therefore, even though the children have their own homes, they frequently follow the same practice of keeping in touch with us whenever they travel. Pam and I shared our experiences about work and other events on a daily basis. The children, while still at home, shared their experiences with the family at our weekly family council on Sunday mornings. If something unusual happened, they communicated it immediately. This provided a measure of security for them as well as for Pam and me. This method of sharing information gave us the opportunity to offer suggestions or support in case of problems at home or at work. Family members usually assist each other financially whenever the need arises, at times without the thought of reimbursement, unless the amount is large. Let's consider other opinions on security within the family.

Security: Its Role

A successful marriage should provide a sense of security and safety for the entire family. The family relationship should be a haven for each member of the family. Usually, the father/husband takes the lead to provide the hedge of safety and security. He should be relied upon for securing the home. Nevertheless, the wife needs to provide comfort for her husband by helping him to feel secure in her love. Oftentimes, he appears so strong that his wife forgets that he needs loving care. Since men and women fulfill their need for security in different ways, it is necessary for each spouse to be aware of the other's need for security and seek to fulfill them.

Nancy Van Pelt pointed out that emotional security is the ultimate goal in a woman's life. Recently, studies have brought to view more clearly that "a woman's need for emotional fulfillment is every bit as pressing as is the male's need for sexual release. It is as unjustifiable for a man to ignore his wife's need for romantic love as it is for her to deny him his sexual urges."[1] Van Pelt discusses this further by adding that she asks him to do small things for her that she can do for herself, and she expects him to know what she wants without telling him. She considers his willingness a measure of his love and regard for her. The woman continually seeks reassurance from her husband. Sometimes this causes confusion for the man since he seeks to please his wife in more practical ways, such as buying a house she likes and purchasing household items. Although she will appreciate his efforts to acquire these things, he must also pay attention to her need for kind words and a loving touch. He must persist in making her feel loved, respected, cherished, and special. Van Pelt added these words: "Because of her capacity for affection, daily expressions of romantic love are vital to a woman's existence. It is the key to her self-worth, her satisfaction with married life, and her sexual responsiveness. If a man feels trapped in a bored, tired marriage, he might look to himself for part of the answer. By consistently and thoughtfully expressing romantic love, many men could melt even the most frigid wife."[2]

> He must persist in making her feel loved, respected, cherished, and special.

A man's love is different. Sometimes, he appears to be more practical than romantic. But his need for romance is very real. The difference between a man and a woman is that his love is not as closely tied to his emotions. He needs to feel secure in his wife's love for him. This is most evidenced when he feels close to her sexually. "The typical wife doesn't understand her husband's deep need for sex anymore than the typical husband understands his wife's deep need for affection."[3] "Affection is the environment of the marriage," declared Willard Harley, and "sex is the event." He proposed the five basic needs of both men and women.

Men's Most Basic Needs	Women's Most Basic Needs
Sexual fulfillment	Affection
Recreational companionship	Conversation
An attractive spouse	Honesty and openness
Domestic support	Financial support
Admiration	Family commitment [4]

Harley claimed that paying attention to these needs would help to build an affair-proof marriage.

Diane and John Rehm wrote *Toward Commitment*, in which they gave their personal views on different aspects of their marital experiences. Addressing the subject of sex and emotional response, John said: "It's like a little island—it removes you from the prevailing problem." Diane, his wife, responded: "As a woman, for me a sexual encounter is very much an extension of the emotional encounter—I am still in the problem and therefore can't move that quickly from the emotional feelings I'm experiencing, turn them off, and move toward becoming a sexual partner."[5] Realizing his predicament, John tried a strategy he called "romantic illusion." He tried "making love as a way of seeking forgiveness, of trying to reconnect" with his wife after a disagreement. He was rebuffed. This resulted in "a bitter feeling of rejection, and, in turn, isolation." He tried relating by withholding sex when she is interested but this approach "boomeranged." Eventually they reconnected. He was expecting a "big bang" in their next encounter: She preferred just to reconnect.[6] This illustrates vividly the real difference between the sexes in dealing with sexual relations and the need for emotional security. Intimacy, the heart of emotional security, must be achieved before sex can be truly meaningful. When an understanding of this key ingredient is added to the spouses' relationship, they will reap positive results. Ellen White, one the most prolific female religious authors of the previous century, penned these lines:

> The courtesies of everyday life and the affection that exist between members of the same family do not depend upon outward circumstances. Pleasant voices, gentle manners, and sincere affection that find expression in all the actions, together with industry, neatness, and economy, make even a hovel the happiest home. The Creator regards such a home with approbation.
>
> There are many who should live less for the outside world and more for the members of their own family circle. There should be less display of superficial politeness and affection toward strangers and visitors and more of the courtesy that springs from genuine love and sympathy toward the dear ones of our own firesides.[7]

Family Interview

How accountable are we for our partner's insecurities?

Whether we like it or not, each partner in the marriage relationship is accountable, in part, for the level of security the other feels. To what extent may be debatable. However, each spouse, through his or her actions, gives cause to the other to either feel a sense of security or a degree of insecurity. This is true in all aspects…emotional, financial or otherwise.

Secretive behavior, lack of communication, and emotional support inevitably lead to distrust and sometimes paranoia. We have found that being forthcoming in our actions has minimized the occurrence of these failures. But there is a point at which the individual is responsible for his or her own responses. Our need to be validated may stem from places that our spouse does not have anything to do with. Our individual past experiences play a part in how we analyze our spouse's actions, but we have to know when we are imposing our past "baggage" on a current situation. We are responsible for keeping ourselves in check. It is tempting to hold our partner responsible for all past wrongs done to us when he or she fails to measure up to our expectations, but this can lead to complications.

Contributed by Sherine and Stephen

12

Spirituality

Spirituality has been a significant part of our family life. The fact that I am a minister does not explain the reason for a strong spiritual emphasis in our home. In fact, I believe we have lived a normal family life, that is, without undue emphasis on the physical, social, mental or spiritual aspects. Our goal was to develop and maintain a balanced life. When Pam and I first met in February 1959, we were committed Christian youths. Our parents had instilled Christian values in our developing characters. Not only were we attracted to each other because of those principles, we were committed to adhere to them faithfully. Our commitment to moral and spiritual values occurred long before I entered the ministry.

Despite the cliché parents tell their children: "When we were young, things were different," I could think of a thousand similarities between secular influences on the youth of our time and the youth of today. Surely there are many differences between the societal influences on youth of these two vastly different eras. Yet there remain several significant similarities: The cultural gap between parents and their children, radical differences in music choices, peer pressure, the attraction of "worldly" influences (such as nightclubs and wild parties), the tension between home training and outside influences, the temptation to experiment with smoking and alcohol (the allure of addictive drugs adds additional pressure), and most of all, the temptation to experience sexual activity at an early age. Granted that the deleterious effects of these forces on today's youth are greater, yet these influences in the earlier period were just as real. Generally speaking, youth in any period must face serious character-building choices.

My Early Experience

After graduating from Knockalva (a male boarding secondary technical school with specialized training in agriculture, woodwork, and mechanics), I spent a few weeks with my father. Doug Archer, a fellow Knockalvarian, and I took up residence in Kingston, in order to seek employment. Doug and I had not seen each other for a year. He had graduated the previous year and returned to his home district where he worked as a supervisor on a dairy farm. We met in Spanish Town by coincidence or more likely by providence. He was nineteen and I was eighteen years old. We were ready to take on the world. That Saturday morning when we met, we sat and talked for several hours. Among the things, we discussed was religion and how we should relate to it. The outcome of that discussion radically altered our lives permanently. What is remarkable is that we even discussed religion at all, since we were graduates of Knockalva, a highly secular boarding school. To their credit, the school administrators did encourage students to attend church services in the community on Sunday mornings and attend the weekly meetings the Students' Christian Movement conducted.

The students, ages fifteen to twenty, had little contact with the public, especially girls for three months at a time. The exception was the permission to attend church for an hour on Sundays or the occasional venture into the nearby villages on Saturdays. Even though the staff provided strict discipline and guidance in most areas of the students' life and development, such as physical training, competitive sports, cadet training, academic preparation, study habits, manual training, and etiquette, the students obtained only a limited exposure to moral and spiritual discipline. Most of the students participated in some activities merely from a sense of duty. It was a common practice for some students to leave campus on Saturdays and walk a few miles to neighboring villages to meet girls. Their sexual conquests were hot topics. These escapades were shared with one another during the ensuing week. Drinking alcoholic beverages and smoking were added to their secret trysts. This left some of us with the feeling that we were missing out on youthful adventure. However, most of the students were cooperative and engaged only in the usual teenage boys' activities. To my knowledge, the students never engaged in taking hard drugs and participating in illegal conduct. Entering the school as a sheltered early teen, I had to develop rapidly into an adult to function effectively in that environment. The most difficult experience was facing the extreme "ragging" or initiation perpetrated on the first-year class (called derogatorily "grubs" by the second-year and third-year students). The initiation was harsh, overpowering, and persistent. It was like being trapped in a fierce battle with no escape route. The senior students used confident authority to cause the new and unsuspecting students to cower and submit to their demands. Next year, though, would be their turn.

On one occasion, I believe a sports event, several buses carrying girls from one of the girls' high schools in Montego Bay arrived on campus for a late-night party and dance. Before the night was over, several pairs of students were dispersed over the two-hundred-acre campus. The rest is left to the readers' imagination. How I managed to avoid this moral morass, I cannot fully explain. Of course, there was sobering influence of some morally upright schoolmates. Strict moral discipline liberally dispensed by my father, my older brother, Keith, and my sister, Violet, whose influence had replaced our long-deceased mother, should be given some credit.

Although I avoided the moral trap into which many of my schoolmates were caught, I yearned for the freedom I would have after graduation. Free from the rules of school and the discipline of home, I expected to experience the fun of dancing in nightclubs, the thrill of sex, and the pleasure of visiting the movie theaters whenever I desired. In retrospect, to discuss religion seriously three months after my graduation was indeed remarkable.

After Doug and I discussed various options for our lives, we concluded that the best choice would be a Christian life. We opted for the Christian values. Since neither of us knew how to proceed, we decided to visit different churches and listen to the different points of view. Thereafter, we would choose a church. That day being Saturday, we started with the Seventh-day Adventists. When we arrived at the church, the minister was just about to begin a baptismal service. After listening to our request for information about his church, he asked one of his local elders to meet with us. The layman sat with us for about three hours explaining why his church was the true church. He was emphatic concerning his belief that Saturday was the true biblical Sabbath. We had attended church on Sundays but never on a Saturday. Doug and I were so convinced that we decided to explore his views further. The following Saturday we visited that church and became convinced that the teachings of Seventh-day Adventists were closest to the biblical requirements. I accepted Christ on October 21, 1957, just months following high school graduation. After further studies, Pastor A. D. Laing baptized Doug and me on December 22, 1957.

Neither of us was prepared for what was to follow. Those experiences would fill the pages of another book. Suffice it to say that for the next two years, 1957 to 1959, we embarked on an incredible period of adventure and hardship brought on because of adherence to our new religious beliefs. I became a voracious reader. I read the entire Bible in just over three months. Several other books written by Ellen White followed, such as *Messages to Young People, Education, Great Controversy Between Christ and Satan and Desire of the Ages* (perhaps the best book ever written on the life of Christ). I also read *Hope of the Race* (written by F. L. Peterson, a Black author, a rarity in those days) and several others. Concurrently with my decision to become a Christian was commitment to become a minister. A deep desire to share my religious faith came upon me with a sense of urgency.

During this period of developing a direction for my life, Pam and I met. Since she was brought up in the Seventh-day Adventist faith, she was fully settled in her beliefs. The principles that shaped her character were already established. I was still searching, sifting, and sorting the principles which would guide my life.

A few weeks prior to meeting Doug in Spanish Town, I had decided to exercise my newly acquired freedom by trying out the pleasures the world had to offer. I delved into the secular music world. My favorites were Laverne Baker, Bill Haley and his Comets, Little Richard, Fats Domino, The Lymann Brothers, and Elvis Presley. Some Caribbean calypsos were also among my favorites. Daring to seek female companionship merely for experimentation, I began a short-lived contact with a young woman in the community. She was much more knowledgeable than I concerning sexual matters. Since I had only sexual relations in mind and she did not seem to resist my advances, the outcome might have been disastrous had it not been for the providential meeting with my friend Doug.

My relationship with that woman began and ended with one encounter, which terminated short of a sexual relationship. Before we had the opportunity for a follow-up date, my entire life had been miraculously transformed. That same weekend Doug moved to Kingston, the capital of Jamaica, to forge new lives and careers. Interestingly enough, I found out soon thereafter that the young lady became pregnant. Since she was involved with another man. I was fortunate to avoid a complicated situation before I even got my life of independence started. A fireman, with whom I had shared my newly acquired religious faith, remarked that since I had given up the normal pleasures sought by most young people, I would not last three months without capitulating.

Today, nearly five decades later, I am still committed to those values and principles.

It was very natural for Pam and me to choose to follow Christian principles. Many of these teachings were rooted in the Protestant tradition. They helped to form the basis of our marriage as well as our personal lives. Seven months after we met, Pam left Kingston to attend West Indies College (now Northern Caribbean University), a Christian coeducational boarding school. At the beginning of the following school year (September 1960), I enrolled in the same college. The school's standard of strict discipline kept us apart for much of the time. During my two years and Pam's three years on the West Indies College campus, we obtained invaluable appreciation for a balanced education, the development of the mental, spiritual, social, and physical powers.

The school's emphasis on morality, self-control, and service was superb. In the cross-cultural milieu on the college campus, we learned to get along with others from different cultures. For the 1961–62 school year, Pam was elected president of the girls' club, Philmelodia, and I was elected president of the boys' club, Excelsior. We were both in our second year of college. These appointments provided us enormous opportunities to develop leadership skills.

Because our religious training forbade sex before marriage, we enjoyed our five years of friendship without the pressure and demand of premarital sex. Both of us knew and accepted this principle. We never even tried kissing and caressing before we were engaged and even then we knew that was as far as we would go before marriage. Regarding health principles, the college program provided excellent exposure to a balanced diet without animal products and a drug-free lifestyle. We learned the value of fresh air, sunshine, water, rest, diet, and exercise in promoting vigorous health. Having accepted these principles for ourselves, we passed them on to our children and subsequently our grandchildren. All of them accept and practice these principles. Let's see how others view the controversial topic of spirituality.

Because our religious training forbade sex before marriage, we enjoyed five years of friendship without the pressure and demand of premarital sex.

Religion in Society

Not many decades ago, religion was entrenched in the heart and homes of people in Western nations. America was a Christian nation and the population was proud of it. Morality was fundamentally acknowledged and practiced in the society, including the workplace. Today, there is a strong anti-Christian movement bent on destroying the very godly foundation on which North American society was built. Yet the form of marriage still accepted and embraced in our society has its roots in Judeo-Christian origins. The concept of the family as the basic unit of our society is still being advanced, despite contrary views and strong opposing forces.

William J. Bennett, former national Education Secretary, has emerged as a voice for morality in America. In his book, *The Broken Hearth*, he described his approach to "reversing the moral collapse of the American family." He pointed out that research has confirmed that in the last four decades marriage and family life have been significantly transformed. The core of his book, Bennett maintained, "is that the nuclear family, defined as a monogamous married couple living with their children, is vital to civilization's success. We may build cities of gold and silver, but if the family fails, fewer and fewer of our children will ever learn to walk in justice and virtue."[1] Armed with information gleaned from the 2000 U.S. Census and other sources, Bennett said:

> Since 1960, fewer people are marrying, they are doing so later in life, they are having fewer children, they are spending less time with the children they do have, and they are divorcing much more frequently. Those who do not marry are having sexual relations at an earlier age and contracting sexually transmitted diseases at much higher rates, cohabiting in unprecedented numbers, and having a record number of children out of wedlock. Finally, more children than ever before live with only one parent.[2]

The U.S. Census recorded the increase of unmarried couples to be nearly 60 percent during the decade, 1990–2000, from 3.2 million to 5.5 million. During that same decade, the number of homes headed by single mothers versus those headed by both mother and father grew nearly five times. The harsh reality is that while most people in the population are alarmed by the trend, others are cheering this collapse and are busy implementing various ways to ensure its ultimate demise and the eradication of the mention of God in the public arena. Speaking about the basic argument of his book, Bennett declared:

It also reflects an understanding of marriage and family life rooted in traditional Christian and Jewish teachings, and, more specifically, in my Catholic faith. One certainly does not have to hold these faiths to agree with the arguments I propounded; there [is] a raft of nonreligious reasons to support marriage and the family. But the effort to pry discussions of these matters away from the religious context altogether is, I believe, both wrong and counterproductive. The Christian and Jewish understanding of family is no myth. Not only does it reflect deep human truths, it contributes to a vital perspective that mere social science is powerless to provide.[3]

Tom Eisenman related his experience of his narrow escape from death by drowning. Following that frightening experience, he was determined to live a purposeful life. But he acknowledged the strong crosscurrent within society against those who want to follow a moral code for their lives. Eisenman recognized that much of the population has grown up in an unchurched culture and do not accept the principle of right and wrong. "The loss of societal support for righteous living means that men and women who choose Christ in our day will have to be part of a counter-culture movement. It is always tough to swim upstream against the prevailing current."[4] The daily temptations we face are difficult to resist because they are "charged with the raw power of advertising and couched in the subtle and perverted genius of worldly persuasion."[5]

Pray and Play Family Style

In an article, "Worship, Family Style," Howard Hendricks, professor of Christian education at Dallas Theological Seminary, told about the value of family devotion in the process of building a happy home. "Worship," he claimed, "is a personal response to a divine revelation. God has revealed himself and I am responsible for responding."[6] Family devotion is absent from most families in America, including Christian families. This lost function has left a void that nothing can fill. Family devotion provides an invaluable opportunity for parents to inculcate in their children the fundamentals of respect for God, country, and neighbors. How many children who had this opportunity to start the day by meeting with God around the family altar with their parents would need illegal drugs and rebellious friends during the day? Think about it.

This principle would be even more effective if parents would include time to play with their children frequently, or even just have fun together. Ken Anderson, president of Ken Anderson Films, who has seven children, supported this view by stating: "You've heard it said, 'The family that prays together stays together.' From rather disheartening observation, however, my wife and I have come to the conclusion that 'the family that prays together may yet go shipwreck unless that family also plays together.'"[7]

This principle also applies to the relationship between husband and wife. Among all the busy activities of life, they should take time to pray and play together. Ellen G. White has written:

> The mission of the home extends beyond its own members. The Christian home is to be an object lesson, illustrating the excellence of the true principles of life. Such an illustration will be a power for good in the world. Far more powerful than any sermon that can be preached is the influence of a true home upon human hearts and lives. As the youth go out from such a home, the lessons they have learned are imparted. Nobler principles of life are introduced into other households, and an uplifting influence works in the community.[8]

Today, religion is either a form without substance in many homes, or worse yet, it is abandoned in favor of a godless home. The consequences are devastating. Children as well as parents are likely to flounder through life without a moral guide or compass. Consequently, they have no moral basis for making decisions or adopting fundamental principles for guiding their actions. The courts used to be the halting point for this reckless conduct in society, but after decades of correcting social injustices, such as discrimination against races, women, the handicapped, and so on, the courts are using their power to swing the pendulum much farther than is healthy for society. In reality, if this trend is not halted by the prevailing positive forces in our society, the destructive forces that led to the fall of the Roman Empire, now at work in our society, will be evidenced in the collapse of our modern society. Ancient Israel obtained sound principles, which could have guided that nation to unsurpassed achievements, but it did not follow its divine mandate. America was founded on the best moral principles that ever guided a nation in all of history. From its inception, America benefited from the experience of other nations' successes and failures. If it collapses as a moral force in the world, to what set of guiding principles could we look for leadership from any other nation? The fundamental principles of freedom embedded in the Constitution that have resulted in unspeakable wealth, power, and prestige are unparalleled in the history of any nation that has existed on the face of the earth. The problem lies in the erosion or misuse of these principles in the Constitution. The Judeo-Christian religious principles have undergirded this society for most of its history. The principle concerning fidelity of partners in the family structure is certainly a part of that heritage.

Our society should be particularly concerned about three aspects of dramatic decline: the abandonment of religious principles on which our moral foundations are based, the destruction of family values, and the lack of respect for authority.

I would be "painting the lily" should I proceed to enumerate the evidence of the attempted overthrow of these three basic pillars of society. To state the obvious, however, I will make one reference. Most of us learn to accept the umpire's decision in a game as final, even if we disagree with the ruling. The same principle holds true in the military or even in dealing with the police. At least if we disagree, we learn to seek justice in an orderly manner. We teach this to our children so that order would prevail in society. We also teach our children to respect authority. Yet after a prolonged process of legal debate over the 2000 presidential election, a ruling of the U.S. Supreme Court prepared the way for the vote count in Florida to be completed according to previously established election laws. George W. Bush was declared the winner. Subsequently, he was slandered daily by a large number of those who disagreed with the outcome. Surely, it would be acceptable to challenge the process and the ruling as much as our freedom allows us. But to hate and slander the president for the duration of his duly elected term in office, despite the fact that he was legally ruled the winner, tends to destroy the very authority that is established by the Constitution to protect us and provide order in the society. Our youth are being taught to ignore the laws and the principles that should guide present as well as future generations. Remember the umpire principle? Even in sports, the designated authority's ruling is final, even if he/she is in error. A process of appeal is established to avoid anarchy and disorder.

Don't similar principles, which prevail in our society, also regulate our homes? In order to have successful marriages and families, we should include morally binding principles. This would aid us in respecting the mutually binding terms of marriage and respect each other in the relationship. Remove the moral basis for marriage, and the relationship will be unstable as a small boat on a vast ocean during a raging storm.

We should acknowledge that as humans we have at least four dimensions within our being: mental, physical, social, and spiritual. The key to happiness and well-being is to develop a harmonious balance of these four dimensions in our lives. Omit or de-emphasize any one of these and our personalities become unbalanced. Nancy Van Pelt agreed. She stated: "Balanced living doesn't come by chance or by wishing for it or by waving a magic wand. It comes as a result of a planned life that progresses in harmony with the development of the physical, mental, social, and spiritual whole."[9] There is a concerted effort in our society today to eliminate the spiritual aspect in our lives, in our homes, and in our society. But just as if we injure our bodies by neglecting its care so we diminish our well-being should we diminish the spiritual aspect. We cannot become whole unless spirituality takes an appropriate place in our lives. "Spirituality constitutes a vital component of balanced living, but we often leave it out of our lives. Love to God and to our fellow man, a clear conscience, and service to others complete the picture, vitalizing all life's activities. This is the formula for balanced living. When life has depth, it will have as a consequence greater breath and greater length."[10]

In the book *A Lasting Promise*, the authors emphasized spiritual oneness and intimacy for couples.[11] They viewed function of spiritual intimacy in a marriage as paradoxical. You need Christ in the center of your life to help other aspects of your life to function better. Yet if other aspects of your life, such as managing conflicts, solving problems as a team, maintaining commitment, and developing a closer friendship bond, are functioning well, spiritual intimacy will thrive. The biblical counsel is for husband and wife to be of the same faith (see 2 Corinthians 6:14). Nevertheless, the Bible counsels that if you find yourself married to someone who does not share your faith, you should remain married (see 1 Corinthians 7: 12-16). Intimacy between husband and wife requires the sharing of each other's deepest feelings, trust, safety, security, hopes, fears, and commitments. Since spirituality requires a serious depth of commitment to God and, most likely, a church with doctrines and duties, it is difficult for one spouse to live such an experience without sharing it unreservedly with the person closest to him/her.

> Intimacy between husband and wife requires the sharing of each other's deepest feelings, trust, safety, security, hopes, fears, and commitments.

This level of intimacy would best be shared or lived together. Spirituality does not guarantee success in your marriage but it offers much aid in the marital journey. Praying together sincerely during times of calm and during times of storm in a couple's marriage can serve to draw them closer together. "We don't know how many Christian couples pray together," the authors of *The*

Lasting Promise said. "We've heard it's pretty rare. Perhaps this is a time we are most authentic; therefore it's most threatening, especially when relationships don't feel completely safe. But we believe that praying together can be an important key to experiencing spiritual intimacy....There's real power in praying together, whether it's silent prayer or verbal prayer, long or short."[12] The entire family should be built on a solid spiritual foundation. T. D. Jakes stated that he "believed God chose the wedding and marriage to illustrate His relationship with His people because it is the most intimate and personal relationship we experience in our natural lives."[13] The Psalmist admonishes: Unless the Lord builds the house, those who build it labor in vain. Unless the Lord watches over the city, the watchman stays awake in vain.[14]

Family Interview

Can spirituality within the family setting make a difference in successfully raising children?

In our experiences we can certainly testify that it made a difference in our upbringing. The awareness of God's omnipotence and watchful care over us served as a constant lighthouse or beacon to redirect our behavior when we might otherwise be influenced by friends who were not always a positive influence. How else could we remain faithful amidst so much pressure to stray from what we knew to be right? After all, you may convince yourself to slip a little once Mom or Dad are out of sight, but you cannot stray from God's loving presence, especially if you are prone to ask, "Would Jesus be pleased?" If through regular prayer and family worship you can establish a healthy knowledge of God's love and create a desire to please him above all else, then many child-rearing challenges are substantially mitigated. Certainly, teaching values like respect, honesty, kindness, and diligence are all strengthened by presenting them within the context of enjoying a Christ-like life. Above all, we have found that learning to love, becoming a Christian, and seeking salvation have been more effective guiding principles than simply living a decent life as its own existential reward.

Contributed by Royland and Shawna-rika

13

Service

Of vital importance to most people are three significant life choices: spouse, service, and spirituality. At least one of these choices is usually made during one's teenage years. It is preferable to wait for one's more mature years to confirm the choice of a spouse since infatuation could be mistaken for true love. Nonetheless, successful life choices can develop particularly in the middle to late teens. These are very important formative years. They serve as a valuable transitional period from childhood to adulthood. This period provides the shift from parent control to personal responsibility. Therefore, to give serious thought to one's lifelong spouse, one's area of service (career), and one's spiritual path may prove crucial to one's future success.

In the foregoing discussion I have dealt with the subjects of spouse and spirituality. Now, let's take a look at how Pam and I considered the matter of service. According to her mother's report, Pam had a desire to be a teacher from preschool. She lined up sticks, gave them names, and proceeded to conduct a class. She has not indicated to me her motivation for becoming a teacher. What seems clear over the years is her selfless commitment to her calling as an elementary school teacher. While in college, I tried to shift her focus from elementary education to secondary education. This appeared to work for a time since she changed from a major in elementary education and obtained a bachelor's degree in secondary education from Andrews University in Michigan in 1967. She even taught English literature for four years in a senior high school. By 1973 Pam returned to her first love—elementary education—and never looked back. While carrying a full-time workload, she attended McGill University in Montreal and obtained a diploma in elementary education in order to qualify for her permanent teaching credentials in the Province of Quebec. Pam then received a diploma in special education at McGill University and later a master's degree in Special Education from the University of Alberta in 1984. She accomplished all this education while raising four children. For several of those years, she cared for five relatives, who came to live with us at various times. Pam's two brothers, Vernon and David, lived with us for four years. Michael, my nephew, lived with us for two years and Kingsley, Pam's nephew, lived with us for one year. My father also lived with us for nine years. During her teaching career, Pam contributed much of her time to enriching the lives of hundreds of youth through voluntary projects. These activities included directing plays, such as *Oliver* and *The Wizard of Oz*; organizing and sponsoring junior youth organizations; forming writing and reading clubs; tutoring slower learners during her spare time; and mentoring at-risk youth. Pam contributed more than forty years to educating youth through the teaching profession. She has adamantly rejected any suggestion to serve as an administrator. (She served as principal of a private school for one year, only by default.) She constantly reaffirms her commitment to the classroom, primarily the fifth grade. Having served in various areas of education for several years, including two years as a high school principal when Pam was on staff as a teacher, I can state confidently that she qualifies as a master teacher. Pam's files are replete with school principal's evaluations in support of that claim.

My experience has been much different from Pam's. Whereas Pam stayed with her teaching career, I served in various aspects of three professions: education, business administration, and Christian ministry. My service spanned four countries, two languages, and many distinct cultural groups. My commitment to service began concomitantly with my conversion to Christ on October 21, 1957. Prior to that time, I could not decide what to do with my life. There was no passion for any particular career, dream to achieve a particular goal, desire to make a contribution to society, or even the aspiration for gaining wealth. The closest I came to being passionate about a career was my desire and my willingness to join the British army and go to war when the Suez crisis erupted in 1957. My three years of training and rank as sergeant in the cadet corps qualified me to be ranked as an officer under the British forces. At the age of eighteen years, I was prepared and ready to take up arms against an enemy I did not know nor cared to know. I never stopped to question which side was right or wrong or even whether I should have a moral response to the purpose of the war. My commitment and loyalty to Britain was all that I felt was necessary at the time. There was an automatic assumption that the British forces would have a just cause for which I was willing to commit my life to defend. I do not recall entertaining the thought about the probability of death. I was motivated to join the army and to go to war without any fear of possible consequences. As history has recorded, the Suez crisis passed without the escalation of serious, sustained armed conflict.

Upon even cursory reflection on my state of mind as a teenager, I am amazed to realize how malleable the young mind can be. This may be the reason a large percentage of our youth are prey to the evils of society. Often parents are not aware of the subtle forces that influence their children to engage in destructive conduct. During the middle to late teen years, young people have a sense of adventure, fearlessness, and even recklessness.

This is not necessarily because they lack proper upbringing, rather the complex psychological and physiological changes occurring in the natural transition from childhood to adulthood create the mood for daring conduct. It is for this reason that especially during this stage teenagers need proper guidance and supervision.

There is no doubt in my mind that my conversion to Christ, and consequently the adopting of Christian values, radically altered my character. From the age of nineteen I was driven to lead a life of service. So strong was the sense of urgency that I began immediately to talk to everyone about my religious faith and their need to accept it. During the fall of 1958, after Doug and I sold the Rainbow Manufacturing Company (a bottling company we started earlier that year) to our other partners, I became a literature evangelist. My new job provided badly needed income as well as the satisfaction that I was engaged in a mission. It gave me a sense of purpose. Becoming a colporteur kept me focusing on future purposeful possibilities rather than drifting back to futile pursuits. Colporteuring also provided the means to earn college tuition funds for the next nine years. Every summer I sold books, such as Uncle Arthur's *Bedtime Stories* (a set of five volumes with only true stories told in such a way that each story teaches a moral lesson), *The Great Controversy* by Ellen White, and the ten-volume set of *Bible Stories* by Arthur Maxwell. (Information about them is displayed in most Doctors' offices).

After graduating from Canadian Union College (now named Canadian University College) in May 1964, Pam and I were invited to serve as teacher and principal of the Grand Bahama Central Academy. It was a newly organized private school, which was organized from the vision of a Bahamian, Leonard Rahming. With his wife, Bernice, they opened an elementary and junior high school in September 1964. The school provided standard educational opportunities for those who wanted to escape the low level of learning in the public schools and could not gain entrance to the only other secondary school on the island. The Freeport Secondary School provided educational opportunities for the elite, which was mainly immigrants who resided exclusively in the town of Freeport. Pam and I served on the staff for two years before returning to continue our studies at Andrews University in Michigan.

Because we shared the same view of service before self-interest, we were highly motivated to support each other. I gave Pam my full support throughout her teaching career. Whereas her career required merely my moral support, my clergy and non-profit administrative assignments were significantly enhanced by Pam's sacrificial participation. There is no doubt that her counsels, suggestions, and actual participation accounted for much of my success. My second administrative appointment at age twenty-nine was treasurer of a large church organization with one hundred and fifty churches, two secondary schools (one of them with more than one thousand students), and sixteen elementary schools, as well as manager of a large book center that had fifty sales employees. My duties also included supervising the auditing of all the schools and churches. I also volunteered for a position as pastor for a sizable congregation, which was in the midst of a church-building project. During this time, I also conducted public religious lecture series annually, which lasted from seven to ten weeks, six nights per week. All my weekends were occupied with various commitments. Some of these were attending church building dedication ceremonies, group functions, speaking assignments, weddings, and board meetings. The most challenging aspect was how to balance these weekend and late-night assignments with attending to my family. That was precisely where Pam's sacrificial participation shone with unusual brilliance.

Pam taught English literature at Harrison Memorial High School and cared for our four small children and her two teenage brothers, who were living with us at that time. During this period we employed a live-in helper for the children. Despite her difficult task, Pam and the six children accompanied me to five to seven different speaking appointments each Sabbath (Saturday). Sometimes we would arrive at the first church service (at times, as far as one hundred miles from home) at nine o'clock in the morning. We frequently finished our last visit after the setting of the sun. This could also be fifty to one hundred miles from home. Since other engagements would occupy my time on Sundays, the effort that Pam made to accompany me on Saturdays helped preserve valuable family time. We got the children ready while they were still very sleepy, and she attended to them as we traveled from one assignment to another for the entire day during four years. To me, that was heroic. Our time together as a family proved to be invaluable, especially since during that period we never took a family vacation. I should mention that personal or family vacations were not a part of the corporate culture at the time. The policy of the organization provided for vacations but an overwhelming workload for most of the staff led to a pattern of ignoring vacation provisions.

From 1973 to 1985, Pam's role shifted from supporting me in my professional duties to sharing actively in them. Upon arriving in Montreal, Canada, to be installed as pastor of the Westmount Seventh-day Adventist Church, we found ourselves in an extremely complex situation. Not only did we have to deal with the complex issue of race relations and linguistic differences, but also like midwives we had to assist the new immigrants from various parts of the world in their struggle to find a place for themselves in the mainly homogeneous Caucasian society.

Until 1968, after Pierre Elliott Trudeau who epitomized the ideal blend of French and English cultures was swept into power, the Canadian immigration policy did not provide for dark-skinned people entering the society as permanent immigrants. With the government policy of relaxing immigration regulation to allow foreigners to visit Canada without a visa and then apply through a point system for permanent residence, Prime Minister Trudeau, perhaps unwittingly, opened the borders to West Indians, Asians, Africans, and South Americans. What the country did not anticipate was the massive movement of people from these countries who would seek to take advantage of the new policy. These large numbers of would-be immigrants created a crisis in the immigration processing system. The applicant who failed to obtain fifty out of a possible one hundred points based on selected criteria, such as language, education, and a family member already a Canadian resident, was afforded the privilege of reapplying up to three times. With the large influx of new applicants taking full advantage of this policy, very few visitors applying for landed status were sent out of the country. Since preference was given to those with family ties in Canada, once a person obtained a permanent visa, several family members lined up for preferential privilege to enter the country. Needless to say, in the 1970s several politicians paid the price of rejection at the polls in the federal elections, which followed a stormy debate over the immigration issue throughout the country.

The policy seemed to have been created for Europeans in order to increase the population in the country, which at the time was about eighteen people to the square mile. But people of other colors and cultures flooded the cities and created a different kind of social problem, that of race relations. It was into this foment that we had arrived. Hundreds of new immigrants endured the displeasure of Canadian citizens that did not understand, nor did they want to understand, the cultural differences that these new residents brought. Prime Minister Trudeau responded with a new social policy called multiculturalism. In contrast to the traditional American melting pot, Canada encouraged the new immigrants to add their culture to the undefined existing Canadian culture. This shifted the focus from resentment of the new immigrants to debate over this new policy. Of course, this concept also fitted the already existing struggle between the French and English cultures. For that Trudeau introduced national bilingualism: French and English languages.

All these political and social dynamics had a profound impact on our family and professional duties. The congregation to which I was assigned as pastor comprised several different racial, ethnic, and linguistic sectors. Although they were members of one congregation, they maintained their diversity. This reality resulted in untold conflicts within the congregation while it maintained a deep distrust for the French and English Canadians, which included the leaders of the Quebec church headquarters to which the congregation owed allegiance through organizational ties.

Among the nearly five hundred members of the Westmount church, there were Filipinos, Hispanics, Yugoslavians, Hungarians, Haitians, Ghanaians, French and English Canadians, and West Indians from various Caribbean islands. Considering the hostile racial and linguistic tensions in Montreal at that time, one should have no difficulty imagining the resulting conflicts. There were many.

My time was absorbed in assisting families that were experiencing enormous adjustment problems. Many individuals were alone while attempting to sponsor their families. Others had their family members but no other relatives from whom they could obtain support. Since most of these new immigrants were people of color, they experienced great difficulty in obtaining or retaining a job. Regardless of their qualifications (and many had solid professional and academic qualifications), they were denied proper employment. Many of them settled for jobs as hospital orderlies, factory workers, office clerks, nursing assistants, and other low-paying jobs. When they went for job interviews, they were told either that they were underqualified or overqualified for the position. The real reason was that they did not fit the racial or language preference of the employer. Even the children had difficulty to enroll in school.

Rene Levesque became premier of Quebec in 1976 by championing the cause of the French Quebecois. His new Quebec government passed a law that every new Quebec student—even a native Canadian from another Province—must provide proof that at least one of his/her parents attended an English elementary school in order for the child to enroll in an English school. Otherwise, the child must attend a French school. A curious fact was that the government schools were divided into two school boards: Protestant School Board of Greater Montreal (English) and the Catholic School Board (French). Hence a committed Protestant was forced to enroll in the Catholic school system if he/she did not meet the legal requirement to attend an English school. To help ease the difficulties facing the new immigrants, I spent much of my energy supporting a viable private school system. Our four children and my nephew, Michael, attended this private elementary and junior high school. During this period Pam taught at Coronation Elementary School, which is within the Protestant School Board of Greater Montreal.

Because the winters were long and harsh, the children and youth needed wholesome entertainment and indoor recreational activities. Not only did I lease large gymnasiums and auditoriums for games and concerts, but I supervised these activities. The advantages were that I could spend long weekend hours with our children and at the same time provide supervision for various activities in which they were happily involved. Therefore, they had no time or desire to engage in deviant behavior. Pam participated in the church programs and the social activities. She did not get involved in the recreational activities. Pam spent much of her time planning social activities such as concerts, banquets, and frequent dinners for various church gatherings in our home. The congregation expected and supported the pastor's wife's leadership in several aspects of the church program. In fact, I believe she is to be credited for much of my success as pastor of the Westmount Church. In the eyes of the congregation, we functioned as a team. To a large extent, the members' fond regard for Pam helped build a stronger bond between the congregation and me.

We had just settled in our new five-bedroom house when I was invited to serve as pastor of a newly organized church in Edmonton, Alberta. This was a difficult decision for the children. Montreal was their home and they liked it. They had no desire to separate from their friends, but they wanted to support my decision as well. Pam was disappointed to leave our new home after only a few months. Nevertheless, she was ready for a change from Coronation Elementary School. The family treated the transfer as an adventure. Only Tamaylia found the experience traumatic. It took her a long time to get adjusted to making new friends and overcoming the loss of her friends in Montreal.

Although my responsibilities in Edmonton were much less complex than those in Montreal, there were many challenges. The most difficult challenge was to provide a church home for this new seventy-three-member congregation. There were three inhibiting factors. The congregation had been recently organized with most of the members being new residents from other parts of Canada. There were limited funds since most of the members had limited income. Most of my time there was during the early to mid eighties, the period of extensive economic downturn in Alberta and much of North America. At one time, most of the men were laid off from their jobs while most of the women remained employed. This resulted in undue hardship for many families. During 1981 and 1982, the expectation of an enormous economic boom in Western Canada was created by several large oil companies planning to run oil pipelines from Alaska to the United States. At the peak of the migration, the viability of this project was evident since much of the infrastructure for the project was being organized. Real estate prices skyrocketed; office spaces were in high demand as companies employed personnel. Oil prices soared. Evidence of the anticipated oil boom could be seen in every aspect of the society. This unexpected economic windfall brought untold millions to the government's treasury causing it both to spend recklessly and to set up a trust fund for the future.

The unrestrained optimism of the promised wealth to come to Alberta was abruptly halted. The two-year squabble between Prime Minister Pierre Trudeau and Premier Peter Laugheed of Alberta over revenue sharing caused the oil companies to abandon the project and withdraw their commitment to the oil pipeline project. The result was devastating, economically and socially. Companies dismantled their businesses and laid off their employees. Real estate plummeted. Unemployment rose to record levels.

Consequently, the impact on the families was enormous. While dealing with my parishioners, I had to give serious thought to an impending problem aimed at my family. We had opted for renting our house in Montreal at a price that would cover the mortgage payments. We bought a large house in Edmonton with borrowed funds. In the light of the economic boom, I concluded that this would be a wise investment. Everything went well for a short while until we received information from the town of Dollard des Ormeaux in Montreal that property taxes would be imposed. I had informed the city that I was no longer living in the house. They withdrew the clergy tax exemption status I had enjoyed for nearly a decade. I would now have to pay nearly two hundred and fifty dollars per month in addition to other expenses on the property. In addition, the interest rate for our mortgage had jumped to an unexpected 18 percent. With five children (including my nephew) in high school and Pam completing requirements for the Alberta teacher certification, we knew a financial crisis had developed. To compound the problem, because of the economic downturn, the properties could not be sold without incurring a loss.

We started to sell our furniture and valuables at auction. This continued for several weeks until most of our possessions were gone. I sold the Ford Marquis I had recently purchased. One of my parishioners noticed that I did not have a car and offered to lend me one she was not using. I politely declined because I did not want to be obligated in any way to my church members. Throughout my professional career, I refused to take money from anyone for personal use. My view was that doing so could compromise my position should that person become involved in a matter requiring my objective opinion. My practice was to donate any monetary gifts to charitable purposes. Taking someone's car in that situation seemed unwise. We had to rely fully on Richard's compact Mercury Capri. When traveling together as a family, Sherine, being the smallest, had to ride in the trunk section of the hatchback. (In the eighties, seatbelt laws were not yet on the books.)

After we surrendered the house to the builder and lost our deposit of fourteen thousand dollars, we rented a two-bedroom apartment. Needless to say, we were grossly inconvenienced. We lacked space and flexibility. We could not make any changes to the property and the sounds from the adjoining apartment were disruptive. When our children practiced on the piano, the neighbor was annoyed and knocked on the wall separating the apartments. Within weeks I gave up and rented a house. The rent being equal to a reasonable mortgage payment caused me to conclude that I should purchase another house. Eventually I found a small ranch-style house recently foreclosed by the bank. After many diplomatic maneuvers, the bank sold the house to me. At first, they declined my loan, but I persuaded the manager to sell the house to me by convincing him that even though I did not have a deposit he could not find a person in the city more committed to his financial obligations. He reversed his decision and sold us the house. We lived there for three years until we left for California in the summer of 1986. Despite the grave difficulties we faced, no one in the family complained. We supported each other and that cooperation lifted the burden posed by financial strains.

Our contribution to the Edmonton community was more extensive than that in Montreal. In Montreal we were functioning in a city of over three million people comprising several ethnic, linguistic, and cultural groups. The church building was located in Westmount. Westmount and Mount Royal, contiguous townships, were regarded as the wealthiest parts of Montreal. The home of Prime Minister Pierre Trudeau was only a few blocks away from the church. Built in 1913, the building is regarded as one of the largest Protestant church buildings in Canada. The gold-leaf dome was one hundred and twenty feet high. Stained glass murals around the building depicted the entire life of Christ. It was designated by the city as a historical monument. It attracted people from various sectors of the community as well as tourists. Several people wanted to be married there or just visit. The needy considered it as a place of refuge and our community services program was quite active.

A major task in Westmount was the renovation of the building, which was sold to us because the Presbyterian congregation found the upkeep too expensive. This proved to be a daunting task as well as an expensive one. In November 1974, the restoration was completed, and the building was dedicated with a community-wide participation.

The situation in Edmonton was much different. There was no immigration problem. However, the members had limited resources and they had no church building. They were worshipping in rented facilities. At first, it did appear that there was little to do. However, the challenge emerged from the desire to develop rapidly into a mature congregation with strong support for youth activities, community outreach, and adequate facilities to accommodate a diversified program for the members.

A decided advantage for our family was the ages of our children. They were in junior high school and senior high school and developing independence and pursuing personal interests. Richard had a car, which provided transportation so they could travel about the city on their own. Pam and I had more time together.

In Edmonton, though still very supportive of my efforts, Pam did not participate in leadership as much as she did in Montreal. Perhaps she needed time to renew her energy and to engage in personal pursuits. Or perhaps, the need was not as great as in Montreal. In contrast, the children were much more active in certain leadership roles. They helped organize recreational activities, joined the newly formed wind instrument band, toured with the youth choir, and supported various social programs. In addition, they were very active in their high schools.

In 1986, we felt that the time had come to relocate. Considering that we were three days of travel by car and one day of travel by air to visit any of our relatives, five years in Alberta was a reasonable time to spend there. The move to San Jose, California, did not take us closer to our relatives, but we felt closer since we were now in the same country.

The family considered California an adventure. We found it much different from any of the places we had lived before. It was a place of contrasts. There were mountains and valleys, congested cities and beautiful suburbs. We experienced the affluence of the Silicon Valley and Beverly Hills and the poverty of Oakland, near San Francisco, and Watts in Los Angeles. We enjoyed the mild temperature but we were nervous about the frequent earthquake tremors. We lived in San Jose for one year. The experience is unforgettable.

Pam taught at Independence High School, which had an enrolment of four thousand students. She considers that year one of the highlights in her career. My experience was different. Because I chose to follow Pam to California after she was recruited at a teachers' recruiting convention held in Vancouver, British Columbia, I did not have employment in advance. I made the decision to go with Pam because she had not hesitated to follow me when I wanted to accept a transfer to another city or even another country.

This decision to move to California had very serious consequences for me. Since I considered my occupation a calling rather than a profession of choice, I refused to seek a job in another career field, at first. We arrived in San Jose during the economic downturn in the States. There were few jobs available during this time of massive corporate downsizing and restructuring. When I realized that no jobs were available in my field, I volunteered to assist the San Jose Seventh-day Adventist Church pastor without remuneration. Our financial challenge was great since three of our children were attending University and Sherine, the youngest, was attending Independence High School. During the previous school year Richard and Tamaylia had attended Andrews University in Michigan, an expensive private university. Since funds were limited, we preferred to have them live at home and attend school nearby. This was a positive decision: All of us enjoyed living together that year for the last time.

Our experience at the church was very positive. There was a vibrant youth sector. In addition to the friendships the children formed, unlike their Edmonton experience where the youth were preoccupied with socializing, they were strongly influenced by creative energy of a more mature and forward-looking nature. Whereas they had an outstanding exposure to uplifting music in Edmonton under the tutorship of Una Marshall and the wind instrument band, in San Jose, the children were surrounded by a wide range of talented musicians. Sherine, who is currently pursuing a musical career, received tremendous inspiration from her California experience. The children and their cousins, Adria and Lisa, toured the gorgeous state with their friends.

After an agonizing twelve months, everything changed when I received an appointment in New York. Although I dislike living in that complex city, I accepted the assignment as manager for the Greater New York Conference Book and Bible House with offices in Manhassett on Long Island and downtown Manhattan. This allowed Sherine to attend Manhassett High School for her senior high school year. Royland attended Atlantic Union College, a boarding school in South Lancaster, Massachusetts. There he met Shawnarika, a Bermudian, whom he later married and accompanied her back to her homeland some years later. In 1988, I accepted an invitation to serve as president for the Seventh-day Adventist Church organization in Quebec. The children had gained their independence, but they had not yet completed college. They still needed guidance and assistance.

As president of the Quebec Conference of Seventh-day Adventists, my commitment to service was sorely tested. By accepting this position, it became obvious that Pam and I would be alone for the first time. Pam teased me that I would not be able to adjust to the "empty nest" easily. Similarly, I thought that she would be depressed after she realized that the children were now living on their own. Knowing how protective she had been, I braced myself for the worst. Both of us surprised each other. We missed the children, but we accepted the change without any major concern. The children made it easy for us. All four of them related to us just as closely as though they were living at home. Richard and Tamaylia attended New York State University on Long Island and lived with their uncle Vernon's family in Freeport. After a brief stay with us in Longueuil, Quebec, Sherine moved to Toronto to attend York University. Interestingly, all four children lived together in Toronto one summer. Royland came home on weekends while attending New York State University, Plattsburg campus, for his final college year. After graduation, he attended Ohio State University in Columbus where he graduated with a doctor of optometry degree.

Serving the constituency in Quebec proved to be personally challenging. It also created complex circumstances for our new family setting. The Quebec population, which was about six million, was sharply divided culturally between the island of Montreal (multicultural) and the rest of the province (mainly unilingual French Quebecois). Whereas in the United States there is a

Black/White racial tension, in Quebec the issue was Quebecois/non-Quebecois, cultural-linguistic conflict.

Before assuming my duties as president in July of 1988, I was invited by the national president of the Seventh-day Adventist Church to attend the plenary session of the Quebec constituency in May 1988. To my amazement, there was serious tension among the delegates because of the proposed organic separation between the Quebecois and the non-Quebecois membership. In fact, the Canadian executive committee and the North American executive committee of the church authorized the separation, but some of the local delegates resisted the decision. The French Quebecois delegates applauded the decision and accepted it as *fait accompli*. The Montreal delegates opposed the move since they viewed it as racially motivated.

Ten years of my previous fourteen years of professional service in Canada were spent in pressing the Canadian Adventist church as well as local governments to change their policies of discrimination. Now that I was in a position of strength, I seized the opportunity to recommend a rejection of the decisions made by the higher organizations to divide the Quebec church organization along racial lines. Citing Article 4 of the Quebec Association constitution, I pointed out that the decision to separate into two administrative bodies in the Province of Quebec would be unconstitutional and illegal. It was unconstitutional because the constitution did not provide for such a separation and illegal because that constitution was established by an act of the Quebec parliament and could not be amended without an act of the Quebec government. Article 4 of the constitution stated that the territory of the Quebec Association was the Province of Quebec.

While this was unexpected good news for much of the Montreal delegation, the Quebecois delegates were irate. They expressed their anger against the leaders that led them to believe that the plenary session was only a formality. They would be allowed to operate their own organization free of racial or cultural diversity. My recommendation to the session provided for the Quebecois sector to develop an operational entity with fraternal relationship to the legal provincial organization and not an organic separation. This recommendation was approved with a large majority vote.

Needless to say, my task as president required tact and temerity. We had to craft the leadership to reflect the diversity of the membership. However, we had to bear in mind at all times that about 80 percent of the population of Quebec was unilingual French Quebecois. Although they had been granted flexibility to operate as a distinct group (an arrangement that was abandoned by the Canadian and North American administrative entities after only two years), they were still a part of a larger whole—the Quebec Conference—of which I was president. We had to relate to each other in many ways. After the two-year experiment with the Quebecois-only project, they were brought back under the general administrative body with much protest. Although I had no decision in the dissolution of the Quebecois Project, I became the object of their opposition.

During the next seven years, Pam and I experienced an unusual and unexpected period in our marriage. We had to make two major adjustments simultaneously. We were alone for the first time since our first year of marriage, and we had to face the difficult challenge of presiding over a church organization that was in dire racial, linguistic, and cultural foment.

These conflicts had furrowed deeply into the psyche of the members of the organization. In addition, I spoke very little French and my wife spoke even less. Within two years, however, I had gained enough proficiency in the French language to deliver speeches in French and participate in French-only meetings. Pam had it far more challenging. She accompanied me to various appointments in which French was the only language spoken. She was always patient and supportive.

The greatest difficulty with respect to the impact of my job upon our marriage was the constant quest of a few disgruntled Quebecois members to unseat me as president. The progress of the organization was remarkable in several aspects, not the least being the near doubling of its assets and membership in seven years. A viable school system for three sectors of the organization—namely, English, French Montreal, and French Quebecois—was developed. Although a reasonably good relationship among the various sectors was fostered, there remained an undermining element against the leadership. At a biennial plenary session of the Quebec Conference held in 1994, this group succeeded in convincing key delegates on the nominating committee to recommend to the constituency that I be replaced. The nominating committee did so. Before bringing their recommendation to the floor for a vote, the chairman called Pam and me aside to inform us that I would be voted out of office. We accepted the news gracefully.

Earlier in the session, we had seen the subtle attempts by a few persons to undermine my leadership in speeches from the floor. Being the chairman of the session, I had the opportunity to call on my executive officers for pertinent information to counter them. Now it appeared that they had won. To my surprise, the recommendation from the nominating committee to the general session entered a marathon debate that persisted intermittently from mid-morning to about eight o'clock in the evening. At that time the chairman was obliged to reveal that unethical activities by some members of the nominating committee had precipitated the decision to recommend my replacement. Upon hearing this revelation from the chairman, a motion was placed on the floor to nullify all proceedings of the day, disband the nominating committee and the organizing committee that nominates the nominating committee, and recall the session for the following Sunday. The following week I was re-elected as president for the third time with an 80 percent vote. Pam supported me throughout this struggle. Today, we feel satisfied that our most productive years were spent in meaningful service to our community and, more importantly, to those who needed help. Our goal was to foster harmony among the racial and cultural sectors and assist families with their social, educational, and spiritual development. In that way, I believe we succeeded.

Our experience was unusual in some respects. Nevertheless, other families can draw lessons from our experiences, especially how we supported each other during the challenging times. Let's see what further clues in the area of service we may discover to aid in our search for enrichment of the family relationship.

The Significance of Service

In reviewing much of the literature on marriage, I have observed a preponderance of emphasis on self-pleasure and a paucity of references to self-sacrifice and service. We have found that our marital difficulties and conflicts were ameliorated when we focused together on something or someone outside our marriage. We developed a positive feeling when we focused more on helping solve someone else's problem or giving assistance.

> We found that our marital difficulties and conflicts were ameliorated when we focused together on something or someone outside our marriage.

In her book, *The Surrendered Wife,* Laura Doyle posited an excellent and, perhaps, controversial strategy for wives to achieve success in dealing with their husbands. As she approached the end of her book, she tackled the issue of what women should do with the surplus energy and time accrued from surrendering the "Needless Emotional Turmoil" or NET with which most wives find themselves preoccupied. "If surrendering makes you feel like you have nothing to do or say anymore, that's a good measure of how much time you spent in 'Needless Emotional Turmoil.'"[1] Doyle explained that most people would agree that some attention should be given to uncovering one's neglected passion. The metaphor of laying down a heavy backpack of NET gives a vivid picture of the experience of weightlessness that would ensue. The spouse is no longer focusing on problems or issues resulting in conflict and tension with his/her spouse or spending energy second-guessing his/her actions and motives but rather shedding that burdensome approach to relationship. Apart from Doyle's mention of pursuing her ambitions, the recommendation emphasized a more introspective and self-satisfying approach to the use of her new energy and time. She even mentions the joy of accomplishing nothing.

At a similar juncture of his book, *The Seven Principles for Making Marriage Work,* John Gottman named his seventh and final principle: Create shared meaning. He did not enumerate the importance of service in creating intimacy and connectedness in a relationship, but he implied it. The emphasis was on developing a family culture. Dr. Gottman pointed out that it is possible to have a successful marriage even if your goals or dreams are different. But there should be meshing. "They find a way of honoring each other's dreams even if they don't always share them. The culture they develop together incorporates both of their dreams. And it is flexible enough to change as husband and wife grow and develop. When a marriage has this shared sense of meaning, conflict is much less intense and perpetual problems are unlikely to lead to gridlock."[2] William Betcher added to the view of the couple finding value in focusing on connections outside the marriage. "No couple can isolate themselves at length from the world of their culture, especially the family-of-origin loyalties and ideas of gender identity."[3]

It is a popular view, especially among female writers, to differentiate between men and women's roles regarding sacrificial service. The general view is that women by nature or historical designation are more caring, nurturing, and giving. Men are more task-and achievement-oriented. Jean Baker Miller argued incessantly that the need for rendering service is psychologically different for men and women. "In our culture 'serving others' is for losers, it is low-level stuff. Yet serving others is a basic principle around which women's lives are organized; it is far different for men. In fact, there are psychoanalytic data to suggest that men's lives are psychologically organized against such a principle, that there is a potent dynamic at work forcing men away from such a goal."[4] Miller considered the internal (psychological) and external (social traditions) pressures to serve as a burden from which modern women are seeking to escape. For many women this need to do good for others has been a "martyr syndrome or the smothering wife and mother." While she does not object entirely to women's serving husband, children, and countless others, she said it should not be done at the expense of their fulfillment or suffocating their identity. "Women do have a much greater and refined ability to encompass others' needs and to do this with ease. By this I mean that women are better geared than men to first recognize others' needs and then to believe strongly that others' needs can be served—that they can respond to others' needs without feeling this as a detraction from their sense of identity."[5] The problem exists only when women are coerced to perform in that subservient role. Miller expressed that men do not share the same psychological burden of service. To the contrary, men are trained to think that service is a lesser role and they should strive for the nobler goal of gaining power over others.[6]

I wonder how Miller's view of men matches with historical examples of prominent people, such as Jesus, Mahatma Gandhi, Albert Schweitzer, Martin Luther King, and countless others who have served as role models for men over the centuries. In fact, Christianity reversed the traditional view of service as subservience. Jesus declared: "He who is greatest among you shall be your servant."[7] I agree with Miller in declaring that "both sexes have been deprived of the possibility of developing as people who have the experience of giving to equals and realizing that such reciprocal kinds of giving are possible and can enhance the development of all."[8] There is no question in my mind that a spirit of service or giving to others as a couple or family could significantly enhance a marriage relationship and concurrently teach children in that home the value of pursuing that course in life. Commenting on this subject, Ellen White has written:

> Those who, so far as it is possible, engage in the work of doing good to others by giving practical demonstration of their interest in them, are not only relieving the ills of human life in helping them bear their burdens, but are at the same time contributing largely to their own health of soul and body. Doing good is a work that benefits both giver and receiver. If you forget self in your interest for others, you gain a victory over your infirmities. The satisfaction you will realize in doing good will aid you greatly in the recovery of the healthy tone of the imagination.
>
> The pleasure of doing good animates the mind and vibrates through the whole body. While the faces of the benevolent men are lighted up with cheerfulness, and their countenances express the moral elevation of the

mind, those of selfish, stingy men are dejected, cast down, and gloomy. Their moral defects are seen in their countenances. Selfishness and self-love stamp their own image upon the outward man.

That person who is actuated by true disinterested benevolence is a partaker of the divine nature, having escaped the corruption that is in the world through lust; while the selfish and avaricious have cherished their selfishness until it has withered their social sympathies, and their countenances reflect the image of the fallen foe rather than that of purity and holiness.[9]

Ellen White's emphasis on the positive outcome of sacrificial service is supported by the result of research reported by Stanley Scott. Researchers found "that people who were most inclined to sacrifice were the happiest in their relationships and the most likely to continue in them. Therefore, sacrificial attitudes and actions were more likely to be found among the happy, committed, and sticking people."[10] Another interesting research finding that supports Jean Baker Miller's view is that while men and women benefited equally from sacrificial giving, giving to their spouse rated differently with husbands sacrifice for their wives and vice versa. Stanley Scott found that "women were somewhat less likely to report getting pleasure from giving sacrificially to their husbands. So, both men and women who felt better about giving sacrificially were more likely to have great marriages, but women found it harder to derive pleasure from giving to their husbands than the vice versa."[11] Scott concluded that in our culture it is more expected that women would sacrifice for their husbands. "Hence when women give, the actions receive less notice and less reinforcement than when men do. Since men sacrifice less on an average, the actions get more attention when they do, and they reap more praise."[12]

The foregoing underscores the need for spouses, especially men, to acknowledge even the small sacrifices done for them and not just take them for granted. They should seek for opportunities to render service for others together.

Family Interview

Considering your differences in upbringing, do both of you share a similar view of service? If not, do your differences affect the harmony of your relationship?

As a child of Pamela and Robert, my orientation for service has been couched in religious and self-sacrificial framework. Growing up, I experienced first-hand the commitment and sacrifice required to give service to the community. I also witnessed, firsthand, its rewards.

We spent hours in church waiting for our father to complete his ministerial duties. I believe that the desire to serve and contribute to society were formed, internalized, and cemented during my formative years. I admired my father's dedication to his profession and my mother's incredible loyalty and dedication to the youth she influenced. My parents' commitment and dedication have left an indelible mark upon my conscience and have sparked my desire for service.

Frank's approach to service is much different. He believes that one should first achieve his goals (his are financially oriented) before considering service to others. He believes we cannot truly serve society until we have taken care of our family's needs. Since he considers himself head of the household, he believes that he must adequately provide for his family. Although he has always provided for his family, he continues to feel pressure to maintain and increase our standard of living.

The differing approaches to service present a source of stress and pressure in our relationship. He believes that the success of our family relies on financial circumstances. In contrast, I believe that defining a family's purpose in terms other than financial achievement would prove more rewarding.

Our differing views of service have driven us to make more opposing than agreeable choices. For example, he has decided to work abroad. This takes him away from his family frequently. I have chosen to seek jobs based on service rather than financial compensation. Frank believes I should capitalize on my Ivy-League education in corporate America, not social services. I am driven by the classic "service" motto to empower the community (specifically youth) and make a difference in their lives.

Some irony exists in that Frank proclaims that he loves and admires me for my generous and giving nature, yet he resents what he perceives as my willful decision not to promote myself in a manner that would give me better financial opportunities.

Where does a couple go from here?

After much discussion, we have arrived at a very delicate solution. Couples in a marriage must respect each other's differences. They should seek to identify a separate new common goal or goals that can be mutually satisfying. We needed to blend service and a mutually acceptable financial compensation. We hope to accomplish this venture by blending our goals. We hope to develop a business project together that will incorporate service to a specific community and generate significant financial income.

We agree that service to each other first is a critical and necessary component to building a healthy marriage and we strive to do so, every day.

Contributed by Tamaylia and Frank

14

Sickness

Coping with Illness

Our marriage vow included the words "in sickness and in health" with reference to our commitment to each other. Of course, when we were taking our vows at the altar, we envisioned only happiness for the future. Regardless of our positive outlook, we've encountered several problems and difficulties. Sickness proved to be the most difficult experience since it threatened our survival. Our family faced six life-threatening illnesses.

The first illness occurred when Richard, our first child, was about a year old. We were living in Freeport, Grand Bahama, about twenty minutes by plane to Nassau, the capital, or to Miami. One morning we noticed that Richard was very weak. Although we were concerned, we expected his condition to improve as the day progressed. To the contrary, his condition worsened. It occurred to us that he had not passed his urine from the previous day. While we were considering what to do, he went limp. We panicked.

Our family doctor, knowing that there was only one clinic on the Island (which did not offer care for serious medical cases), made immediate plans to transport Richard by private plane directly to Nassau. An ambulance met the plane and transported him hurriedly to the hospital. Pam was allowed to accompany him. We were relieved to learn that he was treated successfully. In a few days he was back to normal. Richard had a similar event at about age five. This time he had developed nephritis. The doctor placed him in bed for two weeks during which he was not allowed to eat any protein, especially meat. Even though he recovered completely, Richard did not eat meat for several years following this incident. This demonstrates how children can be affected seriously by certain negative experiences.

The stress caused by facing illness in our family for the first time was enormous. As inexperienced parents, we felt helpless as we watched our precious energetic little toddler fade as though the life was ebbing from his body. Nothing prepared us for such a serious occurrence. The joy we experienced as he recuperated compensated for the deep emptiness we felt when he appeared lifeless.

Apart from the death of my father in May 1978, no single event in our marriage caused me greater trauma than the illness of my wife in 1977. That winter in Montreal was extremely cold. We went to the Fairview shopping mall in West Montreal on a Friday afternoon and found the parking lot crammed with cars. So we had to park several chains from the mall entrance. While returning to our car, the icy wind increased significantly. We walked courageously into the wind, which was so cold that exposed flesh froze in thirty seconds. Apparently, Pam was not sufficiently clothed for such inclement weather. That night she began to experience pain in her forehead. Of course, we didn't make any connections to the earlier experience in the cold. The following day Pam had more intense pains and her vision began to blur so that she became unsure of where she was stepping. A level floor appeared slanted.

When I took her to the Montreal General Hospital and left her after she was admitted, I had the strangest feeling. By that time the pain had become excruciating. Her right eye was so swollen that it was closed as the eyelid drooped. As I walked to my car, I felt a deep sense of loss, not only a loss of companionship but also a gnawing inner feeling that the end had come too soon.

When the first doctor saw her, he blurted out: "Oh my God!" That didn't help the already tense situation. Later, the doctor, believing her case to be a typical case of brain tumor, brought about twenty-five doctors in training to view the examination. But they were mistaken and my greatest fears were relieved. A week later Pam walked out of the hospital to complete her recovery at home. The diagnosis was acute migraine. I still believe the intense cold wind blowing directly at her exposed forehead had done some damage to her blood vessels. We may never really know. That was a scary experience.

Although I have given careful attention to my health and followed reasonably good health practices, I have had two serious illnesses. Neither left any noticeable residual effects. One incident took place at age forty and the other occurred in 1991 at age fifty-two.

Two years before my first illness, I started to lose vital energy. This was very noticeable. Not only did I experience diminished sexual interest, but my body developed different symptoms that clearly indicated that something was wrong with my health. I had been jogging one to two miles three to four times per week since I was twenty-seven years old. I maintained this practice whether the weather was inclement or pleasant. In fact, while living in Montreal I jogged in the snow on cold winter mornings. I enjoyed a good sense of well-being most of the time. Yet I'd developed high blood pressure. I ignored it for a long time because I had no knowledge of how deadly high blood pressure could be. One morning, after taking the children to school, I developed a severe attack of headache and vomiting. I drove to Dr. Emmanuel's office. The doctor was surprised that my heart was not affected since my blood pressure was very high. She told me that high blood pressure is called the silent killer because often there is no symptom until it develops into heart failure or stroke. Frequently, it is observed too late. Only then did I realize the importance of checking my blood pressure occasionally. Since that incident, I have used a personal kit to check my blood pressure once or twice per week.

Following this incident, my health declined rapidly. I had constant headaches, my sleep pattern was often disturbed by frightening nightmares, and whatever I ate seemed to upset my stomach. Worst of all, I could no longer speak in public without a panic attack occurring after three to five minutes. My doctor prescribed Librax to relax my nerves, but it caused me to developed nightmares. I stopped taking them. Thinking that my career was over, I resigned myself to withdrawing from any activities.

Everything changed when a doctor I had consulted for an opinion told me that all the tests were negative therefore nothing was wrong physically. He recommended that I visit a psychiatrist. My sister-in-law, a nurse, suggested that I ignore the crises since there was no physical ailment. Fearing the prospect of having to see a psychiatrist, I decided to take her advice and fight back when a panic attack occurred. Slowly the symptoms disappeared and I recovered fully after three years. Later, I realized that my illness was caused by burnout, a condition about which I had no knowledge. That lasted from 1979 to 1982. It was not until several years later that I had another health crisis.

The morning of April 12, 1991, began the same as any other morning. I had a doctor's appointment for my annual check-up but postponed it in favor of visiting Eudeen, a former parishioner, who had recently undergone surgery and was recuperating in the St. Mary's Hospital in Montreal. Although Pastor Wayne Martin and I had made plans to visit Eudeen, when I arrived at his office, he was very busy. I offered to go on my own. He insisted that I wait for him. We stopped for lunch at a restaurant on Victoria Avenue before proceeding to the hospital. We performed our pastoral duties by reading devotional passages and offering prayer for Eudeen. As we left her room on the fifth floor, I suggested that we walk down the stairs rather than taking the elevator. When we reached the third floor, I turned to go through the door, thinking that was the ground floor. As Wayne pulled me back, he mentioned that we had not yet reached the ground floor.

While walking down the stairs, I lost consciousness. The experience is similar to someone awaking partially from a deep slumber. I kept slipping in and out of consciousness. However, even during that time my mind did not register that something was wrong. My reasoning did not connect with the problems in my body. It was like everything was a dream. I remember just following Pastor Martin mainly by his voice since I was not fully aware of my surroundings. I recall talking to him about the blessing of being a minister and having the satisfaction of helping so many people. Before reaching the revolving door at the main entrance, I slipped back into unconsciousness. I returned to contact with my surroundings as we walked toward my car, which was parked one block away. Pastor Martin said later that it was about this time he observed that my speech was slurred. I recall also that as I came back to consciousness briefly I heard my feet dragging on the pavement. I knew nothing again until we reached the car. Pastor Martin asked two passersby to help me into the passenger side of my car. When they did, I felt I was in the wrong place and tried to climb over the gearshift to go over to driver's side. Pastor Martin pushed me back to the passenger's side as I again slipped back into unconsciousness. He drove one block to the hospital emergency room, and I remember him calling out to an attendant that they should get a wheelchair since I was having a stroke.

Five doctors attended to me immediately. In fact, they watched me having the stroke. They gave me crushed aspirins and took several tests. My stay in the hospital lasted eight days. I really never found out how Pam felt about my illness. The stress caused by my sudden illness must have been enormous. Apart from dealing with my illness as well as teaching full-time, she had to contend with a large number of inquiries daily concerning my health. There were so many visitors that the doctor moved me to a room where only few visitors were permitted. Pam never showed impatience or frustration.

Pam has mentioned frequently that I was impatient and insensitive with her whenever she got sick. I think the opposite. Her observation could be based on my belief that we tend to surrender to our feelings far more than is necessary. Sometimes our feeling can be regulated by our will. For instance, some people decide the time they get out of bed in the morning based on how they feel. I prefer to decide the time to get out of bed in the morning based on my decision the night before. In the morning my body responds to the dictates of my mind and not the opposite. Pam functions more by how she feels in the morning, except when she has an appointment. Of course, I can be somewhat insensitive to her if I feel she is listening to her body too much.

The doctors didn't seem to know what caused my illness. They indicated to me that it could be a blood clot to the right side of my brain. But it was certainly not a heart attack as many people rumored. What was peculiar to me was that for the first three days I did not feel that I was sick. I really questioned the reason I was in the hospital. It was not until the third day, when the doctor permitted me to leave my bed that I saw my twisted face in the mirror. When I asked the doctor the reason my mind failed to alert me to the grave illness of my body, he said that was the nature of a stroke. One could be extremely ill and not know it.

After being discharged from the hospital, the true effects of my illness appeared. Walking was accomplished only with some amount of effort. Strength returned to my body very slowly. My full recuperation took about six months. For several months after returning to work, my energy level declined drastically about two o'clock in the afternoon. Fortunately, there were no noticeable lingering effects apart from writing, which is still not restored to its original level of functioning. There were many anxious moments during the weeks following my release from the hospital when I thought the stroke was returning. On one occasion, Pam had to rush me to the hospital late at night. But it was a false alarm. Fortunately, my health has been restored fully.

Healthful Choices

Speaking generally, our family has enjoyed very good health with the exception of the foregoing incidents and a few other minor ones. The reason may be found in our strong belief in our church's teachings on health principles. Pam was brought up in a home where the health principles of our church were taught and practiced. I was brought up differently. As a youth, I ate anything and everything that did not appear harmful. No creeds or restrictions were involved. Viewing my situation in retrospect, I can see distinct advantageous health practices among the many unhealthy ones. Being brought up in the country where there was easy access to a large variety of fruits, I consumed many of them daily. Most of the time I picked them from the tree fully ripened and ate them immediately. My family did the same regarding our daily meals. We ate very little processed food since we bought very few items from the grocery store. The bulk of our food was reaped from the nearby garden just at the time of cooking. This was the same for meats and fish. Chickens were killed just before cooking, fish was bought when the fishermen came in from the sea, and mutton and beef were bought as soon as the butcher had slaughtered the animals. We prepared our drink from squeezing freshly picked fruits. Most of our diet was fresh and full of natural vitamins. Apart from colds, I was never sick. However, because I ate so many sweet items such as processed sugar, candies, and cakes, and since dental care was rare, I suffered much from toothaches.

The other reason for my reasonably good health was my total disdain for smoking, liquor, and drugs. I even avoided prescription drugs as much as possible. Although I attended a boys' boarding school where it was fashionable to act mature by engaging in illicit sex, smoking, and drinking alcohol, I rejected those activities as irrational even though some of my close friends engaged in them. Now that I am in my senior years, I recognize that my health choices of those early years have produced rich rewards.

Faithful to the Marriage Vow

When conducting wedding ceremonies, I become quite solemn as I utter the words to the bride and groom: "Will you love, comfort, honor, and cherish her/him in sickness and in health, in prosperity or adversity; and, forsaking all other, keep yourself only unto her/him so long as you both shall live?"[1] This section of the vow has two significant aspects: faithfulness to their partner in the changing circumstances of their lives together and remaining committed to their partner only, sexually. However, since the wedding is so positive and festive, it is very likely that the bride and groom will not give much thought to such challenges as illnesses or financial crises during the ceremony. Nevertheless, they will most likely face these challenges as most families do. When illness strikes, it may be sudden and devastating or it may be gradual and burdensome.

Stanley Scott recalled a moving account of Robertson and Muriel McQuilkin's experience with illness, which was reported in *Christianity Today*, October 1990. Robertson was serving as president of Columbia Bible College and Seminary (later named Columbia International University) in South Carolina when he received word from the doctor that his wife, Muriel, had developed Alzheimer's disease. Robertson made the surprising decision of resigning his post at the age of fifty-seven to care for his wife full-time. Not only did he sacrifice his career at its peak, he had to endure observing her gradual decline. Additionally, she was no longer able to fulfill his needs during this painful period. But he maintained his commitment to the end. The oncologist who attended to Muriel remarked to Robertson that in his capacity in dealing with terminal cases, he observed that "almost all women stand by their men; very few men stand by their women."[2] This "doctor who regularly dealt with dying people was plainly saying that men are more likely to desert their wives when their wives are dying. That's partly why Robertson's story is so powerful, because it is about a man choosing to sacrifice dramatically for his wife."[3] What an example for husbands and wives!

> The medical profession has expended a significant amount of effort to alleviate the physical and psychological problems that women experience. I do not believe the same has occurred for men.

Midlife Crisis

While growing up, I heard occasional mention of men's midlife crisis. But I passed it off as another way of talking about men's sexual escapades. Little did I realize that it was as real for some men as menopause is for most women. Much has been written about women's experience in menopause. Women's change of life experience is more dramatic and noticeable, especially since it is closely linked to the cessation of their childbearing years. The medical profession has expended a significant amount of effort to alleviate the physical and psychological problems that women experience. I do not believe the same has occurred for men. Perhaps, the reason is that men's crisis is not defined by a distinct period in their lives. Nevertheless, it is very real for those who experience this physiological change. Of course, some men may not even distinguish this occurrence in order to differentiate it from other physiological changes.

Others may not experience any significant changes. When my midlife change occurred at forty years of age, my system went into crisis. It was not until after I visited two hospitals and four doctors' offices seeking relief from the confusing symptoms that one alert physician and a nurse helped me understand what was really taking place in my body. Armed with the necessary knowledge, I was able to gain the psychological edge, and subsequently, the control over my body that was necessary for me to recover. (I am referring to the same illness previously referred to as burnout syndrome).

In her book *Awakening at Midlife*, Kathleen Brehony explained the issues so many people face at midlife. "Some of us may drift into it unconsciously, barely noticing the effects, while others of us will feel as if we've been knocked over the head with a two-by-four."[4] She claimed that the cultural belief, that only few changes are to be expected in adulthood, is very dangerous. It will cause us to deny that we have to make adjustments throughout our lives. Therefore, just when some people think they are secure and stable, they run the risk of falling in love with someone new or have an affair.

> Therefore, just when some people think they are secure and stable, they run the risk of falling in love with someone new or have an affair.

"Most people experience some physical, relational, professional or psychological changes during their midlife years, often in the form of an unhappy marriage affair; or divorce; anxiety that may have no clear source; depression; dissatisfaction with career or job; disillusionment; or despair."[5] Some people just refer to an emptiness that is deep and inexplicable. James Harnish referred to the midlife crisis as a crash.[6]

Jim Conway described his midlife crisis as hitting a wall. He explained that our society lays out a clear path males are expected to follow. They are expected to start a career, marry, establish a home, and then move up the ladder of success. Theoretically, from age forty, men start to move downhill. "He wonders what hit him and if life is worth living. He may finally rebel against all of this and abandon the two things he thinks are causing his problems—his wife and his work. He will later learn that abandoning these was not a good solution."[7] He will then become depressed, consider himself a martyr, and retreat into silence. At this stage many marriages break up or experience extreme difficulty and their careers are disrupted. "The crisis is a pervasive thing that seems to affect not only the physical, but also the social, cultural, spiritual, and occupational parts of a man's life."[8]

Since the changes occurring with women during menopause have been studied extensively and the information distributed widely, no real purpose would be served in reviewing that subject here. Suffice it to say, many women are deeply distressed during this period. The period of intense changes may last several years. The full unsettling effects on a woman's system physically, psychologically, and emotionally may never disappear completely.

If the couple is aware of this potential crisis, they can better prepare the necessary solutions. One important key could be open and honest sharing of feelings between the partners. Both would be wise to be patient with the other, knowing that their spouse is experiencing turbulent crises over which he/she has little control. Time, however, provides healing. Hence the exercise of patience with one another is crucial.

Family Interview

What is the effect of sickness in your marriage?

One year after I met my husband, we went off to college together. I found him to be curious and quizzical as some males are right around the time of their girlfriend's menstrual cycle. As it was around the fifties and sixties when women were not bold in telling that they were having their "periods," I also was spared from the embarrassment of having to explain how or what I was feeling throughout those five to seven days of menstrual torture—back pains, varicose veins, extreme heavy blood flow. But at that very time as he looked me in the face, he knew; he knew I was having my period and in few words would say: "You look pale." I felt his compassion, although at times I really wished he didn't know. Why, then, after marriage, didn't he have the same sensitivity when I complained about migraines, and about all the other physical pain and discomfort that came along with time? Even worse, he seemed less understanding about sickness during my menopausal years; he just couldn't accept that these changes were causing me unusual discomfort! He seemed judgmental and unhappy with my low response to his sexual needs, and often conflicts began. I became upset because I thought he was misjudging me and not making any effort to understand my feelings while he thought I was "giving way to my feelings" and not considering his needs as a husband.

Days of malice would follow; the children saw us being unhappy and it made them unhappy, too.

Ten or twelve years ago, I sensed that my husband has changed into a more understanding, sensitive, and compassionate individual. He volunteers his help with a better attitude, although at times I see a little of that "old boy attitude" return but it doesn't last. He doesn't complain as much when he has to put aside for a moment something he desperately wants to do whether it's watching the playoffs in sports or going to play golf. He has begun to appreciate my words when I express that I am not well. He is beginning to show the compassion that I think a husband or wife should show when a spouse is sick even though it may be for the long term. I must feel this way too, and I must expect to reciprocate and be fair to my spouse as I expect him to be fair to me. Sickness should not alter love neither should it cause the marriage to fall apart.

It seems almost true that when a husband or wife goes through sickness either of them is in a better position to empathize or be less critical of the other. This is not to say that we wish sickness upon our spouse or children so that they will understand what sickness is, but I have observed that after my husband had his stroke twelve or more years ago while he was visiting one of his parishioners in the hospital, he could better understand sickness. Until my husband was in his late thirties he was never sick; he never took a tablet, and he was never hospitalized. Then one day he was diagnosed with hypertension. He was overworked on the job having held several positions, including school principal, school board chairman, church pastor, conference treasurer, and Conference president.

Sickness in the marriage has led husbands to neglect their marriage, sometimes ending in separation or divorce. If the marriage vow, "…for better or worse…" is not binding enough, love should be.

Contributed by Pamela

15

Support for In-Laws and Parents

Without any direct discussion, Pam and I accepted our parents' security as our responsibility. Both of us accepted each other's family as our own. In many ways Pam's family members and relatives have been closer to us than my family members have been. The reason might be found in the physical closeness to her family before and after marriage. Apart from family members who lived with us, we have not had the privilege of living near my relatives. Consequently, Pam and the children did not have the opportunity to be as close to my relatives as I have been to hers.

When we first met in 1957, I was residing in the same city as Pam's family. My family was scattered in other towns and abroad. From the outset, I made contact with Pam's family and remained close to them over the years. They became increasingly a part of our family. Five of them lived with us for extended periods. Her two younger brothers lived with us for four years while they completed high school. They became as older siblings to our four children. One of Pam's sisters also lived with us two different times. Her mother stayed with us twice. Our children had close bonds with two cousins (Adria and Lisa). Kingsley and Michael, who lived with us for a while, are as brothers to our children. Our children consider them as part of our family. On my part, only Michael, apart from my father, lived with us. One of my sisters and my brother visited only occasionally.

We have treated our parents on both sides as our own. My mother passed away when I was four and Pam's stepfather passed away during the first year of our marriage. So both of us had a mother and a father after we were married. We just accepted our new parents as gifts to our marriage. My father lived with us for nine years. It would have been difficult for an observer who does not know our family connections to determine the real blood relations. Pam treated him as her own father. The children were very happy to have him so close to them, especially Sherine, who had him as her guardian. He walked her to and from kindergarten one block away from home.

Pam and I were very pleased that Papa, my father, never interfered with our marriage or attempted to discipline the children. We felt he was the perfect father-in-law. In 1978 Papa became ill. Persistent high blood pressure had taken its toll on his heart. In May of that year he passed away. Our family was deeply affected by his passing. His death was only one of two our family has experienced. The only other was Lisa, a daughter of my wife's sister. The children were very close to her. They were traumatized when word reached our family that she had passed away suddenly in Miami. She was only thirty years old.

Aunt Sada, as we call Pam's mother, has been very close to us. Although we have invited her to live with us in her later years, she refused. Perhaps, she feels that her married children should not have parents living with them. She has expressed her discomfort in that regard. However, she has spent extended periods in our home, particularly when Pam had our babies. We have accepted our responsibility to make sure our mother, who is in her late eighties, has the security and care she needs. She has lived for many years with one of Pam's sisters, who is a nurse. We are very close to our mother. We are constantly in close contact with her. Contrary to the popular view of a mother-in-law's relationship to married couples, our relationship over the years has been cordial.

In-laws have been the source of irritation for many married couples. The following are some additional counsels concerning relationship with in-laws.

Wellington Boone observed quite correctly that in the wedding ceremony the only part the bride and groom's parents have is for the bride's father to say: "I do," when the minister asks: "Who gives this woman to be married to this man?" Boone remarked that sometimes the father does not even have the opportunity to give the bride away because the groom does not ask him for the hand of his daughter. "Nobody consulted Daddy about the marriage. The speech by the father of the bride is just a formality. The wedding was all set up between his daughter and some guy she met."[1] The father is like a farmer who plants a field, only to have it snatched from him just as it becomes productive. Boone is concerned that the custom, which required the girl's suitor to seek her parents' consent, has been lost, to a great extent, in our culture. Under that system the parents, particularly those of the bride, were very involved in the wedding ceremony. Wellington Boone would like to see that system restored. He bemoaned: "How things have changed since those days. Now the father not only doesn't receive a dowry, he usually has to bear the full cost of the wedding—and still not get to say anything but 'I do.'"[2]

> **The couple, however, is not free from responsibility to support their two sets of parents, according to their ability and their parents' needs.**

Regardless of the changing times and customs, two very important biblical injunctions remain binding on us whether Christians or non-Christians.[3] These two principles simply make sense if society would function effectively. When two people marry, they form a new home and, therefore, are free of parental authority and unsolicited influence. The couple, however, is not free from responsibility to support their two sets of parents according to their ability and their parents' needs. Harold Shryock explained that the solution to the delicate problem of parent-in-law relationships requires the steering of a narrow course between the respect, which a child owes to his/her parents, and the obligation to his/her spouse. The fifth commandment does not set a limit on one's responsibilities to his/her parents. However, the Scripture is clear that a person's spouse is his/her first responsibility. "There can be no mistaking that the Scriptural admonition enjoins a first consideration of those factors which make harmony in the home, even though this involves a separation from the parents. Such separation, however, does not excuse negligence of the parents or a disregard for their comfort once their time of life or their circumstances have brought about a decrease of their vital forces."[4]

Parental Involvement

The interference of in-laws in their children's affairs after they are married has become proverbial. Just say "mother-in-law," and the first relationship that comes to most people's mind is meddling. "Marriage is a merger—not just of a man and a woman but also of their two families. Marriage should be an extension of both family trees, with both sets of parents as full participants. Grandparents and great-grandparents back through the generations all contributed something to what they are today."[5]

Therefore, the newly married couple should leave room in their relationship for their parents to give counsel and suggestions. It is then left to both partners to decide the level of involvement they require from their parents and whether to accept any input they make. The parents should refrain from being too involved in the lives of their children, regardless of their concerns, except if they suspect a crisis emerging, and even then they should proceed with caution. The new couple should handle such challenges as financial difficulties and having children without undue interference. Developing a reasonable balance between the couple's privacy and the parents' involvement will emerge after some time, providing a concerted effort is made on both sides.

In their article "Ins and Outs of In-laws," Gordon and Dorothea Jaeck wrote that of all the problems faced in a marriage, studies show that with both newly married couples and couples married for a long period, "in-law problems rank first or second. Our culture's negative conditioning toward mothers-in-law must take some responsibility for this. Studies reveal other interesting characteristics of the in-law interactional pattern. For one thing, it seems to be predominantly feminine. Seldom do male members of the two families find themselves at odds. Also, studies show that parents, rather than brothers or sisters, are the focus of fractured relationships."[6] To the surprise of many couples, despite the rumors about in-laws, they soon discover that the relationship with their in-laws proves meaningful and enriching. Although these relationships need to be guarded (since each partner may tend to cling more to his/her side of the family), both should bear in mind constantly that they have two sets of parents.

> Both should bear in mind constantly that they have two sets of parents.

Young couples that choose to live with one set of parents or depend on them for financial assistance should not be surprised if these parents appear to interfere. They may even have good intentions, but the reason for the problem may be that they are directly involved with their children's life and being human as well as having much more experience, especially with raising children, they feel constrained to get involved. When such problems begin to recur, it may be a signal to change the arrangement that places the new family in that situation. Michael Broder made a valid point: "If you've been depending on parents for financial support or assistance with some expenses, don't blame them completely if they try to be too 'helpful.' They may genuinely believe that you need emotional and moral support as well. It's your responsibility to separate emotionally from your family of origin—not their responsibility to 'free' you! And what applies to parents often applies to stepparents, other relatives, and even close friends."[7]

Respect and concern for the well-being of both sets of parents should be developed from the beginning of the couple's relationship. Once animosity and resentment surfaces, it is difficult to rebuild the relationship. Even if your partner's parents resented the marriage, every effort should be made to build trust and eradicate any cause for concern they may have for your happiness in the future. Any sacrificial effort made to develop a good relationship with your parents-in-law could redound to your benefit in the future. Remember that you are dealing with your spouse's parents and, regardless of whether your strong bond together seems to exclude your partner's parents, eventually that family bond between your spouse and parents will likely resurface. You want to be on the right side when it does. Always remember the biblical command to honor your father and your mother so that your days may be long and blessed.

Family Interviews

Did your commitment and relationship to your parents and in-laws change after marriage?

Our love remains the same for our parents, but the nature of the relationship with our parents has changed because our priorities have changed. Of course, we love our parents just as we did before we got married. But, whereas our parents and siblings were previously our first priorities, we are now each other's first priority except for our relationship to God. We aim to reserve the better part of our allegiance, time, and confidences for each other and our children.

Nevertheless, we still feel a moral obligation to our parents in terms of making sure that they have the necessary care and comfort. Because our marriage has made us one, we have stepped into each other's shoes in that regard. For example, each of us has assumed the responsibility of loving, supporting, and caring for our parents and parent(s)-in-law as if they were our biological parents. We are also committed to communicating, bonding, and visiting with our in-laws.

Contributed by Richard and Alicia

16

Conclusion: Making Marriage Successful

Recently, my wife, Pam, and I went to Myrtle Beach, South Carolina, for Thanksgiving. We stayed in a hotel room that had an excellent view of the beach. In fact, we could lie in bed and see the waves breaking gracefully on the sandy shores. We could also view the gorgeous sunrise and sunset casting their iridescent rays on the palm trees and glistening ocean. For the first four days, our emotional energy flowed freely between us as though it was a never-ending stream. I felt as if we were in the first year of marriage rather than the fortieth. However, I made a minor blunder that had a major effect. Without describing the specifics of the issue, let me attempt to summarize the effects.

Before I realized what was happening, the flow of emotional bonding between us had been frayed on the final day of our vacation. There were no harsh words or open conflict, but we both knew that things were not the same between us. We continued communicating in a friendly manner, despite the full consciousness that we had to repair the strained emotional connection. As the week progressed, I felt all was forgiven and forgotten. However, on Friday evening, a week later, I decided to share with Pam my feeling about how our relationship could improve. I took what I considered the necessary precaution to avoid placing any demands on Pam or give her the impression that she was at fault in any way. Suffice it to say, I failed miserably. At first, Pam listened without interrupting me. But as I proceeded, she got involved until it became a dialogue. Thereafter, for the next one and one-half hours, my wife recounted my failings over the decades of our marriage. She was direct, detailed, and dramatic. From my recollection of the occurrences recounted, her presentation was precise and persuasive.

I listened, only interrupting occasionally to get clarification or to utter expressions, indicating that I was listening in earnest and was not disapproving. To be truthful, it was painful to listen to the scathing recounting of the many ways I had made her unhappy over the years. When she was finished, I made a few comments acknowledging that I was wrong and reminded her that I had changed. I made sure to tell her plainly and unequivocally that I love her and I am greatly privileged to have her as my wife. Immediately thereafter, our spirits merged into a beautiful flow of passion for each other.

The recounting of the foregoing episode, although personal and private, has been done to demonstrate the purpose and essence of this book. The key to a successful marriage is not the absence of conflict or problems, but the presence of the strategies to resolve them. Before writing this book, I could not have made that statement with the conviction and certainty I am doing now. Let me make three bold confessions that should serve to clarify the profound impact the research for this book had upon me.

> The key to a successful marriage is not the absence of conflict or problems, but the presence of the strategies to resolve them.

I Did Not Understand the Meaning of Love

Before I started writing this book, if someone had asked me if I love my wife, I would have responded affirmatively, but I would not have known for sure. The reason is that despite my professional training and experience, I did not know for certain what love really was. Like most people, I had a feeling about what it was, but I had an uneasy feeling about whether I understood it fully. After this extensive study of love and marriage, I can say without reservation, not only that I love my wife, but that I am in love with my wife, Pam.

> I did not allow myself to be vulnerable. I felt that I had to be in control at all times.

I Did Not Understand Women

The other critical matter for me was my constant dissatisfaction with how little I understood women. I have said frequently that the longer I live the less I understand women, including my wife. That was the primary reason for most of our marital conflicts. It was not so much that I didn't understand women as much as I refused to understand them. Obviously, I had to deal with women on a professional level throughout my career. I had to counsel engaged couples and husbands and wives for decades. I understood theoretically about husbands and wives so that I could function on the level needed in my career. What is at stake here is that I did not take the time to internalize the reason women think and act so differently from men. I was acquainted with many books (e.g., John Gray's *Men Are from Mars and Women Are from Venus*), but my views concerning women were never altered substantially. I accepted their differences but still expected my wife to be different from other women. For instance, my wife cried sometimes during our arguments in the early and middle years of our marriage. I did not have the level of sensitivity then to see how to bring about a resolution to the concern that brought her feelings to overflow because she was unfulfilled. Instead, the more she cried, the further I would distance myself emotionally from the cause of her hurt. I did not allow myself to be vulnerable. I felt that I had to be in control at all times. My approach caused her to be insecure in our relationship at times. Obviously, I was oblivious to that at the time. How tragic!

As the episodes regarding our Thanksgiving vacation revealed, we found a way to express our feelings honestly and openly in a protected and safe environment. Pam did not hesitate to tell me how she felt, and fortunately for me, due to my recent exposure to viable strategies for resolving conflict, I was able to keep the dialogue real but without my usual withdrawal into silence or feeling hurt or misunderstood. I was able to keep my focus on her feelings as well. During Pam's expression of her feelings about me, I tried to introduce a bit of humor; she was not amused. She was beginning to feel that I was making light of her concerns, so I retreated hastily to being an active listener.

I Did Not Understand Intimacy

It is not that I didn't know what intimacy was but I didn't understand how to achieve and maintain it. From time to time, I achieved intimacy with my wife. However, I never figured out why or how we achieved it. It just happened.

Now I feel more confident that I understand the process that leads to intimacy and that which prevents it. I always respected my wife, but I was not careful to let her feel cherished at all times. Most women regard being respected and feeling cherished as the most important factors affecting their response to achieving intimacy. During the years of our marriage, I reacted to defend my position, which, from my perspective, seemed to be right. Now I try to surrender earlier, whether I am right or wrong on an issue, to listen more engagingly to Pam, not only for understanding her point of view but to better understand her and what she is feeling.

> Most women regard being respected and feeling cherished as the most important factors affecting their response to achieving intimacy.

This includes sexual intimacy. During the recent dialogue referred to earlier, Pam shared something about her feeling that never registered with me before. I knew that after menopause her body changed as it does for most women and I tried to adjust to her new moods sexually. Having made allowance for these changes, I felt that Pam and I had found a comfortable sexual arrangement. I was surprised when she told me, while sharing her feelings, that my relationship to her during our earlier years of marriage still affects her sexual relationship with me. If I did not have a fuller understanding of intimacy, my natural inclination would be to think that she was vindictive and that would likely lead me to retaliate emotionally. Now it is easier for me to empathize and to be determined to make up for the past, in which I was often insensitive to her true feelings. Changing my approach to our relationship is a serious challenge. Sometimes, I react reflexively to a comment or an action from Pam. I then hastened to do damage control, but quite often I had to let time do the healing. I still struggle with my own negative feelings during that process. And Pam is now an expert at reading my expressions, even if I try to mask my struggles with these negative moods. My tone of voice and passionless expressions usually betray me. However, I think I am winning the battle. Currently, we connect intimately for much longer periods and with far less effort.

To a great extent, our marriage survived because of our commitment to each other. Both of us accepted each other without reservation. We believed in marriage for life and we still do. So the problems that developed did not bring the future of our relationship into question. We dealt with them, not the future of our relationship. A significant element that contributed to our success was our deep and abiding faith in God. We have regular devotions together. And we attend church together frequently. I treasure the past few years of my sabbatical, when we could dress for church in our own time and sit together during the service. Prior to this, we had to rise early in the morning and drive long distances to meet speaking appointments and return home often late at night. Obviously, we were separated during the service since I was the speaker.

My challenge for the future is to continue to learn to love, respect, and cherish my wife. I trust all those who read this book will strive to achieve the same in their friendships or marital relationships.

References

Chapter One

1. Eva Marie Everson, *True Love*, p.223

2. Theodor Bovet, in J. A. Petersen, *For Men Only*, p.58

3. Theodor Bovet, Ibid., p.58

4. Theodor Bovet, Ibid., p.59

5. Theodor Bovet, Ibid., p.60

6. Theodor Bovet, Ibid., p.60

7. C. J. Jung, *Women in Europe*, (Zurich Rasler, 1932), quoted in J. A. Petersen, *For Men Only*, p.67

8. Nancy Van Pelt, *We've Only Just Begun*, p.98

9. Nancy Van Pelt, Ibid., p.98

10. Kevin Howse, et al., *Family Matters*, p.36

11. Nancy Van Pelt, *We've Only Just Begun*, pp.87-89

12. "*Christianity Today*," February, 2003, p.80

13. Nancy Van Pelt, *We've Only Just Begun*, p.90

14. Quoted in Nancy Van Pelt, *We've Only Just Begun*, p.158

15. Ann Landers, in "*The Montreal Gazette*," September, 1980

16. Tom Eisonman, *Temptations Men Face*, p.55

17. William J. Bennett, *The Broken Hearth*, p.12

18. Eric Cohen and Sterling Gregory, *You Owe Me*, p.1

19. *Songs of Solomon* chapter 8: 6,7 (All biblical quotations are from The Revised Standard Version Common Bible, National Council of Churches (1973), except where noted).

Chapter Two

1. Nancy Van Pelt, *We've Only Just Begun*, p.208

2. Nancy Van Pelt, Ibid., pp.208,209

3. Nancy Van Pelt, Ibid., p.209

4. Nancy Van Pelt, Ibid., p.20

5. Nancy Van Pelt, Ibid., p.21

6. Eric J. Cohen and Gregory Sterling, *You Owe Me*, pp.18,19

7. Eric J. Cohen and Gregory Sterling, Ibid., p.8

8. Jim Conway, *Men In Midlife Crisis*, pp.209,210

9. Jim Conway, Ibid., pp.211,212

10. John Townsend, *What Men Want-What Women Want*, p.165

11. John Townsend, Ibid., p.165

12. Judith Wallerstein and Sandra Blakeslee, *The Good Marriage*, pp.3,4

13. Alistair Begg, *Lasting Love*, p.72

14. Alistair Begg, Ibid., p.72

15. Alistair Begg, Ibid., p.72

16. Alistair Begg, Ibid., p.73

17. Fred Lowery, *Covenant Marriage*, p.109

18. Scott Stanley, et. al., *A Lasting Promise*, p160

19. Scott Stanley, et. al., Ibid., p.164

20. *Genesis* chapter 1: 26

21. *Genesis* chapter 2: 24

22. Fred Lowery, *Covenant Marriage*, pp.42,43

23. *Hebrews* chapter 13: 5

24. Fred Lowery, Ibid., p.12

25. Catherine Musco and Joseph A. Garcia-Pratts, *Good Marriages Don't Just Happen*, pp.10,11

26. Iris Krasnow, *Surrendering to Marriage*, p.3

27. Iris Krasnow, Ibid., p.3

28. Iris Krasnow, Ibid., p.3

29. Shere Hite, *The Hite Report*, p.279

30. Shere Hite, Ibid., p. 279

31. Stephen Carter and Julia Sokol, *Men Who Can't Love*, p.4

32. Scott Stanley, *The Heart of Commitment*, p.144

Chapter Three

1. William Betcher and Robie Macauley, *The Seven Basic Quarrels of Marriage*, p.3

2. John Gottman, *Why Marriages Succeed or Fail*, p.14

3. Bill Knott, article, *"Safety and Sanctuary,"* in journal, *"Advent Review,"* July, 1997, p.14

4. John Gottman, *Why Marriages Succeed or Fail.*, p.23

5. John Gottman, Ibid., p.24

6. John Gottman, Ibid., p.58

7. John Gottman, Ibid., p.28

8. John Gottman, Ibid., p.57

9. William Betcher and Robie Macauley, *The Seven Basic Quarrels in Marriage*, p.12

10. William Betcher, Ibid., p.16

11. William Betcher, Ibid., pp.19,20

12. William Betcher, Ibid., p.19

13. William Betcher, Ibid., p.259

14. William Betcher, Ibid., p.274

15. Judith Wallerstein and Sandra Blakeslee, *The Good Marriage*, p.145

16. Charlie W. Shedd, article, *"Seven Rules for a Good Fight,"* in *The Marriage Affair*, p.286

17. John Gottman, *Why Marriage Succeed or Fail*, p.159

18. John Gottman, Ibid., p.161

Chapter Four

1. *Ephesians* chapter 5: 22-24

2. William Hulme, *"The Head of the House,"* in J. A. Petersen, *The Marriage Affair*, p.70

3. William Hulme, Ibid., p.74

4. William Hulme, Ibid., P.74

5. Neil Boyd, *The Beast Within*, p.60

6. Deborah Blum, *Sex on the Brain*, p.xiv

7. Anne Campbell, *Men, Women, and Aggression*, p.20

8. Anne Campbell, Ibid., p.15

9. Anne Campbell, Ibid., p.69

10. Anne Campbell, Ibid., p.1

11. Anne Campbell, Ibid., p.74

12. Anne Campbell, Ibid., p.75

13. Anne Campbell, Ibid., p.45

14. Anne Campbell, Ibid., p.105

15. Scott Wetzer, *Living with the Passive-Aggressive Man*, p.14

16. Scott Wetzer, Ibid., p.15

17. Scott Wetzer, Ibid., p.15

18. Scott Wetzer, Ibid., p.22

19. Scott Wetzer, Ibid., p.52

Chapter Five

1. James Dobson, *Marriage and Family*, p.308

2. James Dobson, Ibid., p.306

3. John Bradshaw, *Bradshaw on: The Family*, pp.186,187

4. Denis and Barbara Rainey, *Starting Your Marriage*, p.6

5. John Bradshaw, *Bradshaw on: The Family*, p.187

6. John Bradshaw, Ibid., pp.187,188

7.   Larry Crabb, *Men and Women: Enjoying the Difference*, p.27

8.   Jean Baker Miller, *Toward a New Psychology of Women*, p.49

9.   Jean Baker Miller, Ibid., p.49

10. Jean Baker Miller, Ibid., p.49

11. Jean Baker Miller, Ibid., p.50

12. Laura Doyle, *The Surrendered Wife*, p.23

13. Laura Doyle, Ibid., p.24

14. Laura Doyle, Ibid., p.24

15. Judge Judy Sheindlin, *Keep It Simple, Stupid*, p.42

16. Andrew J. Dubrin, *The New Husbands and How to Become One*, p.30

17. Andrew J. Dubrin, Ibid., p.155

18. Judith Wallerstein and Sandra Blakeslee, *The Good Marriage*, p.239

19. Judith Wallerstein, Ibid., p.239

20. Judith Wallerstein, Ibid., p.60

21. Judith Wallerstein, Ibid., p.60

22. Judith Wallerstein, Ibid., p.62,63

Chapter Six

1.   William Betcher and Robie Macauley, *The Seven Basic Quarrels of Marriage*, p.91

2.   James Dobson, *Love for a Lifetime*, p.67

3.   Wallace Denton, article, *"Money and Meaning,"* in *For Men Only*, p.144

4.   William Betcher and Robie Macauley, *The Seven Basic Quarrels of Marriage*, pp.105,106

5. Andrew Dubrin, *The New Husbands and How to Become One*, p.109

6. Andew Dubrin, Ibid., p. 109

7. Jean L. Potuchek, *Who Supports the Family?* p.2

8. Jean L. Potuchek, Ibid., p.4

9. Jean L. Potuchek, Ibid., p.5

10. Randi Minetor, *Breadwinner Wives and the Men They Marry*, p.27

11. Randi Menetor, Ibid., p.26

12. Randi Menetor, Ibid., p.7

13. Laura Doyle, *The Surrendered Wife*, p.91

14. Laura Doyle, Ibid., pp.90,91

15. Laura Doyle, Ibid., p.91

16. Laura Doyle, Ibid., p.96

17. Laura Doyle, Ibid., p.96

18. Laura Doyle, Ibid., p. 97

19. See the book, Dave Ramsay, *Financial Peace*.

20. James Dobson, *Marriage and Family*, pp.339,340

21. James Dobson, Ibid., p.340

Chapter Seven

1. Khalil Gibran, quoted in Helen Arnstein, *Getting Along with Your Grown-up Children*.

2. Leslie Flynn, article, *"Like Father, Like Son,"* in J. A. Petersen, *For Men Only, p. 85*

3. John Bradshaw, The Family, p.159

4. Oswald Hoffman, article, *"The Crime Against Children," The Marriage Affair*, p.146

5. Oswald Hoffman, Ibid., p. 146

6. Oswald Hoffman, Ibid., pp.46,47

7. James Dobson, *Marriage and Family*, pp.81,82

8. Oswald Hoffman, article: *"The Crime Against Children," The Marriage Affair*, pp.81,82

Chapter Eight

1. Albert Ellis and Ted Crawford, *Making Intimate Connections*, p.28

2. Nancy Van Pelt, *To Have and to Hold*, p.77

3. Nancy Van Pelt, Ibid., p.110

4. Eric J. Cohen and Gregory Sterling, *You Owe Me*, p.3

5. Eric J. Cohen, Ibid., p.6

6. Nancy Van Pelt, *To Have and To Hold*, p.109

7. Claire Etaugh and Judith Bridge, *The Psychology of Women*, p.294

8. Claire Etaugh, Ibid., p.285

9. John Gray, *Men Are from Mars, Women Are from Venus*, p.52

10. Shere Hite, *The Shere Hite Report on the Family*, p.411

11. John Gray, *Men Are from Mars, Women Are from Venus*, p.53

12. John Gray, Ibid., p. 53

13. Barbara DeAngelis, *What Women Want Men to Know*, pp.243

14. Barbara DeAngelis, Ibid., p.258

15. John Gray, *Men Are from Mars, Women Are from Venus*, p.52

16. Paul Tournier, article: *"Listen to Understand," The Marriage Affair*, p.31

17. Barbara DeAngelis, *What Women Want Men to Know*, p.266

18. Michael Broder, *The Art of Staying Together*, p.65

19. Louise Ferrebee, *The Healthy Marriage Handbook*, p.5

20. Louise Ferrebee, Ibid., p.5

21. Kathy Dawson, *Diagnosis: Married*, p.21

22. Kathy Dawson, Ibid., p.23

23. Maurice Taylor and Seana McGhee, *The New Couple*, p.125

24. Maurice Taylor, Ibid., p.126

25. Michael S. Broder, *The Art of Staying Together*, p.74

26. Michael S. Broder, Ibid., p. 74

27. Kathy Dawson, *Diagnosis: Married*, p.1

28. Kathy Dawson, Ibid., p.1

29. Nancy Van Pelt, *To Have and To Hold*, p.78

30. Steve and Cathy Brody, *Renew Your Marriage at Midlife*, p.122

31. Robert S. Cohen, *Reconcilable Differences*, p.34

32. Robert S. Cohen, Ibid., p.34

Chapter Nine

1. Sandra Leiblum and Judith Sachs, *Getting the Sex You Want*, p.2

2. Sandra Lieblum, Ibid., p.2

3. Louise Ferrebee, editor, *The Healthy Marriage Handbook*, p.85

4. Louise Ferrebee, Ibid., p.86

5. Billy Graham, *"Discovering Sexual Intimacy,"* J. A. Petersen, *The Marriage Affair*, pp.369,370

6. *Songs of Solomon* chapter 7: 1-4

7. Op. cit., p.370

8. I *Corinthians* chapter 7: 3,4

9. See such passages as *Romans* chapter 1: 18-32; I *Corinthians* chapter 6: 9-20; *Ephesians* chapter 5: 3-14

10. Linda Dillow and Lorraine Pintus, *Intimate Issues*, p.15

11. Linda Dillow, Ibid., p.15

12. Linda Dillow, Ibid., p.15

13. Linda Dillow, Ibid., pp.18,19

14. Nancy Van Pelt, *To Have and To Hold*, p.168

15. Nancy Van Pelt., p.168

16. Samuel and Cynthia Janus, *The Janus Report*, p.228

17. Samuel Janus, Ibid., pp.227-261

18. Samuel Janus, Ibid., p.260

19. James Dobson, *Marriage and Family*, p.350

20. James Dobson, Ibid., p.351

21. Clifford and Joyce Pener, article in the *Healthy Marriage*, p.90

22. Clifford Pener, Ibid., p.91

23. Claire Etaugh and Judith Bridges, *The Psychology of Women*, p.167

24. Claire Etaugh, Ibid., p.168

25. *The Paducah Sun*, Kentucky, August 25, 2003, p.13A

26. Claire Etaugh, Ibid., p.169

27. William Masters and Virginia Johnson, *Human Sexual Inadequacy*, pp.12,13

28. Andrew Dubrin, *The New Husbands and How to Become One, p.109*.

29. Samuel and Cynthia Janus, *The Janus Report on Sexual Behavior*, p.27

30. Samuel Janus, Ibid., p.21

31. James Dobson, *Marriage and Family*, p.322

32. David Schnarch, *Passionate Marriage*, p.76

33. David Schnarch, Ibid., p.78

34. Robert Butler and Myrna Lewis, *Love and Sex After 60*, p.4

35. Robert Butler, Ibid., p.10

36. Robert Butler, Ibid., p.10,11

37. Robert Butler, Ibid., p.25

38. Shere Hite, *The Hite Report on the Family*, p.20

39. The Tormont Webster's Illustrated Encyclopedic Dictionary

40. Catherine and Joseph Garcia-Pratts, *Good Marriages Just Don't Happen*, p.132

41. Catherine Garcia-Pratts, Ibid., p.133

42. William Masters and Virginia Johnson, *Sex and Human Loving*, p.233

43. Barbara DeAngelis, *What Women Want Men to Know*, p.309

44. Barbara DeAngelis, Ibid., pp.309-311

45. Barbara DeAngelis, Ibid., p.312

46. Kim Cattrall and Mark Levinson, *Satisfaction*, p.13

47. Harville Hendrix, *Getting the Love You Want*, p.208: cf pp.80,81,247 ff.

48. Harville Hendrix, Ibid., pp.208,209

49. Steve and Cathy Brody, *Renew Your Marriage at Midlife*, p.18

50. Steve Brody, Ibid., p.17

51. David Schnarch, *Passionate Marriage*, pp.38,39

52. David Schnarch, Ibid., p.41

53. David Schnarch, Ibid., p.41

54. David Schnarch, Ibid., p42

55. David Schnarch, Ibid., p.43

56. David Schnarch, Ibid., p.43

57. David Schnarch, Ibid., p.153

58. David Schnarch, Ibid., p.190

59. Ibid., p.190, cf Stephen George, *A Lifetime of Sex*, p.2

60. Neil Wertheimer, introduction, Stephen George, et. al., *A Lifetime of Sex*.

61. Barbara DeAngelis, *What Women Want Men to Know*, p.327

62. James Dobson, *Marriage and Family*, pp.319,320

63. James Dobson, Ibid., pp.323,324

64. Robert Butler and Myrna Lewis, *Love, and Sex After 60*, p.172

65. Robert Butler, Ibid., p.172

66. Robert Butler, Ibid., p.173

67. Linda Dillow and Lorraine Pintus, *Intimate Issues*, p.48

68. Valerie Raskin, *Great Sex for Moms*, p.227

69. Barbara DeAngelis, *What Women Want Men to Know*, p.316

70. Barbara DeAngelis, Ibid., p.317

71. Barbara DeAngelis, Ibid., p.318

72. Barbara DeAngelis, Ibid., p.324

73. Dr. James Dobson, *Marriage and Family*, p.319

74. James Dobson, *Marriage and Family*, p.321

75. Nancy Van Pelt, *To Have and To Hold*, p.164

76. 1*Peter* chapter 3:7 (King James Version).

Chapter Ten

1. *Proverbs* chapter 29: 11 (King James version.)

2. Andrew Weiner, *"New Scenes from a Marriage,"* published in *"Quest Magazine,"* Sept., 1978

3. Andrew Weiner, Ibid., p.35

4. David Augsburger, article: *"Should I Confess,"* J. Allan Petersen, *The Marriage Affair*, p.293

5. Anita Diggs and Vera Paster, *Staying Married*, p.5

6. Laura Schlessinger, *Ten Stupid Things People Do To Mess Up Their Relationships.*

7. Nancy Van Pelt, *We've Only Just Begun*, p.187

8. Nancy Van Pelt, Ibid., p.187

9. William Betcher, *The Seven Basic Quarrels of Marriage*, p.205

10. William Betcher, Ibid., p.205

11. Alexander Lowen and Robert Levin, article: *"The Case Against Cheating in Marriage," "Redbook,"* June, 1969 (Quoted in *"Advent Review,"* May 30, 1974.)

Chapter Eleven

1. Nancy Van Pelt, *To Have and To Hold*, p.31

2. Nancy Van Pelt, Ibid., p.30

3. Willard Harley, Jr., *His Needs Her Needs*, p.43

4. Willard Harley, Ibid., 43

5. Diane and John Rehm, *Toward Commitment*, p.54

6. Diane Rehm, Ibid., 55

7. Ellen White, *The Advent Home*, p.422

Chapter Twelve

1. William J. Bennett, *The Broken Hearth*, p.12

2. William J. Bennett, Ibid., p.14

3. William J. Bennett, Ibid., p.5

4. Tom Eisenman, *Temptations Men Face*, p.17

5. Tom Eiseman, Ibid., p.17

6. Howard Hendricks, *"Worship Family Style,"* J. Allan Petersen, *The Marriage Affair*, p.187

7. Ken Anderson, *"The Family That Plays Together,"* J. Allan Petersen, *The Marriage Affair*, p.198

8. Ellen White, *Messages to Young People*, p.328

9. Nancy Van Pelt, *To Have and To Hold*, p.177

10. Nancy Van Pelt, Ibid., p.177

11. Scott Stanley, et. al., *The Lasting Promise*, p.261

12. Scott Stanley, Ibid., p.267

13. T. D. Jakes, *Celebrating Marriage*, p.7

14. *Psalms* chapter 127: 1

Chapter Thirteen

1. Laura Doyle, *The Surrendered Wife*, p.265

2. John Gottman, *The Seven Principles of Making Marriage Work*, p.244

3. William Betcher and Robie Macauley, *The Seven Quarrels of Marriage*, pp.267,268

4. Jean Baker Miller, *Toward A New Psychology of Women*, p.60

5. Jean Baker Miller, Ibid., p.61

6. Jean Baker Miller, Ibid., p.51

7. Matthew chapter 23: 11

8. Ellen White, *Messages to Young People*, p.51

9. Ellen White, Ibid., p.209

10. Scott Stanley, *The Heart of Commitment*, p.191

11. Scott Stanley, Ibid., pp.191,192

12. Scott Stanley, Ibid., pp.191,192

Chapter Fourteen

1. *Manual for Ministers*, General Conference of Seventh-day Adventists, p.41

2. Scott Stanley, *The Heart of Commitment*, p.196

3. Scott Stanley, Ibid., p.196

4.   Kathleen Brehony, *Awakening at Midlife*, p.2

5.   Kathleen Brehony, Ibid., p.3

6.   James Harnish, *Men at Midlife*, p.19

7.   Jim Conway, *Men at Midlife*, p.26

8.   Jim Conway, Ibid., p.21

Chapter Fifteen

1.   Wellington Boone, *Your Wife Is Not Your Momma*, p.157

2.   Wellington Boone, Ibid., p.158

3.   References are made to *Genesis* chapter 2; 24; *Exodus* chapter 20; 12

4.   Harold Shryock, *Happiness for Husbands and Wives*, p.76

5.   Wellington Boone, *Your Wife Is Not Your Momma*, p.163

6.   Gordon and Dorothea Jaeck, "*In and Out of In-laws*," J. Allan Petersen, *The Marriage Affair*, p.306

7.   Michael Broder, *The Art of Staying Together*, p.77

Bibliography

Anand, Margot. *Sexual Ecstasy*. New York: Putnam Press, 2000.

Begg, Alistair. *Lasting Love*. Chicago: Moody Press, 1997.

Bennett, William J. *The Broken Hearth*. New York: Doubleday, 2001.

Betcher, William. *Intimate Play*. New York: Viking Penguin Inc., 1987.

Betcher, William and Macauley, Robie. *The Seven Basic Quarrels of Marriage*. New York: Villard Books, 1990.

Blum, Deborah. *Sex on the Brain*. New York: Penguin Books, 1997.

Boone, Wellington. *Your Wife Is Not Your Mamma*. New York: Doubleday, 1999.

Boyd, Neil. *The Beast Within: Why Men Are Violent*. New York: Greystone Books, 2000.

Bradshaw, John. *Bradshaw on: The Family*. Deerfield Beach, FL: Health Communications, 1996.

Brehony, Kathleen A. *Awakening at Midlife*. New York: Riverhead Books, 1996.

Broder, Michael. *The Art of Staying Together*. New York: Hyperion, 1993.

Brody, Steve and Brody, Cathy. *Renew Your Marriage at Midlife*. New York: G. P. Putnam's Sons, 1999.

Brown, D. Anne. *You Can Get There from Here*. New Jersey: Bryant & Dillon Publishers, 1995.

Campbell, Anne. *Men, Women and Aggression*. New York: Basic Books, 1993.

Carter, Stephen and Sokol, Julia. *Men Who Can't Love*. New York: Berkley Publishing Group, 1988.

Cohen, Eric J. and Sterling, Gregory. *You Owe Me*. New Jersey: New Horizon Press, 1999.

Cohen, Robert Stephen. *Reconcilable Differences*. New York: Pocket Books, 2002.

Conway, Jim. *Men in Midlife*. Colorado: Chariot Victor Publishing, 1997.

Crabb, Larry. *Men and Women: Enjoying the Difference*. Grand Rapids, MI: Zondervan Publishing House, 1991.

Dawson, Kathy. *Diagnosis: Married*. New York: The Berkley Publishing Group, 2000.

De Angelis, Barbara. *How to Make Love All the Time*. New York: Dell Publishing, 1987.

De Angelis, Barbara. *What Women Want Men to Know*. New York: Hyperion, 2001.

Diggs, Anita Doreen and Paster, Vera S. *Staying Married: A Guide for African American Couples*. New York: Kensington Publishing Corp., 1998.

Dillow, Linda and Pintus, Lorraine. *Intimate Issues*. Colorado: Waterbrook Press, 1999.

Dobson, James. *Love for a Lifetime*. Oregon: Multnomah Publishing, Inc., 1998.

Dobson, James. *Marriage and Family*. Wheaton, IL: Tyndale Publishing, 2000.

Douglas, Marcia and Douglas, Lisa. *The Sex You Want*. New York: Marlowe & Co., 1997.

Doyle, Laura. *The Surrendered Wife*. New York: Simon & Schuster, 2001.

Dubrin, Andrew J. *The New Husbands and How to Become One*. Chicago: Nelson-Hall, 1976.

Eisenman, Tom L. *Temptations Men Face*. Illinois: Intervarsity Press, 1991.

Ellis, Albert and Crawford, Ted. *Making Intimate Connections*. California: Impact Publishing Inc., 2000.

Emerson, Richard. *The Best Sex You'll Ever Have*. London: Carlton Books, 2001.

Etaugh, Claire A. and Bridges, Judiths. *The Psychology of Women*. Massachusetts: Allyn & Bacon, 2001.

Everson, Eva Marie. *True Love*. Ohio: Promise Press, 2000.

Fausto-Sterling, Anne. *Myths of Gender*. New York: Basic Books, Inc., 1985.

Ferrebee, Louise general editor. *The Healthy Marriage Handbook*. Tennessee: Broadman & Holman Publishing, Co., 2001.

Friedman, Betty. *The Feminine Mystique*. New York: W. W. Norton & Co., Inc., 1963.

Garcia-Pratts, Catherine Musco and Joseph A. *Good Marriages Don't Just Happen*. Texas: Thomas More, 2000.

George, Stephen C. et al. *A Lifetime of Sex*. Pennsylvania: Rodale Press, Inc., 1998.

Glasser, William and Carleen. *Getting Together and Staying Together*. New York: HarperCollins, 2000.

Goldburg, Herb. *What Men Really Want*. New York: Penguin Putnam Inc., 1991.

Gottlieb, Daniel. *Family Matters.* New York: Penguin Books, 1991.

Gottman, John. *Why Marriages Succeed or Fail.* New York: Simon & Schuster, 1994.

Gottman, John. *The Seven Principles for Making Marriage Work.* New York: Crown Publishers, Inc., 1999.

Gray, John. *Men Are from Mars, Women Are from Venus.* New York: Harper Collins Publishing, Inc., 1992.

Hakim, Lawrence S. *The Couple's Disease.* Florida: DHP Publishers, LLC., 2002.

Harnish, James. *Men at Mid-Life.* Nashville, Tennessee: Dimensions for Living, 1993.

Harley, Jr., Willard F. *His Needs Her Needs.* Grand Rapids, MI: Fleming H. Revell, 1994.

Hendrix, Harville. *Getting the Love You Want.* New York: HarperPerennial, 1988.

Hite, Shere. *The Hite Report.* New York: Grove Press, 1995.

Howse, Kevin; Dunton, Hugh and Marshall, David. *Family Matters.* Grantham, UK: The Stanborough Press, 1989.

Huyse, Elizabeth Cody Newen. *Sometimes I Feel Like Running Away from Home.* Minnesota: Bettany House Publishers, 1993.

Jake, T. D. *Celebrating Marriage.* Oklahoma: Albury Publishing, 2000.

Janus, Samuel S. and Janus, Cynthia L. *The Janus Report.* New York: John Wiley and Sons, Inc., 1993.

Kantor, David. *My Lover, Myself.* New York: Penguin Putnam, Inc., 1999.

Kimball, Gayle. *The 50-50 Marriage.* Boston: Beacon Press, 1983.

Krasnow, Iris. *Surrendering to Marriage.* New York: Hyperion Press, 2001

LaHaye, Tim and LaHaye, Beverly. *The Act of Marriage*. Grand Rapids, MI: Zondervan Publishing House, 1998.

Landers, Ann. New Jersey: Prentice-Hall, Inc., 1968.

Lowery, Dr. Fred. *Covenant Marriage*. West Monroe, LA: Howard Publishing Co., 2002.

Masters, William H. and Johnson, Virginia E. *Human Sexual Inadequacy*. London: J. & A. Churchill Ltd., 1970.

McDonough, Yona. *Between "Yes" and "I Do"* New Jersey: Carol Publishing Group, 1998.

Miller, Jean Baker. *Toward A New Psychology of Women*. Toronto: Fitzhenry & Whiteside Ltd., 1976.

Minetor, Randi. *Breadwinner Wives and Men they Marry*. Far Hills, NJ.: New Horizon Press, 2002

Napa, Amy. *A Woman's Touch*. Louisiana: Howard Publishing Co. Inc., 2001.

Oates, Wayne E. and Rowatt, Wade. *Before You Marry Them*. Nashville: Broadman Press, 1975.

Petersen, J. Allen. *For Men Only*. Wheaton, IL: Tyndale House Publishers, 1973.

Petersen, J. Allan. *The Marriage Affair*. Wheaton, IL: Tyndale House Publishers, 1971.

Potuchek, Jean. L. *Who Supports the Family?* Stanford: Stanford U. Press, 1997

Rainey, Dennis and Rainey, Barbara. *Starting Your Marriage Right*. Nashville: Thomas Nelson Publishers, 2000.

Ramsay, Dave. *Financial Peace*. New York: Viking Penguin Books, 1995.

Raskin, Valerie Davis. *Great Sex for Moms*. New York: Simon and Schuster, 2002.

Rehm, Diane and Rehm, John. *Toward Commitment*. New York: Alfred K. Knoff, 2002.

Roiphe, Anne. *Married*. New York: Basic Books, 2002.

Schlessinger, Dr. Laura. *Ten Stupid Things Couples Do To Mess Up Their Relationships*. New York: HarperCollins Publishers, 2003.

Schnarch, David. *Passionate Marriage*. New York: Henry Holt & Co., 1997.

Sheindlin, Judge Judy. *Keep IT Simple, Stupid*. New York: HarperCollins Publishers, Inc., 2000.

Shryock, Harold. *Happiness for Husbands and Wives*. Mountain View, CA: Pacific Press Publishing Association, 1949.

Stanley, Scott, et al. *A Lasting Promise*. San Francisco: Jossey-Bass Publishers, 1995.

Stanley, Scott. *The Heart of Commitment*. Nashville: Thomas Nelson Publishers, 1998.

Stark, Marg. *What No One Tells the Bride*. New York: Hyperion Press, 1998.

Taylor, Maurice and McGee, Seana. *The New Couple*. San Francisco: Harper Collins Publishing, 1997.

The Tormont Webster's Illustrated Encyclopedic Dictionary. Montreal: Tormont Publications, 1990.

Van Pelt, Nancy. *To Have and To Hold*. Nashville: Southern Publishing Association, 1980.

Van Pelt, Nancy. *Train Up A Child*. Hagerstown, MD: Review and Herald, 1984.

Van Pelt, Nancy. *We've Only Just Begun*. Hagerstown, MD: Review and Herald, 1985.

Wallerstein, Judith S. and Blakeslee, Sandra. *The Good Marriage*. New York: Houghton Mifflin Co., 1995.

Westheimer, Dr. Ruth. *Dr. Ruth's Guide to Good Sex*. New York: Warner Books, 1983.

Wetzler, Scott. *Living with the Passive Aggressive Man*. New York: Fireside Publishing, 1992.

White, Ellen G. *Education*. Mountain View, CA: Pacific Press, 1952.

White, Ellen G. *Child Guidance*. Nashville: Southern Publishing, 1954.

White, Ellen G. *Messages to Young People*. Nashville: Southern Publishing, 1974.

Yates, John and Yates, Susan. *What Really Matters at Home*. Dallas: Word Publishing, 1992.

Other Sources

"Advent Review"(periodical). Hagerstown, MD.
"Celebration"(periodical). Published by Advent Review. Hagerstown, MD.
"Christianity Today"(periodical). Carol Stream, Illinois.
"Quest" Canada's urban magazine.
"Red Book"(periodical). New York, New York.
Statistical Abstract of the United States, U.S. Census Bureau, 2004–2005.
"The Montreal Gazette"(newspaper). Montreal, Canada.
"The Paducah Sun"(newspaper). Paducah, Kentucky.
U.S. Census Bureau, 2000.
Vital Statistics of the United States. U. S. Department of Health and Human Services, 1985.

Robert O.A. Samms, Ph.D.
www.makingmarriagemeaningful.com

978-0-595-34289-1
0-595-34289-2

Printed in the United States
35365LVS00007B/70